Oliver Parodi / Ignacio Ayestaran / Gerhard Banse (eds.)

Sustainable Development – Relationships to Culture, Knowledge and Ethics

Karlsruher Studien Technik und Kultur
Band 3

Herausgeber:
Prof. Dr. Gerhard Banse
Prof. Dr. Andreas Böhn
Prof. Dr. Armin Grunwald
PD Dr. Kurt Möser
Prof. Dr. Michaela Pfadenhauer

Eine Übersicht über alle bisher in dieser Schriftenreihe erschienenen Bände finden Sie am Ende des Buchs.

Sustainable Development – Relationships to Culture, Knowledge and Ethics

Oliver Parodi
Ignacio Ayestaran
Gerhard Banse
(eds.)

Umschlaggestaltung: Christian-Marius Metz
Satz: Waltraud Laier

Impressum

Karlsruher Institut für Technologie (KIT)
KIT Scientific Publishing
Straße am Forum 2
D-76131 Karlsruhe
www.ksp.kit.edu

KIT – Universität des Landes Baden-Württemberg und nationales
Forschungszentrum in der Helmholtz-Gemeinschaft

KIT Scientific Publishing 2011
Print on Demand

ISSN: 1869-7194
ISBN: 978-3-86644-627-4

Content

Part 1
Methodological Questions, Conceptual Debates and Frameworks

Part 2

Epistemic Topics, Knowledge and Ethical Dilemmas

Editorial

Mutual relationships between technology and culture are as old as mankind itself. Technical achievements have influenced culture and cultural patterns and practices have influenced technology and its development, modification, dissemination, and use. Theoretical reflections about this relationship, however, are not so old. Numerous approaches, concepts and reports only recently referred to this relationship between both areas. Meanwhile, this relationship has been subject of reflection in various disciplines. Major questions are:

- How can the relationship between culture and technology be described conceptually?
- To what an extent can the relationship of technology and culture in connection with communication media (book, image, film, radio, TV) be understood as a specific one?
- Which relevance do innovations have in the interdependence of culture and technology and which relevance does this interdependence have to innovations?
- In which way does our culture design "future", i.e. which technical, social, and cultural circumstances of the presence are considered in an extrapolating manner?
- In which way is culture "objectified" in technology, to what an extent is the handling of technology influenced by cultural aspects, and how do cultural aspects influence technology and design it?

These few questions illustrate that "technology and culture" is a field of work that can and has to be further developed in a perspective manner. Moreover, the relevance of this field of research is presently growing with globalization, due to technology transfer and intercultural communication. It becomes increasingly obvious, however, that this area can only be studied successfully by a joint effort of humanists, social scientists, cultural scientists, and engineers. Hence, it is required to integrate and structure the existing disciplinary approaches and results.

The "Karlsruher Studien Technik und Kultur" (Karlsruhe Studies on Technology and Culture) wish to further this development and structurization work.

*

The idea of the present third volume of *Sustainable Development – Relationships to Culture, Knowledge and Ethics* was developed in the course of the international conference "Sustainability 2010: The Cultural Dimension", which took place in July 2010 in Berlin.

The emergence of a global and technological world and its accelerating, dissemination before the beginning of the 21st century does not only give rise to technological, economic, social, environmental, political, and educational tasks. Significant philosophical questions, epistemic reflections, and cultural debates result. In this connection, we, mankind, have special information processing capabilities Aristotle called "theoretical and practical reasoning". Presently, we are needing discussions about new contexts and contests not least, because our planet is a global and technological network of living information. The aim of this book is to provide information about epistemic, ethical, and cultural implications of contemporary changes and emerging challenges on an interdisciplinary and international level.

The Editors

Preface

Looking back, in 1987 the World Commission on Environment and Development (the Brundtland Commission) published a global report – *Our Common Future* – that analysed the links between development and environment, and challenged policy-makers to consider the global interrelationships among environment, economic and social issues. The report examined emerging global challenges in six issues: population and human resources, food security, species and ecosystems, energy, industry, and urbanization. The Brundtland Commission recommended institutional and legal changes in six broad areas to address these challenges: getting at the sources, dealing with the effects, assessing global risks, making informed choices, providing the legal means, and investing in our future. The report of the Brundtland Commission defined sustainable development internationally as "development that meets the needs of the present generation without compromising the ability of future generations to meet their own needs". The commission further explained that, "the concept of sustainable development implies limits – not absolute limits but limitations imposed by the present state of technology and social organization on environmental resources and by the ability of the biosphere to absorb the effects of human activities".

In 2007 the United Nations Environment Programme published the *Global Environment Outlook 4: Environment for Development (GEO-4)* report 20 years after the Brundtland Commission produced its seminal work. This work was a comprehensive UN report on the environment, prepared by about 390 experts and reviewed by more than 1,000 others across the world. The GEO-4 report assessed the current state of the global atmosphere, land, water and biodiversity, described the changes since 1987, and identified priorities for action. It examined institutional developments and changes in thought since the mid-1980s, and explored the relationships involving environment, development and human well-being. This inquiry reviewed major environmental, social and economic trends, and their impacts on environment and human well-being, and provided options to help achieve sustainable development.

According to GEO-4, over the past 20 years, the international community has cut, by 95 per cent, the production of ozone-layer damaging chemicals; created a greenhouse gas emission reduction treaty along with innovative carbon trading and carbon offset markets; supported a rise in terrestrial protected areas to cover roughly 12 per cent of the Earth, and devised numerous important instruments covering issues from biodiversity and desertification to the trade in hazardous wastes and living modified organisms. But today humanity uses the equivalent of 1.3 planets to provide the resources we use and absorb our waste. This means it now takes the Earth one year and four months to regenerate what we use in a year. Moderate UN scenarios suggest that if current population and consumption trends continue, by the mid 2030s we will need the equivalent of two Earths to support us. And of course, we only have one: one planet and many people; one world and many cultural issues.

GEO-4 recalls the Brundtland Commission's statement that the world does not face separate crises: the environmental crisis, the development crisis and the energy crisis are all one. In this way, the idea of 'sustainability culture' is not a peripheral consequence of the philosophy and management of sustainable development; it is, rather, of central importance to it. The environmental crisis is a cultural crisis. Environmental change and development challenges are caused by the same sets of drivers. They include population change, economic processes, scientific and technological innovations, distribution patterns, and cultural, social, political and institutional processes. To be able to determine more precisely the role and function of the idea of sustainability, we need to get to the core of cultural practice and identity; and to get there, we need to consider first of all the interest underlying cultural reality and secondly the fundamental assumptions motivated by that interest in our (un)sustainable societies.

We still lack analysis of the role and significance of the culture for sustainable development. To anticipate hypothetically and empirically such analyses, we may, however, present several scholars who have studied and investigated issues concerning this realm. The aim of this book is to provide information about the epistemic, ethical and cultural implications of those contemporary changes and emerging challenges. The emergence of a global and technological world and its accelerating dissemination at the beginning of the 21st century not only raises technological, economic, social, environmental, political and educational tasks. Significant philosophical questions and epistemic reflections also arise, designing a new paradigm for sustainability. We – *homo sapiens* – recognize that we are no longer, and never really were the biological masters and possessors of Nature that Descartes imagined for our role in the world. At the present time we need new epistemic contexts and contests not least because our planet is covered by a global and technological network of living information.

Concerning the cultural dimension of sustainable development we need a better understanding in two directions: first, culture as a condition for sustainable development, and second, culture as an aim of sustainable development. And: The cultural dimension of sustainable development includes two different main topics, cultural heritage on the on side and specific (sustainable!) patterns of action (patterns of consummation, of traffic, ...) on the other side.

First analyses in the field of the relationships between sustainable development and culture have two conclusions as a result:

- there is a necessity of a "culture of sustainable development";

- there is a necessity of a cultural change in the direction of sustainable development.

This is the background of this book which consists of two sections: section 1 treats of methodological questions, conceptual debates and frameworks around culture and sustainability, Section 2 presents epistemic topics and ethical dilemmas.

This book has been facilitated by the Research Project UNESCO 08/20, supported by the UNESCO Chair for Sustainable Development and Environmental Education at the University of the Basque Country (UPV/EHU). It was also facilitated and supported by the Karlsruhe Institute of Technology (KIT), Institute for Technology Assessment and Systems Analysis (ITAS). To all these institutions and the contributors we – the editors – present the most sincere expressions of thanks for the publication of this volume. We all are grateful and appreciative for their work and ideas.

Donostia-San Sebastián/Karlsruhe, June 2011

Ignacio Ayestaran
Gerhard Banse
Oliver Parodi

Part 1

Methodological Questions, Conceptual Debates and Frameworks

Conflict-resolution in the Context of Sustainable Development

Naturalistic versus Culturalistic Approaches

Armin Grunwald

1 Introduction

The imperative of sustainability has often been criticized to the effect that too much is read into it, that it does not exclude anything, that it permits no differentiation, and that it generates a false sense of harmony. In this paper, the thesis is proposed that, in contrary, conflicts arise on all of the levels of making the concept of sustainable development work – not only when concrete political measures are put to debate but already in making the first steps to clarify the meaning of sustainable development.

Conflicts, however, are mostly not an issue in debates on sustainable development. Recent papers and books (cf. Krainer/Trattnigg 2007; Parodi et al. 2010) include a lot of valuable contributions and reflections on culture and sustainability but non-intendedly seem to exclude the issue of conflict. Even in the context of decision-making (cf. Krainer 2007) where conflicts occur as a rule no emphasis is given to them. Only the fields of politics and governance conflicts and conflict-solving are thematized, even regularly only along the well-known tensions between economy and ecology, or between economy and the social.

On the contrary, I will put the issue of conflicts around sustainable development into the heart of this paper. My main message is that conflicts are not to be avoided but to be managed in a civilian way in order to push societal developments towards sustainable development. In my perception sustainable development is too often related with issues of consensus – which of course is wishful but which is only seldom achievable in modern pluralistic societies.

Several types of conflict will be uncovered and distinguished in this paper.[1] Such conflicts are, regularly, rooted in plural societal values, different images of humankind and nature, and different ideas about future society. The paper suggests that these conflicts could and should be used to define the more concrete societal understanding of

---

1   This paper draws on earlier work (cf. Grunwald 2005) and uses several text passages from that paper.

sustainability and ways to approach it. Therefore, such conflicts are to be made transparent. The approach of settling them should be understood as an essential component of the societal constitution of the content and the interpretation of sustainability. It is stated and argued for that new cultures of conflict-solving should be established across existing cultures and traditions. This would lead to the result that, in the scientific occupation with sustainability, a new field of activity is opened up for those disciplines which can contribute to this objective, such as the cultural, social, and political sciences, jurisprudence, psychology, and ethics, while, on the other hand, it can be shown that there are limitations to the conflict-solving capacities of natural sciences and earth systems analysis.

2   Sustainability as a Conflict-generating Vision

Sustainability as a societal vision is, on the one hand – at least on the political-programmatic level – not only potentially acceptable, but does, in fact, meet with correspondingly broad approval across all societal groups and political positions, nationally and internationally. The number of nations which have signed and ratified the documents of Rio 1992 and the corresponding follow-up papers and the numerous local or regional activities are impressive.

On the other hand, sustainability's conflict potential cannot be overlooked. As soon as relatively concrete goals or even strategies of societal action for attaining sustainability are put on the agenda – at the latest – it becomes obvious that the usual antagonistic societal values and interests are lurking behind the programmatic consensus.

Due to this fact, the opinion is often expressed that sustainability is a concept without content, or that sustainability is a harmonistic wrapper (meant here in an analogous sense to that of the definition in the field of biblical hermeneutics. The harmonistic tradition smoothes the disparities in the biblical text in a manner that imposes greater strain on faith than do the disparities themselves, i.e.: sustainability is, according to this objection, supposed to create a harmoniousness which in reality does not exist) over heterogeneous and incompatible goals, and can therefore only have rhetorical functions. It has sunken, so some people argue, to the level of arbitrariness, and no longer has any power to "make a difference". In order to refute these contentions, it would be necessary, on the one hand, to make clear what the concept of sustainability comprises and what not. On the other hand, the principle of sustainability should not appear to be merely a plaything of conflicting interests, but has to demonstrate and realize possibilities for settling such conflicts in a constructive and, optimally, in a "sustainable" manner.

The objection that nothing more than harmonistic meaninglessness is hidden behind the concept of sustainability, that talking about sustainability would therefore either be of no consequence, or could be arbitrarily instrumentalized or misused, can be interpreted in a number of ways which allow a better understanding of that objection:

- *Sustainability as mere design*: The postulate of sustainability has, in this version of the objection, no content. Of course, nobody can be opposed to a person's pursuing his or her economic interests in a sustainable manner which "satisfies the needs of the present generation without compromising the ability of future generations to satisfy their own needs" (Brundtland Commission 1987, p. 24, no. 27), but acceptance of this understanding says nothing specific regarding content. People who can all generally agree with this statement can still compete further for diametrically opposed aims.
- *Sustainability as an ideological illusion*: The concept of sustainability conceals in this manner the conflicts of interests among the real actors and the actual power constellations. It is instrumentalized as an ostensible legitimization of power and of particular vested interests, for instance, in the question of the relationship between securing continued affluence in the industrialized nations and the perspectives for the developing countries. The danger is that each social actor or group may define its "own" sustainability – the farmers, the industry, social movements, political parties, authorities or others. All of them could then claim to promote sustainable development but with using diverging or contradictory understandings of sustainability.
- *Sustainability as a utopian hope*: A further point of critique is that the concept of sustainability is overtaxed, in any case, whenever more than ecological sustainability only is subsumed under it (cf. Knaus/Renn 1998). If sustainability should be used as a collective designation for everything "noble, helpful, and good", then this would be impracticable, could lead to arbitrary conclusions, and would arouse expectations which cannot be fulfilled. The concept of sustainability as an integrative-utopian aspiration is, according to this contention, a harmonistic illusion which blocks the view onto the real problems.

These doubts have to be taken seriously – at least for the time being. A theory of sustainability which lays claim to relevance in practice and to presenting contributions towards solving societal problems has to make clear how it reacts to these objections. The concept, theory, and operationalization of sustainability have to fulfil at least the following requirements in order to avoid slipping into arbitrariness:

- *Specification of the fields of application*: exactly what they apply to, and what not must be stated, i.e., a field of responsibility for sustainability must be delimited from questions for which sustainability is not relevant.

- *Unambiguous judgements*: distinctions must be made between "sustainable", and "unsustainable" or "less sustainable" possibilities within the areas concerned.
- *Operationalizability*: concrete ascription must be made of these judgements (sustainable/unsustainable) to societal circumstances or possible developments (e.g., by means of indicators to be derived from the concept and theory of sustainability but also by using explanatory cause/effect knowledge about the developments under consideration).

It turns out that conflicts over sustainability do not first arise – as has often been maintained – at the point when concrete measures are discussed. Rather conflicts are unavoidable as early as on the conceptual level where the basic understanding of sustainable development has to be clarified. At least the following types of conflict can break out at this stage:

(1) *Conflicts of demarcation*: What belongs to the subject area that the principle of sustainability should be applied to, and what does not? Is it solely a matter of responsibility for the future or of distributive justice in the present? Is it a question of conservation, or of development? What should be protected or developed under the banner of sustainability? Which legitimate societal goals are there beyond or outside of the concept of sustainability? In the integrative concept of sustainability (cf. Kopfmüller et al. 2001, p. 172) the field of application is defined, for example, so, that the sustainability rules are formulated not as the sum total of all desirable societal goals, but as minimum requirements for a lastingly humane existence. Societal goals which extend above and beyond this level no longer belong to sustainability's areas of study and evaluation. The exact determination of this line of demarcation is, however, obviously connected with societal conflicts, because it is neither on the national nor on the global level at all clear what should be included in these minimum requirements, what the attribute "humane" includes, and what it excludes.

(2) *Conflicts about the substitutability of different parts of the overall societal capital*: Every generation disposes over a certain productive potential, which is made up of various factors (natural capital, real capital, human capital, knowledge capital). Sustainable development demands in general that the stock of capital which exists within a generation be handed down as undiminished as possible to future generations – whereby, however, two fundamentally different alternatives are conceivable (cf. Daly 1999, pp. 110ff.). On the one hand, one could stipulate that the sum of natural and human-made capital be constant in the sense of an economy-wide total; on the other hand, one could require that every single component of itself has to be preserved intact. The former path is sensible if one assumes that natural and human-made parts of the overall capital are completely interchangeable (weak sustainability). The latter path is advisable if one assumes that human-made and

natural capital stand in a complementary relationship to one another (strong sustainability). The controversy over both of these strategies, that is, over the question, how the heritage which is to be handed down to future generations should be composed, is one of the central problems of the sustainability debate (cf. Ott 2001). There are also intermediate positions, sometimes designated as "sensible sustainability" (cf. Serageldin/Steer 1994). Due to this approach, the substitution of natural capital by human-made capital is held to be admissible to a limited extent, as long as nature's basic functions (the immaterial ones as well) are maintained.

(3) *Conflicts over priorities*: Whenever it is a question of the mutual relations of the various (ecological, economic, social, and political) dimensions of sustainability, or of the relation between inter- and intragenerational justice, careful consideration and weighing of priorities are imperative. The proposed approaches to sustainability in the various dimensions will not always mutually reinforce each other and lead to "win-win"-situations. For instance, the precept of conserving landscapes of a particularly characteristic nature and beauty can come into conflict with the need for securing an independent livelihood, as far as the local population is concerned – a classical conflict in environmental conservation policy. It is then necessary to weigh up goals and values and to set priorities which, as a rule, quite obviously give rise to societal conflicts.

(4) *Conflicts over the choice of indicators*: Appropriate and meaningful indicators for sustainability cannot be derived logically and deductively from the sustainability rules. Rather, different indicators are conceivable, which respectively set different accents. The determination of indicators influences further questions, such as, which parameters should be chosen for long-term observation, or for which parameters targets should be set and commitments be made. Because the choice of indicators is, therefore, not value-neutral, it can be fraught with conflicts – and often is, as the pertinent discussion shows. These conflict levels make clear that conflicts over sustainability not only occur, as is often discussed, on the strategic level of concrete measures and their realization, but that they are inherent in the very conceptualization of sustainability. In addition, the usual conflicts arise in the further strategic operationalization of sustainability whenever it is a question of specific measures or their consequences. The distribution of the burdens and risks of measures for promoting sustainability is, as a matter of course, conflict-laden in a pluralistic society.

(5) *Conflicts of distribution*: Further conflict potentials can arise on the strategic level when it comes to translating the principle of sustainable development into concrete responsibilities of action for societal actors. When, for example, one has to decide which contribution the transportation industry and which the power supply industry should bring toward realizing a national CO_2-reduction target. When the contributions of various nations to common goals are set, quite substantial conflicts

of interests flare up (as could be observed, for instance, in the Kyoto follow-up conferences). On the one hand, conflicts of distribution arise because of the winner-loser problems, and on the other hand, due to the finiteness of scarce resources, such as drinking water or soil.

These different types of sustainability conflicts mentioned have their origin in the diversity of the conflicts inherent in a pluralistic society (as, for example, differing conceptions of justice, of responsibility, of the role of the welfare state, or of the economic system). Different and contradicting interests between social actors, between NGOs and industry, between political parties, or between developed and developing countries are leading to such conflicts. These conflicts do not just vanish into thin air by their common relevance for sustainability, but come into play again when sustainability is to be made operable. This is in no way surprising.

Of greater interest with respect to this paper is the fact that not only already existing societal conflicts play a role, but that the imperative of sustainability itself is also the source of additional conflicts. As soon as the question of justice – and this is the essence of sustainability – is extended beyond the small national or regional circle of the present generation to the global scale and to future generations, completely new questions and additional distributive problems arise – with the corresponding lines of conflict. In this category belong questions of the sort whether and how much abstinence can be expected of those presently living (in the western nations) in the interest of future generations, and if so, how this abstinence should be distributed among and within nations. This situation is the clearest proof of the fact that the principle of sustainability is anything but harmonic, and can even be the origin of conflicts.

It is the extension of the time and space dimension inherent to the imperative of sustainable development which leads to new types of challenges in the reflections on justice and equity. Conflicts between the assumed needs and interests of future generations – obviously, there is already a problem of knowing enough about them – and the interests of people living today arise. Why should we renounce on realising certain needs in favour of future generations which we will never meet? The global dimension of sustainability (cf. Kopfmüller 2003) leads to a more narrow contact of different traditions and cultures in attempting to arrive at a common understanding of sustainable development. Different concepts of nature, different views of the relationship between the individual and society, different religious and cultural traditions, different conceptions of justice enter into the sustainability conflicts. Solutions in this respect will require identifying the explicit and implicit contradictions and divergencies between different cultures in the five fields of conflict mentioned above and dealing with them in a constructive way.

It therefore becomes apparent that conflicts are an inseparable constituent of discussions on sustainability, of the way to make it more concrete, and of its societal implementation. It would be "harmonistic" to ignore this fact. The reproach of har-monism rightly draws our attention to the fact that disclosure of the lines of conflict is necessary in order to be able to talk "honestly" about sustainability and in order to avoid the above mentioned dangers of instrumentalization. But in order to refute this contention successfully, it would be necessary to offer advice and strategies how the various types of conflict can be settled constructively.

3 Approaches to Conflict Resolution

In the following, the conceptual question on which cognitive and conceptual basis these conflicts can and should be settled in the interest of sustainability stands in the foreground. In the form of an exaggerated confrontation (cf. on this subject in general Hartmann/Janich 1996), we distinguish between a

- naturalistic conflict management in which, with scientific methods, optimal and, in a certain sense, "objective" paths to sustainability are determined, and a
- culturalistic conflict management, in which, besides scientific knowledge, societal discourses and normative reflection would play an important role.

3.1 Naturalistic Approach

The naturalistic concept is based on the assumption – to put it simply – that sustainability means lasting stability in the relationship between society and the environment (cf. Schellnhuber/Wenzel 1999). It would then be science's responsibility to determine the carrying capacity and the critical loads of natural systems (cf. Kates et al. 2001). Because tolerance limits can hardly be defined empirically without exceeding them, and because this sort of empirical "test" rules out itself (because of its negative and possibly irreversible consequences in the sense of global change), a key role is ascribed to the integrative modelling and simulation of interactions between humankind and the environment (cf. Alcamo 2002; Rotmans 1999). In this manner – one hopes –, "objective" standards for sustainability could be formulated, which would make the societal conflicts – at least in the questions treated by scientific methods – unnecessary. The conflicts, with their subjective and ideological aspects, would be decided virtually "objectively".

One has also tried to transfer the concept of "carrying capacity", which has been adopted from the ecological debate, into the societal sphere: "[…] the insight has been gaining ground that, in the areas of the economic and social systems as well, there are limits of load capacity, which – in the case of overtaxing – can lead to similar consequences (from loss of productivity to the collapse of the system concerned)" (DBT 1998, p. 17; critique of this standpoint in Kopfmüller et al. 2001, chap. 4.1.2). The latitude left for humanity would, according to this conception, in principle have to be defined by the "objective" load-carrying capacity of the ecological, economic, and social systems. The determination of these limits would be science's responsibility, which could therefore decide the resulting conflicts objectively. Making sustainable development work would be a task for optimising the future path of more or less calculable natural and social systems. For the role of societal and therefore "non-objectivizable" conflict management, there would remain only the task of setting the safety margins in a so-called "guard-rail" concept.

The question is to what extent the expectations set in the naturalistic approach – to decide societal conflicts scientifically – are justified. The following problems present themselves:

- Load limits and carrying capacities can, as a rule, not be determined solely by the natural sciences (for the case of ecological problems). The problems are often of a character other than the eutrophication of a body of water by phosphates (in which case there actually is a clear limit of carrying capacity), but are rather a question of a more or less moderate increase of the risk of biohazard by certain anthropogenically-influenced input without a sharply-defined limit of load factor. For the limits of carrying capacity of social or economic systems, this holds true to a much greater extent.
- The intergenerational aspect of sustainability confronts the present generation with questions of long-term responsibility, and therefore with the question of an equitable distribution of the use of the natural and social resources through time. Questions of distributive justice cannot be decided by reference to results of earth systems analysis.
- Questions of the just distribution of chances for making use of the various types of capital, especially natural resources, cannot be decided naturalistically, because they involve ethical problems and concern internal questions of societal organization on the global level.
- The incompleteness and the provisional nature of (scientific) knowledge lead to the fact that societal actions with regard to sustainability always include risk. The resulting conflicts over risk acceptance cannot be decided naturalistically, but require societal discourses.

It therefore turns out that the naturalistic attempt at conflict management by giving an "objectively" best solution according to sustainability aspects encounters limits at several points. The conclusion is, therefore, that exactly the central conflicts of sustainability – questions of the just inter- and intragenerational distribution of chances for utilizing natural resources, questions of priorities in conflicts inherent in sustainability, as well as questions of handling the inevitable problems of dealing with risk – cannot be answered by the naturalistic approach. Knowledge and values cannot be kept distinctly separate (cf. Funtowicz/Ravetz 1993), but rather, societal values pervade even the results provided by a "sustainability science". Lines of conflict have their effects on these results – for this reason, scientific findings cannot even logically be used to solve the societal conflicts.

Therefore it does not seem surprising that, in discussions on and around the subject of "sustainability science", the level of political and normative conflicts is barely even mentioned. In the original manifest on "sustainability science" (cf. Kates et al. 2001), the word "conflict" does not even occur. If the purpose is seen as providing systemic knowledge so that "different social actors to work in concert, even with much uncertainty and limited information" (Kates et al. 2001, p. 641), then the plane of legitimate political negotiation and of ethical reflection is ignored. The background assumption is presumably that the "systemic knowledge" as a result of scientific research on the relationship between the environment and society (e.g., in the form of integrative modelling within earth systems analysis Schellnhuber/Wenzel 1999) decides in a naturalistic manner which actors are in the right in cases of conflict. This orientation has been tempered in further development of the concept; nonetheless, this question still has to be discussed further (cf. Grunwald/Lingner 2002).

3.2 Culturalistic Approach

This brings up the question of the culturalistic approaches to conflict management. Here, we can distinguish at least three different schools of thought:

(1) the *political-decisionistic approach* leaves the decision in societal conflicts to the political system;
(2) the *discursive-participative approach* relies on organizing broad societal communication;
(3) the *ethical/justice-theoretical approach* offers conflict management on the basis of universal ethical principles.

These approaches have their respective strengths and weaknesses, which cannot be discussed here in detail (cf. Grunwald 2000 for the case of engineering ethics). We only want to call to mind the facts that the decisionistic approach contradicts the polycentric self-understanding of modern societies, that the ethical/justice-theoretical approach is fraught with problems of implementation, and that, with regard to the discursive-participative approach, the question poses itself, why societal dialogues, in which decisions about acceptability are made, and in which power and interest constellations build the foundations, should work to the advantage of sustainability, if the actors' egoism and preoccupation with the present play a decisive role (cf. Brand/Fürst 2002, pp. 32ff.) There is no royal road to the solution of these problems, but their solution would require a combination of different approaches from one case to another.

In particular, it is insufficient, even in the culturalistic perspective, merely to refer to the societal dialogue on sustainability. Leaving this dialogue to itself would mean refraining from doing everything in one's power to make use of available potentials for rationality in acquiring knowledge and in seeking orientation. The societal dialogue and its organization, down to the establishment of formal, legitimized decision-making procedures, determine, in the final analysis, in which manner the lines of conflict within the concept of sustainability can be broken up. What is decisive, however, is that these processes are not run "blindly", but are "informed": informed by the results of interlinked models, by knowledge about the systems involved, by the knowledge about the impacts of human activities; informed, too, about the "culturalistic" components of the conflicts, namely by ethics, by the theory of justice, and by the social sciences.

The question is therefore not that of an objective-naturalistic transition to sustainability (cf. Kates et al. 2001), but of the scientific accompaniment of a societal process of gaining awareness, opinion formation, conflict management, and decision-making, in which sustainability is, normatively, first constituted – with observance of the ethical dimension of responsibility for the future. In order to be able to propose some more concrete ideas to enter this way of proceeding, it is necessary to explain the basic understanding of sustainable development in more detail.

4   Conclusions

Constructive conflict management is, obviously, a communicative endeavour. Conflict management can be made by argumentation or by bargaining, by different forms of negotiation and mediation, by participative approaches and by broad debate. In this respect the integrative concept of sustainable development (cf. Kopfmüller et al. 2001) provides some advice in which direction such communicative procedures should be developed and applied for sustainability conflicts and for institutions supporting those types of "sustainable communication patterns". The following issues are relevant in this respect:

- Society's ability to respond;
- society's reflexivity;
- self-organization;
- balance of power.

It is of crucial importance that the impacts and consequences of approaches to make sustainability work are uncovered (reflexivity) and that an open debate is possible (balance of power). Furthermore, it has to be ensured that the results of those reflexive processes can be taken into account in the relevant decision-making processes (ability to respond). The solution of conflicts at the level of people directly concerned is preferred compared to top-down-approaches (self-organization, subsidiarity).

In this way, it becomes clear that approaching sustainable development is a societal endeavour for which cultural resources are needed in a double manner. At first, they are needed as inputs to the debates, as standpoints and experiences in the conflicts and discussions about sustainability. At second, a new "culture" of conflict resolution is required which extends existing experience because of the extension of the scope of sustainability in time and space, compared to other issues in ongoing debates. This situation forms a formidable challenge for all societal groups.

This has considerable consequences, amongst others, for the role of the humanities and for the need for further research. Obviously, deficits of knowledge about the relationship between humankind and the environment have to be filled, systemic relationships of the human economic system have to be investigated, the foreseeable effects of societal-political interventions in even more complex cause-and-effect relationships have to be studied, modelled, and simulated, in order to make forecasts about the potential success of measures under the aspect of sustainability possible. All of this knowledge, which can often only be provided by integrative modelling, is indispensable for a policy of sustainability.

But – and the deliberations on sustainability conflicts and how to manage them point to this insight – this alone is not enough. Many, if not the majority, of the sustainability conflicts on the various levels mentioned cannot be decided naturalistically (cf. part 3.1). They much rather require an open societal discussion, informed by the sciences and the humanities. As soon as it is a question of conflicts based on divergent conceptions of humanity, plans for the future, and ideas of a good society, ethics as well as the social and the political sciences are called for (on the level of negotiations) to contribute to successful and peaceable conflict management.

Conflict management on the levels of the sustainability discussion can itself be understood as a process oriented on the imperative of sustainability. The instrumental rules of sustainability (cf. Kopfmüller et al. 2001, chap. 6) show that demands for self-organization, reflectiveness, and the balance of power have consequences for the manner in which the corresponding conflicts should be settled (these rules are obviously far removed from any sort of naturalism). Sustainability's demands for equal opportunity and participation are in this respect also not inconsequential.

In sum, the following requirements for the formulation of a culturalistic concept for the management of sustainability conflicts follow out of the above discussion:

- Conflict management has to be carried out in a participative and discursive manner, in keeping with the corresponding provisions of the Rio documents. This requirement forms an inseparable component of sustainability.
- In accordance with the instrumental rules of sustainability, the appropriate instrumental and political frameworks have to be established for this purpose. Espe-

cially, this leads to the requirement that societal processes of decision-making have to ensure that enough time and resources are available to the effect that careful reflection ex ante is possible and that there are opportunities to feed the results of that reflection back into the decision-making process.

- Negotiation of the conflicts has to be informed by comprehensive knowledge of the consequences (e.g., of the foreseeable effects of unsustainable developments, of the implementation of measures, or of societal transformation, and be based on knowledge. This implies an important role for the sciences and humanities.

- In normative respects, they also have to be oriented on ethical advice (e.g., with regard to responsibility for the future, justice, and distributive problems): the co-operation between philosophical ethics, the social sciences dealing empirically with conflict management, and extra-scientific actors in the field becomes more important.

- Input from and engagement by the various societal groups is indispensable. Especially the world religions are obliged to bring their experience concerning humankind and history into such conflict-solving processes.

These requirements indicate the dimensions of the challenges – challenges to societal communication and to the societal dialogue as well as to its comprehensive, interdisciplinary scientific support, which extends from research on natural systems and anthropogenic influences on them to ethics and conflict research.

References

Alcamo, J. (2002): Three Issues for Improving Integrated Models: Uncertainty, Social Science and Legitimacy. In: Gethmann, C. F.; Lingner, S. (eds.): Integrative Modellierung für Nachhaltige Entwicklung. Heidelberg, pp. 3-14

Brand, K.-W.; Fürst, V. (2002): Voraussetzungen und Probleme einer Politik der Nachhaltigkeit. In: Brand, K.-W. (ed.): Politik der Nachhaltigkeit. Voraussetzungen, Probleme, Chancen – eine kritische Diskussion. Berlin, pp. 15-110 (in German)

Brundtland Commission (1987): World Commission on Development and Environment: Our Common Future. Oxford

Daly, H. (1999): Wirtschaft jenseits von Wachstum. Die Volkswirtschaftslehre nachhaltiger Entwicklung. Salzburg (in German)

DBT (1998): Abschlußbericht der Enquete-Kommission "Schutz des Menschen und der Umwelt – Ziele und Rahmenbedingungen einer nachhaltig zukunftsverträglichen Entwicklung". Konzept Nachhaltigkeit – Vom Leitbild zur Umsetzung. Bundestagsdrucksache 13/11200. Bonn (in German)

Funtowicz, S.; Ravetz, J. (1993): The Emergence of Post-Normal Science. In: Schomberg, R. von (ed.): Science, Politics and Morality. Scientific Uncertainty and Decision Making. Dordrecht a.o., pp. 85-123

Grunwald, A. (2000): Against Over-Estimating the Role of Ethics in Technology. In: Science and Engineering Ethics, Vol. 6, pp. 181-196

Grunwald, A. (2005): Conflicts and Conflict-solving as Chances to Make the Concept of Sustainable Development Work. In: Wilderer, P. A.; Schroeder, E. D.; Kopp, H. (eds.): Global Sustainability. The Impact of Local Cultures. A New Perspective for Science and Engineering, Economics and Politics. Weinheim, pp. 107-122

Grunwald, A.; Lingner, S. (2002): Nachhaltigkeit und integrative Modellierung. In: Gethmann, C. F.; Lingner, S. (eds.): Integrative Modellierung für Nachhaltige Entwicklung. Heidelberg, pp. 71-106 (in German)

Hartmann, D.; Janich, P. (1996): Methodischer Kulturalismus. In: Hartmann, D.; Janich, P. (eds.): Methodischer Kulturalismus. Zwischen Naturalismus und Postmoderne. Frankfurt am Main, pp. 9-69 (in German)

Kates, R. W.; Clark, W. C.; Corell, R.; Hall, J. M.; Jaeger, C.; Lowe, I.; McCarthy, J. J.; Schellnhuber, H. J.; Bolin, B.; Dickson, N. M.; Faucheux, S.; Gallopin, G. C.; Grübler, A.; Huntley, B.; Jäger, J.; Jodha, N. S.; Kasperson, R. E.; Mabogunje, A.; Matson, P.; Mooney, H.; Moore, B.; O'Riordan, T.; Svedin, U. (2001): Environment and Development: Sustainability Science. In: Science, Vol. 292, No. 5517 (27 April), pp. 641-642

Knaus, A.; Renn, O. (1998): Den Gipfel vor Augen. Unterwegs in eine nachhaltige Zukunft. Marburg (in German)

Kopfmüller, J. (ed.) (2003): Den globalen Wandel gestalten. Forschung und Politik für einen nachhaltigen globalen Wandel. Berlin (in German)

Kopfmüller, J.; Brandl, V.; Jörissen, J.; Paetau, M.; Banse, G.; Coenen, R.; Grunwald, A. (2001): Nachhaltige Entwicklung integrativ betrachtet. Konstitutive Elemente, Regeln, Indikatoren. Berlin (in German)

Krainer, L. (2007): Nachhaltige Entscheidungen. Zur Organisation demokratisch-partizipativer Entscheidungsfindungsprozesse. In: Krainer, L.; Trattnigg, R. (eds.): Kulturelle Nachhaltigkeit. Konzepte, Perspektiven, Positionen. Munich, pp. 169-199 (in German)

Krainer, L.; Trattnigg, R. (eds.) (2007): Kulturelle Nachhaltigkeit. Konzepte, Perspektiven, Positionen. Munich (in German)

Ott, K. (2001): Eine Theorie „starker" Nachhaltigkeit. In: Natur und Kultur, Vol. 2, pp. 55-75 (in German)

Parodi, O.; Banse, G.; Schaffer, A. (eds.) (2010): Wechselspiele: Kultur und Nachhaltigkeit. Annäherungen an ein Spannungsfeld. Berlin (in German)

Rotmans, J. (1999): Global Change and Sustainable Development. Towards an Integrated Conceptual Model. In: Schellnhuber, H.-J.; Wenzel, V. (eds.): Earth Systems Analysis. Integrating Science for Sustainability. Berlin a.o., pp 421-450

Schellnhuber, H.-J.; Wenzel, V. (eds.) (1999): Earth Systems Analysis. Integrating Science for Sustainability. Berlin a.o.

Serageldin, I.; Steer, A. (1994): Epilogue: Expanding the Capital Stock. In: Serageldin, I.; Steer, A. (eds.): Making Development Sustainable. From Concepts to Action. Washington, D.C. (World-Bank), pp. 30-32

Culture and Culturality
Approaching a Multi-faceted Concept

Robert Hauser, Gerhard Banse

1   Concepts of Culture – The Plurality of the Concept of Culture

As early as in classical antiquity, culture occupied a central position in occidental thought.[*] Culture, in its original classical meaning, i.e. the Latin *cultura*, refers to cultivating fields (cf. "agriculture"), meaning tilling, cultivating, planting, as well as mental care and education of intellectual capabilities (cf. Pfeiffer 1997, p. 743). In the Middle Ages, the term hardly played a role in the "Germanic" language area. Only towards the end of the 17th century culture, after having appeared in German texts in its Latin form, became integrated into German, achieving greater significance as a concept (though with partly very different meanings).

This highlights the first difficulty when dealing with the concept of culture. As a consequence of its long tradition, the subdisciplines of the humanities and social sciences now feature a multitude of concepts of culture side by side, all of them defined and used in different ways (cf. Gerhards 2000, p. 16). As a consequence, the concept of culture is far from being sharply defined even in the literature of the field. Disciplines as different as philosophy, sociology, anthropology, and interdisciplinary schools, such as "cultural studies", attempted to describe and characterize what "culture" means from their points of view. Epistemological research in this area is multi-faceted, historically speaking, and continues to grow.

This multiplicity is so pronounced also because, depending on the purpose, object and method of a study, it may make sense to opt for a different concept of culture. Generally, concepts of culture can be distinguished with respect to access (qualitative and quantitative or mixed forms) and level of a study (micro-, meso-, macrolevels). However, even within specific disciplines, the concept of culture often remains vague and ambivalent. Theoretical difficulties begin with the many forms culture can assume, and they end with the paradoxes invariably encountered when looking at the phenomenon of culture from a scientific point of view.

---

[*]   This contribution is based in large parts on Hauser 2009.

Especially three (seemingly) conflicting characteristics of culture cause difficulties (cf. Demorgon/Molz 1996, pp. 43f.):

(1) *Continuity and change:* While culture, on the one hand, ensures the preservation of cultural heritage by means of tradition (holidays, memorial days, etc.), lasting new patterns, techniques, and practices of culture keep arising, often as a result of specific influences.
(2) *Standardization and differentiation:* Culture is frequently described as orientation or standardization of values or patterns of behaviour, thus as uniform; on the other hand, however, there are also individual variations, subcultures, and miniature collectives making cultures appear divergent.
(3) *Openness and boundaries:* Cultures, seen as national cultures, on the one hand, are open to other cultures and cultural patterns (which can also cause them to change) but, at the same time, also represent boundaries of a community: Only those knowing and understanding the common symbols, such as language, history, and institutions, can find orientation and behave accordingly. Behaviour adequate to a culture indicates who belongs and who does not.

2   History – The Genesis of the Concept of Culture

While the classical concept of culture implied cultivation (of soil, plants) or education (of persons), it became broader and was redefined in part from the 17th century onward. Over the following periods of time, the concept of culture was related to the three major concepts of enlightened thought: culture/nature (cf. Pufendorf 2002), culture/civilization (cf. Kant 1977), and culture/life (cf. Freud 1989) (cf. Reckwitz 2000, pp. 66ff.; cf. also Hubig 2010). In its definition relative to those concepts, and in comparison with them, it acquires different meanings. The resultant definitions of culture may also be referred to as concepts of culture "in the narrow sense". They do not point to an ontic difference but merely to different aspects of the same object (cf. Janich 2005, p. 21).

In the period of Enlightenment, the concept was popularized by Immanuel Kant and Johann Gottfried Herder, becoming a buzzword in philosophical thought. The very civilizatory concept of culture can still be found in the everyday meaning of culture. To this day, the "achievements of civilization", such as theatre, movies, or books, are referred to as cultural products or even high culture. This also reflects Western European thought of the late 19th century, when peoples were still judged by their civilizatory achievements, of course always against the backdrop of one's own "cultural achievements" for comparison: Accordingly, there were highly developed cultures and cultures which were less developed or not developed at all – as a rule, this referred to African or American aborigines. Those were not only devoid of religion, i.e. they were heathen, but also of culture, i.e. civilization.

While Kant "charged" the concept of culture normatively in connection with morals, coupling it to civilization, Herder used concepts of popular psychology to develop the historic-holistic concept of culture, thus recontextualizing it (cf. Herder 1989): "The holistic concept of culture de-universalizes the concept of culture, contextualizing and historicizing it. Culture is no longer a distinguished form of life, cultures rather are specific ways of life of individual collectives in history, and the concept of culture logically occurs in the plural form, referring to the diversity of the totalities of human forms of life in various 'peoples', 'nations', 'communities', 'cultural areas'" (Reckwitz 2005, p. 95).

This makes Herder the first author to establish a broad understanding of culture related neither only to man and nature nor, chiefly in a normative way, to civilization: "*The culture of a people is the bloom of its existence through which it manifests itself in a pleasant but also frail way.* Like human beings coming into this world and knowing nothing – needing to learn what they want to know –, a crude people learns from practice for itself or through contacts with others. However, every kind of human knowledge has its own ambience, i.e. its nature, time, place, and period of life [...]" (Herder 1989, p. 571; original italics, R.H./G.B.).

Culture as used by Herder refers, in a neutral way, to the totality of a historically specific contextualized way of life of a collective in contrast to other collectives. This becomes apparent also in the criticism of contemporary concepts of culture, where he complains: "Nothing is less defined than this word, and nothing is more delusive than its application to entire peoples and periods of time" (Herder 1989, preface, p. 39). The concept of culture coined by Herder in this way had a special impact on the discipline of anthropology, which was still young at that time. In their studies of so-called natural peoples, anthropologists found that some of those not only had produced differentiated societies, but also had many rites, traditions, ceremonies, interpretations of the world, and "cultural products", such as carvings, or the like. Accordingly, they did have culture(s), even if those functioned by different mechanisms, and other values and norms influenced activities. The interpretation of culture began to change with these research findings.

The concepts of culture developed in anthropology, also influenced by the emergence of cultural studies, then more and more resembled the meaning of the Anglo-Saxon term "culture" – in the sense of "everyday culture" – thus establishing a broader concept of culture. To this day, this has incorporated everything of importance to human everyday life. Things mental and things material are regarded as culture or are influenced by culture. This enlarged concept of culture (referred to below as the "broader" concept of culture) is used epistemologically chiefly in a reflexive way, i.e., it serves primarily to compare everyday cultures. Culture as defined in this sense is what distinguishes people's ways of life. Accordingly, it is based mainly on the finding that people developed different ways of life by which they are distinguished (cf. Cappai 2005, pp. 50ff.; Reckwitz 2005, p. 95). This gives rise to a pluralistic concept of culture not referring to *culture* per se, but differentiating between equivalent, yet different cultures in contradistinction to civilizational/normative interpretations. Any culture in this sense seems to be anchored in three units: "[…] in a collective of persons (frequently thought of as a *community), in a shared* space – cultures are associated with geographic spaces – and in a continuity of time – cultures appear to be bound to a *historic tradition"* (Reckwitz 2005, p. 95; emphasis and brackets in the original, R.H./G.B.).

Parallel to the "narrow" and "broad" concepts of culture, a concept of culture developed in the 20th century according to theories of differentiation which strongly influenced especially the social sciences. As a full-blown systematic concept, this concept of culture was found for the first time in systems theory constructivism as described by Talcott Parsons in his evolution theory treatise about functional differentiation in modern societies (cf. Reckwitz 2005, p. 95). This shows culture as a functional societal subsystem, a "fiduciary system", institutionalized mainly in the arts and in education and with the duty of handing down and newly developing interpretations of the world (cf. Parsons 1977).

In the mid-20th century, the "linguistic turn" in linguistics was followed by the "cultural turn": a move away from the narrow normative concept of culture towards a broader concept of culture focusing on associations of meaning. In everyday usage, a very narrow concept of culture can still be found (especially in the public and on the feature pages of newspapers), which is associated mainly with the representatives of culture and, in this way, cultural artefacts, such as books, movies, but also dramas, operas, etc. In this case, the concept of culture, following Kant's interpretation, is linked to civilization and the achievements of civilization, respectively.

In the humanities, this concept of culture was discarded around the middle of the 20th century. This break, which is seen in various scientific disciplines under different names, became apparent first in the linguistic papers by Ludwig Wittgenstein. His work shows him in an epistemological position between studies in the early period (cf. Wittgenstein 2003) and the late period (cf. Wittgenstein 2001), expressed in linguistics in the term "crises of representation" (cf. also Mersch 1999). The fundamental difference lies in the fact that it had been recognized that words, as elements of linguistic systems, derive their significance not from any direct correspondence to the objective world to the elements of which they refer, but rather from their position and their relation with other elements of language. This major difference, which is considered the epistemological turnaround and later referred to as "linguistic turn" (cf. Rorty 1967), means that the meaning of words is detached from concrete representatives, instead emphasizing contexts and reference associations within a linguistic system.

This break also occurred with regard to the concept of culture and was expressed in the term "cultural turn" (cf. Reckwitz 2000, 2005, and others). This means that the concept of culture as civilization or high culture, which used to be associated with the material or immaterial products of these high cultures, is replaced by a concept of culture in which culture means context- or meaning-dependent practices of knowledge, communication and, thus, social and cultural practices, respectively (cf. Reckwitz 2005, p. 96). These practices interact with the environment of human life and existence.

3   Concepts of Culture – Cultural Concepts in Current Research Practice

Current research practice in cultural studies as well as in interdisciplinary and trans-disciplinary research, provided that culture is interpreted as a concept, defines three methodological lines or types of concepts of culture of the "broad" variety according to Jürgen Bolten: *"Material" theories of culture* are mainly based semiotically on the totality of artefacts as meaningful real achievements of a society. Artefacts encompass memorials and monuments as well as factory buildings, tools, or clothes (cf. Bolten 1997, p. 488). *"Mentalist" approaches*, employing cognitive anthropology (cf., e.g., Goodenough 1971), consistently consider culture immaterial. Their interest is devoted less to cultural "perceptus" than to cultural "conceptas". "'Conceptas' means collectively shared values, attitudes, and norms which cannot be described directly as causes of actions and behaviour, but require conclusions drawn, for instance, on the basis of observable reality. In a way, this is the 'cultural memory' or 'knowledge pool', used by communicating parties to obtain interpretations by agreeing on something in the world" (Bolten 1997, p. 488; cf. also Reckwitz 2005, p. 97). *"Functionalist" theories of culture* emphasize the aspect of "making oneself understood". This already denotes a functionalist perspective from which the meaning of the concept of culture again changes – culture is given a foundation in action theory. "Culture" in its functionalist interpretation consequently can be regarded as a system of orientation constitutive of, and necessary for, the social practice of a society, organization or group. This is closely related to the concept of "normality" in the group: Only the existence of specific conventions of social action allows concrete everyday actions to invoke assumptions of normality which are presupposed without being queried (cf. Bolten 1997, p. 488).

The macro-theoretical approaches described above (provided they can be assigned unequivocally) can be summarized as type 3. On the other hand, the micro-theoretical approaches tend to be type 2, relating culture to values and norms as interpretations of systems of symbols. The three variants of the broader concept of culture must not be considered mutually exclusive; on the contrary: "Nowadays, an integrating perspective is preferred in which culture is perceived as a system of interaction and orientation which can be described by 'perceptus' and explained as 'conceptas'" (Bolten 1997, p. 489).

In scientific theory, the basic problem of the theory of culture in the humanities and social sciences lies in an exact definition of what precisely is to be understood by cultural differences in the light of existing historical circumstances (cf. Reckwitz 2005, p. 96). The question how to define differences conceptually can be answered only once the basis of comparison, i.e. the element to be compared, has been defined. According to Andreas Reckwitz, mainly three different discourses can be distinguished, which will be outlined briefly below as a summary and for classification (cf. Reckwitz 2005).

The *"social theory" discourse* tries to express the differences in "theories of culture" (cf. Reckwitz 2005, pp. 93ff.). These are mostly approaches of social constructivism formulating a general theory of the origins of social order in human thought and action (cf., e.g., Berger/Luckmann 2000). In this approach, action, thought, and perception are based on symbolic orders which, at the same time, are constitutive to the perception of reality and, ultimately, also to the design of (social and cultural) reality. This group includes approaches from social phenomenology to Pierre Bourdieu, Michel Foucault, and symbolist ethnology to the systems theory constructivism of Parsons and Niklas Luhmann.

The methodological and *science theory discourses,* respectively, concentrated in particular on the specific conditions of, and obstacles to, an external understanding of culture. Above all, the discussions in ethnology, especially the "writing culture" and post-colonialism debate (cf. Clifford/George 1986), and socio-philosophical hermeneutics provided important impulses.

In the context of *social science theory*, the question of cultural differences most recently has been studied especially in the theories of globalization (cf., e.g., Castells 2001; Giddens 1990). With regard to conditions in the Western world, cultural differences were also shown in theories of lifestyles (cf. Hradil 1997) and subcultures as well as gender identities. In the more recent post-Foucaultian cultural history these problems were also addressed with a view to cultural disruptions in history. The question about the differences of, and limits to, cultures is discussed in all these discourses, which cannot be clearly separated from each other, in connection with the abstract problem of the "essence of culture" and "what culture is made up of".

The concepts of culture in anthropology, which are based on the broader pluralistic concept of culture, particularly influenced the genesis of the concept of culture. Especially the arguments of the U.S. anthropologist Florence Kluckhohn exerted much influence, who thought that all cultures in the world concealed basic problems of human existence which could be summarized in dimensions and categories, respectively: "All cultures constitute [...] answers to essentially the same questions posed by human biology and by the generalities of the human situation. [...] Every society's pattern for living must provide approved and sanctioned ways for dealing with such universal circumstances as the existence of two sexes; the helplessness of infants; etc." (Kluckhohn 1962, pp. 17f.).

This definition by Kluckhohn was broad enough to be filled in different ways by different cultures. Macro-theoretical approaches, building on this principle, tried first to determine the most important dimensions of human existence and then show in various empirical studies by comparison that these dimensions are filled differently in different cultures, and that cultures vary within these dimensions, respectively.

4   Concepts of Culture at the Macro- and Microlevels

These approaches, which have remained influential to this day and are being used especially in empirical studies of culture or comparisons of cultures, will be briefly examined below for their epistemological potential in a comparison of cultures. The best known macrotheories of culture include those by Harry C. Triandis (cf. Triandis 1975, 1984), John Galtung (cf. Galtung 1988), Edward T. and Mildred Hall (cf. Hall 1969; Hall/Hall 1983, 1990), Geert Hofstede[1] (cf. Hofstede 1980, 1993), and Robert Hettlage (cf. Hettlage 1990). In these and other macro-theoretical approaches, the concept of culture typically is reduced to a few categories or dimensions. The reason frequently given is that culture (in the above comprehensive meaning of the broad concept) as a subject of research can hardly be captured completely because of its complexity (cf. Bolten 2001, p. 128). These dimensions or categories, thus the idea, are to make cultures comparable with each other. As a consequence, many macro-theoretical approaches try to develop various cultural dimensions and find epistemological reasons for the choice and weighting of the aspects dominating in a specific case. Although these models seem to be quite appropriate in comparing cultures (which is what most of them were designed for), major objections can be raised against such concept of culture. Thus, critics frequently maintain that this kind of macro-theoretical model resulted in a high degree of stereotyping and, hence, simplification, which prevented many phenomena from being included (cf. Bolten 2001, p. 130).[2] In the attempt to force culture into a manageable number of categories or dimensions, merely part of the "surface" of cultures becomes visible as a function of the dimensions chosen. As a result of these macro-theoretical considerations, only abstract averages are obtained in most cases which say little or nothing about the specific actions of individuals (cf. Bolten 2001, p. 130). The relation between the individual and culture as part of everyday experience remains underinvestigated in

---

1   For criticism of Hofstede, cf. Bolten 2001, pp. 130f., and Hansen 2003, pp. 281f.
2   For criticism of macro-theoretical concepts of culture, cf. Bolten 1997 and Demorgon/Molz 1996.

this case, and the question often arises about the criteria by which the categories or dimensions were chosen.

The macro-theoretical perspective is contrasted with various concepts abstracting cultural characteristics from detailed analyses, i.e. proceeding deductively from the microlevel. These concepts therefore can be called micro-analytical and micro-theoretical, respectively. They include concepts, such as the "Dense Description" by Clifford Geertz (cf. Geert 1987), which see culture as a "text" one must be able to "read", and the "Cross Cultural Psychology", inter alia in Alexander Thomas (cf. Thomas 1993), and the "Activity Theory"[3] and the "Cognitive Traits" concept developed in cultural studies. Other concepts of this type stem from the (cross-sectional) area of economics and are often summarized under the heading of "intercultural communication".

However, this perspective, too, entails ontological problems. Thus, deductive models often provide very little information, as findings based on them cannot be generalized. As Bolten puts it, the "more detailed the studies of (sub)cultures are, the less complex they may be if any information about them is to be produced at all" (Bolten 2001, p. 131). According to Bolten, such microanalyses can be used optimally for intercultural coaching or mediation, but not to generate theories (cf. Bolten 2001). Often, approaches based on individual cases are unable to describe adequately cultural contexts in which the culturally specific elements appear, e.g. in the "text" (in the sense of culture as a text, see above) (cf. Bolten 2001). This entails the hazard that the broad context is neglected for assessments of cultural details. Another difficulty connected with micro-analytical approaches is seen in their emphasizing only the dynamic aspect of culture. For that reason, they tended to overemphasize the "change" pole (over "persistence" as the opposite pole) in the sense "that man could develop into anything, given the strong will to do so" (Demorgon/Molz 1996, p. 69).

As has been shown in this brief summary and in the equally brief (and, because of that brevity, often sweeping) criticism, neither the macro-theoretical nor the micro-theoretical concepts are able to describe culture in the most differentiated way possible and in as complex a fashion as necessary, at least for an empirical comparison of cultures. Hence, current empirical cultural research often shows mixed types of various macro- or microapproaches. The anthropological theories of culture described above (cf., e.g., Hall/Hall 1983, 1989; Hofstede 1993; Kluckhohn 1962) are partly modified and expressed in different connotations, recontextualized, and arranged in a structure of meanings corresponding to current development. Mixing and combining different concepts of culture are meant to, if not repair, then at least diminish the deficits referred to above in both the macro- and the micro-theoretical perspectives.

---

3   For the Activity Theory, see Engeström et al. 1999.

This technique of mixing various approaches is problematic, however, as it requires the systems to be greatly modified conceptually. It entails the hazard that the original intention of a concept may be lost. The consequence would be that many research projects which (ought to) deal with the concept of culture retract to an interpretation broad enough to encompass the variety of human actions in specific fields, such as communication, behaviour, consumption, knowledge, technology, etc., but then must try, by using props from other cultural models or conceptual building blocks, to adjust this concept of culture so as to match the actual object (cf. e.g. Paschen et al. 2002).

5   An Evolutionist Concept of Culture

Another branch of understanding culture, influenced mainly by anthropology, sees culture as a strategy of humans living in groups adapting to their environment. In this case, "environment" is not only the natural environment, nature, but also man-made social, material and symbolic environments. Also the evolution of social aggregations up to complex functionally differentiated societies consequently is a cultural act facilitating, or making possible, life and survival by adaptation. The "environments", in which people live and which they partly created by culture, show clear differences, as do the cultures which are in a dialectic relation to those environments.

This concept of culture is guided mainly by the praxeological concepts of culture which consider culture a "theory of practice" dependent on the environment and on knowledge – as described by Bourdieu and others (cf., e.g., Bourdieu 1979) – in which the social and symbolic environment is seen as a man-made cultural product and, at the same time, appears as knowledge-dependent, action- and awareness-related objectivity (cf. Schütz 1974 and, based on this, Berger/Luckmann 2000). Practical action and knowledge in this case depend on communication and its (partly technical) media which simultaneously are both the main prerequisite and the main function of cultures. In this concept, human beings develop cultural habits in line with their environment and knowledge which are useful in their closer or more distant living environments. This also includes the way in which technology is used.

Human beings as incomplete beings, "deficient beings", finding their way into life nearly without any instincts, compared to animals (cf. Gehlen 1941, pp. 34ff.), need to produce a technical culture in the sense of creation, i.e. an artificial world or environment (such as housing, roads, bridges) which holds symbolic meanings, but is made by means of technical artefacts (tools, equipment, machines, etc.), in order to survive under the natural conditions encountered and other environmental states (cf. Metzner 2002, p. 231). The huge flexibility this ensures in processes of adaptation to the environment in this case not only allowed human beings to penetrate nearly all over the world and develop new living space, but also, thanks to the feedback this produced of the different natural conditions encountered, led to a high contingency of cultural developments, such as different cultural practices and languages or, as far as socialization is concerned, manifold social structures. Cultures seen as "evolutionary" in this sense, therefore, in a first approximation, can be defined as follows: They are the outcome of the ways in which human beings cope with life and existence in a community of action and communication within a specific "environment" (cf. Banse/Metzner-Szigeth 2005, p. 33).

As a consequence of this evolutionist understanding of culture, culture can be considered an expanded context of human existence. This covers the whole range of human adaptation reactions. The contexts created in this way are too manifold and too complex to be transferred into a concept which could be operationalized. However, the most important contexts are condensed in three human products: language, history, and institutions. They must be considered functional because they allow groups of human beings to be distinguished by these categories. Consequently, a slightly more concrete, but still quite general, definition of culture can be formulated as follows: Culture becomes visible and plays a role when various groups of persons act differently and their reasons for doing so can be attributed to differences in history, language, and (social) institutions of these groups.

The concept of culture underlying this definition by Klaus P. Hansen (cf. Hansen 1995, 2003) will be described in greater detail below to show that culture, despite all conflicts and complexity, can be incorporated in a differentiated, operational concept (for empirical coverage) of culture(s).

6   The Difference-based Concept of Culture by Hansen

Culture is frequently described as orientation by, or standardization of, values or patterns of behaviour, i.e. uniform or holistic. On the other hand, however, there is also room for individual variation, there are subcultures and miniature collectives which make cultures appear divergent (cf. Demorgon/Molz 1996, pp. 43ff.). Instead of considering culture a holistic entity, Hansen designs a concept of culture which is able to resolve the conflicting ideas of unity and differentiation of culture (cf. Hansen 1995). Consequently, his concept of culture is termed difference-based. Hansen explains it by the example of "Germany": Within German culture, one finds a multitude of different ways of life. Considering, e.g., the way a carpenter in Lower Bavaria lives compared to a manager working at the Frankfurt Stock Exchange, it would be difficult at first sight to find many common features in their everyday life. It would be easier, in fact, to describe the differences. Yet, although the ways of living and everyday activities of the two persons are so different, there are certain commonalities which characterize them as members of the very same culture. These commonalities, which Hansen refers to as "putty", promote cohesion within a national culture and delimit it towards the outside. These are the common history they experienced, or the history handed down, their common language, and the institutions they share (cf. Hansen 1995, p. 179).

These three constitutive elements of national culture and their importance as cultural dimensions within the framework of the difference-based[4] concept of culture will be described in more detail below. History constitutes a separate sphere of importance. "Human societies must be able to reproduce both materially and symbolically to guarantee their continued existence over time. Symbolic reproduction poses the problem for societies to absorb their cultural contents, practices, languages, institutions, norms, work of earlier generations and pass all of this on to the next generation. This requires not only the indispensable assistance of nature, but also personal 'cultural strategies of permanence'" (Assmann 1999, p. 88).

These "cultural strategies of permanence" are strategies of tradition. In the format of traditions and collective or individual histories handed down, history affects the reality of life, strongly influencing the thinking and action of the people identifying with these traditions. Accordingly, Aleida Assmann defines tradition as "a permanent cultural design of identity. This permanence must continuously be wrung from time as a dimension of destruction, forgetting, change, or relativation" (Assmann 1999, p. 90). A common history (historical facts) does not necessarily result in common views about that history, but constitutes the point of departure and a common point of reference or framework of evaluation for and of these views (cf. Hansen 1995, p. 146).

Language is not just a medium of transmission enabling verbal communication to take place, but is closely connected to perception and reason. Every language community has its individual perception of the meaning of the reality of life achieved through its language (cf. Berger/Luckmann 2000, pp. 24ff.; Hansen 2003, pp. 73ff.). This promotes cohesion of this community and acts as the criterion of inclusion and exclusion. History and language are interdependent, on the one hand, because history is handed down by language and, on the other hand, because language also grew historically and is modified and formed by events in history. Despite their differences, cultures can be described by means of their language and their history as an entity in the sense of natural cultures. These natural cultures are a function not so much of national borders but rather of a common area of language and history (cf. Hansen 2003, p. 179), which can differ greatly from the area defined by national borders.[5] This constitutes a first background moulding the individual, albeit "involuntarily" in most cases, because it is defined by birth. At a later point in time (again mostly involuntarily), the socialization of individuals takes place. Socialization, i.e. education, teaches the indi-

---

4   For more details about this concept, see Drechsel et al. 2000, pp. 16ff.
5   National borders are arbitrary political structures which do not necessarily define cultural spaces, as can be seen in the Balkans or in Africa, for instance.

vidual his or her native language and something of the specific history related to the community in which he or she lives. Language, once learnt, plays a key role in this process. It provides the individuals newly born into a society or a communication space with "prefabrications" of objectified human experience, in this way simultaneously empowering the individuals socialized in this way to create their own objectivations (cf. Berger/Luckmann 2000, pp. 40ff.). Socialization also achieves the introduction to, and inclusion into, societal organization and its institutions.

The term "institutions" as used by Hansen was taken from Arnold Gehlen (cf. Gehlen 1962) and is defined very broadly. In the broadest sense, it means stabilized and, hence, institutionalized habits: "It is quite possible to say that animal groups and symbioses are held together by triggers and instinctive movements while humans achieve this by institutions and quasi-automatic habits, established therein, of thought, feeling, evaluation, and action which become specific, habitual and stable only when institutionalized. Only in this way can they be considered habitual and halfway reliable, i.e. predictable in their onesidedness" (Gehlen 1962, p. 79).

Consequently, our institutions are no longer seen as merely governmental or societal institutions but also as social and symbolic institutions, such as Christmas or birthdays. In the concept of institutions by Berger and Luckmann (cf. Berger/Luckmann 2000), institutionalization processes can be described in steps. Institutions can be described epistemologically as objectivations of a higher order. Objectivation is at the beginning of institutionalization. This is achieved by language and action, respectively, habitualized by repetition. In a second step, these actions are further stabilized by typification of behaviour (for instance in social roles). At the end of this process, there is standardization of typified behaviour, which makes it institutionalized. Consequently, Berger and Luckmann offer this definition of institutionalization: "Institutionalization occurs as soon as habitualized actions are typified reciprocally by types of players. Any typification achieved in this way is an institution" (Berger/Luckmann 2000, p. 58).

When a specific collective habitualizes a specific action, the players (as a community) and the habitualized action (as a developing convention) reinforce each other (reciprocal typification), which means that action is institutionalized. The joint action of various institutions in a community develops and, at the same time, structures its type of organization. Although institutions are the outcome of collective action, they basically are opposites of the individual as objective facticities (unavoidably), exerting direct influence on everyday life (cf. Berger/Luckmann 2000, pp. 49ff.).

According to this concept of institution also persons in the real world, imaginary or historical persons can act as institutions. Such a person may have the function of an institution if he or she exerts – due to the importance ascribed to him or her by others, as a result of his or her action or fate – a significant influence on areas of society or groups and thus, in a way, acts like an institution (such as Rudi Dutschke for the student movement in the 1960s). History, language, and institutions ensure continuity in a community through the process of socialization. They are the externally visible and thus empirically detectable signs of the action of culture(s). They are hallmarks of culture(s) and (functional) poles of identification for its/their members.

7   Areas of Standardization

The core of Hansen's concept of culture are standardizations which, in principle, can be considered conventions.[6] It subdivides the different cultural standardizations into four areas for analytical distinction: communication, thought, feeling, and behaviour and action. Cultural standardizations or conventions are bound to collectives; on the other hand, collectives constitute themselves through standardizations. One exception to this rule are overarching collectives defined much more by a common language, history, and institutions. Initially, collectivity in a quite general sense can be taken as a feeling of community generated by living in line with common conventions which thus constitute a collective. The need to be part of a community, both physically but also psychologically (cf. Tomasello 2007), is one of the prime movers specifically of human living together, or even its source. In addition, collectives offer possibilities to individuals to identify, thus creating identity. This commonality of conventions makes communities confirm purpose; their members feel secure (cf. Hauser 2007, p. 682). In sociology, this is described by the term "assurance of expectation" (cf. Bonß 1995, p. 90).

This can be linked to Gehlen's concept of institutions, which relates to the removal of behavioural uncertainties by establishing norms of behaviour (cf. Metzner-Szigeth 2004, p. 392). This results in more assumptions about the importance to collectives of cultural standardizations: "(1) Efficiency: Tried and tested behaviour implies a lower risk of failure. (2) Acceptance: Standardized behaviour entails no [or fewer; authors' comment – R.H./G.B.] negative sanctions. (3) Anticipation: Conformity makes my behaviour and the behaviour of others possible to anticipate. (4) Normality: Existing conventions simplify the complexity of the environment, thereby reducing the cognitive burden. (5) Creation of meaning: If several people behave the way I do, my behaviour most probably is meaningful. (6) Collectivity: When I behave like others do, I feel a member of the group" (Hauser 2007, p. 682).

---

6   Although Hansen uses the term conventions but rarely, standardizations in principle can be seen as conventions. While the standardization concept may be more precise, but also too technical or too abstract, convention is more illustrative but not nearly well defined. For epistemological considerations it is therefore better to use the term standardization, while illustrations by way of example should use really existing conventions. For cultural conventions, cf. also Hauser 2007; for detailed criticism, cf. Altmayer 1996.

Establishing collectives thus has subjective and objective advantages for the individual. Various collectives can be distinguished by the standardizations encountered, which appear as common features of the individuals making up these collectives. This means that the subdivision into different collective relations (within one overarching collective) is derived directly from the range of the standardizations encountered in each case. Wherever similar standardizations occur there is probably also a collective relation (at the level of mono, multi or overarching collectives). The range of standardizations which, at the same time, marks the borders of collective relations, can be termed "degree of partiality" (cf. Hansen 2004) after Hansen. Thus, particular standardizations apply only within specific mono collectives, while other standardizations extend to the level of multi collectives or even global collectives. Consequently, there are universal standardizations which are global in scope and by means of which global collectives can constitute themselves.

However, as standardizations are subject to the change of times and to many influences both within collectives and external environmental influences, standardizations as such and their degree of partiality can change, and so can the borders of segmentation. Standardizations understood as conventions do not arise spontaneously, but develop over a specific period of time and under specific environmental or framework conditions as negotiating processes both within a collective and among several collectives. Communication, thought, action, and feeling of individuals therefore are determined not only by the collective or collectives in which these individuals participate, but also historically, linguistically, and institutionally, in summary, by "cultural spaces and thus understandable only against the cultural background" (Holz-Mänttäri 1984, pp. 32f.). However, the individual is aware of these cultural influences only in part, and they are controllable only to that extent. They have to be that way so that the individual may adapt (and thus participate) in different, or also new, collectives. The spectrum and the variance of the conventions managed in each case thus depend strongly on socialization of the individual, his or her education, and other environmental factors.

8   Culture and Sustainability

Without wanting to anticipate other contributions to this volume, a few general ideas and comments about the relation between culture and sustainability will be made in this last paragraph from a point of view of cultural studies. The first question arising is whether culture(s) is/are sustainable and can be sustainable at all. Cultures are sustainable first and foremost in the sense that they function very effectively and are extremely long-lived. Cultural mechanisms are designed to promote stability and cohesion. Now, this would be an absolutely neutral concept of sustainability more in line with everyday thinking and often used in the media as well. However, if a normative concept of sustainability is used as a basis, such as the integrative sustainability concept of the Helmholtz Association (cf. Kopfmüller et al. 2001), in which desirable sustainable development can only be achieved when manifold normative indicators are met, cultures and cultural mechanisms cannot be sustainable *per se*. This problem will be illustrated by a brief example: The culture of a people living in unison with nature for centuries, and using natural resources only to such an extent that these can regenerate, can be considered sustainable if the value of resource protection and use, respectively, is used as a yardstick. For comparison, Western cultures are not sustainable because they claim or exploit natural resources to an extreme degree, pollute their environment, and thus increasingly destroy the basis of their life. However, if values such as life, infant mortality, nutrition, or the ability to adapt to changing environmental conditions are used as indicators of sustainability, the fictitious people living close to nature probably would not compare well with Western cultures. The answer to the question whether cultures are sustainable in a normative sense therefore very strongly depends on the concept of sustainability used. Thus they cannot be called sustainable *per se*. Applying yardsticks of value to cultures entails another problem: It cannot be harmonized with a contemporary concept of culture. Contemporary concepts of culture emphasize the very neutrality, in terms of value, of cultures in order not to end up in outdated Western hegemonial categories, such as civilization or high culture, putting their own culture above those of other peoples (cf. above for the "narrow" concept of culture).

Yet, thinking about the relation between culture and sustainability can be fruitful in two ways: *On the one hand*, it can be taken in such a way that the generation of normative sustainability concepts has given rise to a cultural trend which, as an institution (according to Hansen's concept), is part of the respective culture and influences it. The question how such trends or movements gradually gain ground as cultural institutions and become a determining element of culture, raises interesting aspects and questions of further research from the perspective of cultural studies. The *second* line – more relevant to this study – would be to ask how cultural aspects can be integrated into existing normative concepts of sustainability. This has hardly happened so far: Although the concept of culture often appears in the concepts as a relevant element of sustainable development, it very rarely is made explicit (see also the contribution by Jürgen Kopfmüller to this volume). The high relevance of cultural contexts to the establishment of problem solutions (e.g. of a technical or organizational type) which are to promote sustainable development has hardly been reflected upon in the specialized community of "researchers of sustainability". A brief look into cultural and technology studies would show that technical systems are embedded in cultural contexts and interact with them (cf. Hauser 2010). Examples from the field of technology transfer in particular show that, when these contexts are taken into account not at all or insufficiently, this frequently causes partial or complete failure of a technology (cf. Hermeking 2001). In a similar way, this certainly applies also to organizational structures, though this question has not yet been studied sufficiently well.

That cultural factors so far have emerged in sustainability concepts only as "spacers" may be due partly to the fact that the field of concepts of culture is too broad and the time of researchers is too limited. On the other hand, there have been hardly any convincing attempts to date to conceptualize culture in such a way as to make it operationalizable for integration into existing sustainability concepts. The concept of culture by Hansen presented in this article and the conceptualization of culture as a context and as conventions of action, seem to offer better preconditions for this step. Yet, there is still an interdisciplinary job to be done, namely to integrate cultural aspects meaningfully into concepts of sustainability.

[This article has already been published in German in Parodi, O.; Banse, G.; Schaffer, A. (eds.): Wechselspiele: Kultur und Nachhaltigkeit. Annäherungen an ein Spannungsfeld. Berlin: edition sigma 2010, pp. 21-41.]

References

Altmayer, C. (1996): Rezension: Klaus P. Hansen. Kultur und Kulturwissenschaft. Eine Einführung. Rezensiert von Claus Altmayer. In: Zeitschrift für Interkulturellen Fremdsprachenunterricht [Online] 1(2). – URL: http:/; http://spz1.spz.tu-darmstadt.de/projekt_ejournal/jg-01-2/beitrag/altmeenh.htm [26.10.2008] (in German)

Assmann, A. (1999): Zeit und Tradition. Kulturelle Strategien der Dauer. Cologne (in German)

Assmann, J. (2007): Das kulturelle Gedächtnis. Schrift, Erinnerung und politische Identität in frühen Hochkulturen. 6th ed. Munich (in German)

Banse, G.; Metzner-Szigeth, A. (2005): Veränderungen im Quadrat: Computervermittelte Kommunikation und moderne Gesellschaft – Überlegungen zum Design des europäischen Forschungs-Netzwerks „Kulturelle Diversität und neue Medien". In: Banse, G. (ed.): Neue Kultur(en) durch Neue Medien (?). Das Beispiel Internet. Berlin, pp. 17-46 (in German)

Berger, L.; Luckmann, Th. (2000): Die gesellschaftliche Konstruktion der Wirklichkeit. 17th ed. Frankfurt am Main

Bolten, J. (1997): Interkulturelle Wirtschaftskommunikation. In: Walter, R. (ed.): Wirtschaftswissenschaften. Eine Einführung. Paderborn, pp. 469-497 (in German)

Bolten, J. (2001): Kann man Kulturen beschreiben oder erklären, ohne Stereotypen zu verwenden? Einige programmatische Überlegungen zur kulturellen Stilforschung. In: Bolten, J.; Schröter, D. (eds.): Im Netzwerk interkulturellen Handelns. Theoretische und praktische Perspektiven. Sternenfels, pp. 128-142 (in German)

Bonß, W. (1995.): Vom Risiko. Unsicherheit und Ungewißheit in der Moderne. Hamburg (in German)

Bourdieu, P. (1979): Entwurf einer Theorie der Praxis (auf der ethnologischen Grundlage der kabylischen Gesellschaft). Frankfurt am Main (in German)

Bourdieu, P. (1987): Die feinen Unterschiede. Kritik der gesellschaftlichen Urteilskraft. Frankfurt am Main (in German)

Cappai, G. (2005): Der interkulturelle Vergleich. Herausforderungen und Strategien einer sozial-wissenschaftlichen Methode. In: Srubar, I.; Renn, J.; Wenzel, U. (eds.): Kulturen vergleichen: Sozial- und kulturwissenschaftliche Grundlagen und Kontroversen. Wiesbaden, pp. 48-79 (in German)

Clifford, J.; George E. M. (eds.) (1986): Writing Culture. The Poetics and Politics of Ethnography. Berkeley, CA

Demorgon, J.; Molz, M. (1996): Bedingungen und Auswirkungen der Analyse von Kultur(en) und interkulturelle Interaktion. In: Thomas, A. (ed.): Psychologie interkulturellen Handelns. Göttingen/Bern, pp. 43-80 (in German)

Drechsel, P.; Schmidt, B.; Gölz, B. (2000): Kultur im Zeitalter der Globalisierung. Von Identität zu Differenzen. Frankfurt am Main (in German)

Engeström, J.; Miettinen, R.; Punamäki-Gitai, R.-L. (1999): Perspectives on Activity Theory. Cambridge

Freud, S. (1989): Das Unbehagen in der Kultur [1930]. In: Freud, S.: Studienausgabe in zehn Bänden. Vol. 9. Frankfurt am Main, pp. 191-270 (in German)

Galtung, J. (1988): The Peace Movement: A Structural-Functional Exploration. In: Galtung, J.: Transarmament and the Cold War. Copenhagen, pp. 322-342

Galtung, J. (1998): Frieden mit friedlichen Mitteln. Friede und Konflikt, Entwicklung und Kultur. Opladen (in German)

Geertz, C. (1987): Dichte Beschreibung. Beiträge zum Verstehen kultureller Systeme. 5th ed. Frankfurt am Main (in German)

Gehlen, A. (1941): Der Mensch. Seine Natur und seine Stellung in der Welt. 2nd ed. Wiebelsheim (in German)

Gehlen, A. (1953): Die Technik in der Sichtweise der Anthropologie. In: Merkur, No. 7, pp. 626-636 (in German)

Gehlen, A. (1956): Urmensch und Spätkultur. Bonn (in German)

Gehlen, A. (1962): Der Mensch. Seine Natur und seine Stellung in der Welt. 7th ed. Frankfurt am Main (in German)

Gerhards, J. (2000): Die Vermessung kultureller Unterschiede. Deutschland und USA im Vergleich. Opladen (in German)

Hall, E. T. (1969): The Hidden Dimension. New York

Hall, E. T.; Hall, M. R. (1983): Verborgene Signale. Studien zur internationalen Kommunikation: Über den Umgang mit Amerikanern. Hamburg (in German)

Hall, E. T.; Hall, M. R. (1990): Understanding Cultural Differences: Germans, French and Americans. Yarmouth

Hansen, K. P. (1995): Kultur und Kulturwissenschaft. 1st ed. Tübingen/Basel (in German)

Hansen, K. P. (2003): Kultur und Kulturwissenschaft. 3rd ed. Tübingen/Basel (in German)

Hansen, K. P. (2004). Die Kulturen der Beschäftigung mit Nationalkultur. – URL: http://www.germanistentag2004.unimuenchen.de/abstracts/wslandeskunde/hansen.doc. [13.06.2007] (in German)

Hauser, G. (2007). Ein Kulturmodell für Translatoren. In: Schmitt, P. A.; Jüngst, H. E. (eds.): Translationsqualität. Frankfurt am Main, pp. 680-695 (in German)

Hauser, R. (2010): Technische Kulturen oder kultivierte Technik? Das Internet in Deutschland und Russland. Berlin [zugleich Dissertation. Karlsruhe (Universität) 2009] (in German)

Herder, J. G. (1989): Ideen zur Philosophie der Geschichte der Menschheit [1784/91]. Frankfurt am Main (in German)

Hermeking, M. (2001): Kulturen und Technik. Techniktransfer als Arbeitsfeld der Interkulturellen Kommunikation. Beispiele aus der arabischen, russischen und lateinamerikanischen Region. Munich a. o. (in German)

Hettlage, R. (1991): Rahmenanalyse – oder die innere Organisation unseres Wissens um die Ordnung der Wirklichkeit. In: Hettlage, R.; Lenz, K. (eds.): Erving Goffman – ein soziologischer Klassiker der zweiten Generation. Bern/Stuttgart, pp. 95-156 (in German)

Hofstede, G. (1993): Interkulturelle Zusammenarbeit. Kulturen – Organisation – Management. Wiesbaden (in German)

Holz-Mänttäri, J. (1984): Translatorisches Handeln. Theorie und Methode. In: Annales Academiae Scientiarum Fennicae, Helsinki, B 226 (in German)

Hubig, Ch. (2010): Kulturbegriff – Abgrenzungen, Leitdifferenzen, Perspektiven. In: Banse, G.; Grunwald, A. (eds.): Technik und Kultur. Bedingungs- und Beeinflussungsverhältnisse. Karlsruhe, pp. 55-71 (in German)

Janich, P. (2005): Beobachterperspektive im Kulturvergleich. In: Renn, J.; Srubar, I.; Wenzel, U. (eds.): Kulturen vergleichen. Sozial- und Kulturwissenschaftliche Grundlagen und Kontroversen. Wiesbaden, pp. 18-37 (in German)

Kant, I. (1977): Idee zu einer allgemeinen Geschichte in weltbürgerlicher Absicht [1784]. In: Kant, I.: Werkausgabe in zwölf Bänden. Hg. v. W. Weischedel. Vol. XI. Frankfurt am Main, pp. 33-41 (in German)

Kluckhohn, C. (1962): Universal Categories of Culture. In: Tax, S. (ed.): Anthropology Today. Chicago

Kopfmüller, J.; Brandl, V.; Jörissen, J.; Paetau, M.; Banse, G.; Coenen, R.: Grunwald, A. (2001): Nachhaltige Entwicklung integrativ betrachtet. Konstitutive Elemente, Regeln, Indikatoren. Berlin (in German)

Mersch, D. (1999): Das Sagbare und das Zeigbare. Wittgensteins frühe Theorie einer Duplizität im Symbolischen. In: Prima Philosophia, No. 4, pp. 85-94 (in German)

Metzner, A. (2002): Die Tücken der Objekte. Über die Risiken der Gesellschaft und ihre Wirklichkeit. Frankfurt am Main/New York (in German)

Metzner-Szigeth, A. (2003): Zwischen Systemkomplexität und Akteursverantwortung. In: Kornwachs, K. (ed.): System – Technik – Verantwortung. Münster/London, pp. 391-409 (in German)

Parsons, T.; Toby, J. (1977): The Evolution of Societies. Englewood Cliffs, NJ

Paschen, H.; Wingert, B.; Coenen, Chr.; Banse, G. (2002): Kultur – Medien – Märkte. Medienentwicklung und kultureller Wandel. Berlin (in German)

Pufendorf, S. von (2002): Eris Scandica [1686]. In: Pufendorf, S. von: Gesammelte Werke. Ed. by W. Schmidt-Biggemann. Vol. 5. Ed. by F. Palladini. Berlin

Rammert, W. (1999): Technik. Stichworte für ein Lexikon. – URL: http://www. hyperkommunikation.ch/literatur/texte/rammert_technik.htm [22.11.2007] (in German)

Reckwitz, A. (2000): Die Transformation der Kulturtheorien. Zur Entwicklung eines Theorieprogramms. Weilerswist (in German)

Reckwitz, A. (2005): Kulturelle Differenzen aus praxeologischer Perspektive: Kulturelle Globalisierung jenseits von Modernisierungstheorie und Kulturessentialismus. In: Srubar, I; Renn, J.; Wenzel, U. (eds.): Kulturen vergleichen. Sozial- und kulturwissenschaftliche Grundlagen und Kontroversen. Wiesbaden, pp. 92-112 (in German)

Schütz, A. (1974): Der sinnhafte Aufbau der sozialen Welt. Eine Einleitung in die verstehende Soziologie. Frankfurt am Main (in German)

Thomas, A. (ed.) (1993): Kulturvergleichende Psychologie. Eine Einführung. Göttingen (in German)

Tomasello, M. (2007): Personal Communication. Leipzig (in German)

Triandis, H. C. (1975): Culture Training: Cognitive Complexity and Interpersonal Attitudes. In: Brislin, R. W; Bochner, S.; Lonner, W. J. (eds.): Cross-Cultural Perspectives on Learning. New York, pp. 39-77

Triandis, H. C. (1984): A Theoretical Framework for the More Efficient Construction of Culture Assimiliator. In: International Journal of Intercultural Relations, No. 8, pp. 301-330

Wittgenstein, L. (2001): Philosophische Untersuchungen [1935/1949]. Kritisch-genetische Edition. Ed. by J. Schulte, H. Nijman, E. v. Savigny, G. H. v. Wright. Frankfurt am Main (in German)

Wittgenstein, L. (2003): Tractatus logico-philosophicus. Logisch-philosophische Abhandlung [1921]. Frankfurt am Main (in German)

Habitats – Habits – Inhabitants
A Biocultural Triad to Promote Sustainable Cultures

Ricardo Rozzi, Alexandria Poole

1   Introduction

We prefer to refer to *sustainable cultures* rather than to a singular culture of sustainability, in order to make explicit the plurality of languages, ecological worldviews and practices that unfold in contrasting ecoregions. The shift helps to acknowledge the existence of diverse sustainable communities around the world, and highlights the need to integrate both biological and cultural diversity into the concept of a global, still heterogeneous mosaic of forms of ecological knowledge, ethics and cultures of sustainability. In this chapter we emphasize that sustainable cultures co-evolve while inhabiting specific habitats, developing idiosyncratic behaviours or ways of inhabiting. The biocultural units formed by unique *habitats* where *inhabitants* develop recurrent ways of inhabiting or *habits* that shape their identities constitute triads of systemic interrelations that are core to a sustainability *ethos*. We argue that better understanding about these biocultural interrelations, and the specificity of each triad of habitats, habits, and inhabitants, can help implement educational, administrative, and economic systems that better support the well-being of the human and non-human participants in these biocultural units, which provide a foundation for achieving global sustainability.

Focusing on biocultural diversity also contributes towards the assessment of a major driver of global environmental change: biocultural homogenization. This process often undermines regional sustainability because it entails simultaneous losses of native biological and cultural diversity, and their replacement by cosmopolitan species, languages, and cultures. This substitution entails both the extinction of native languages, cultures, and biological species, and the loss of interrelation between cultures and their habitats, which are essential for the sustainability and well-being of regional communities of human and other-than-human co-inhabitants. In spite of its widespread character and its detrimental effects on regional human communities, their traditional habits, and habitats, biocultural homogenization remains largely unaddressed by conservation and sustainability sciences (cf. Rozzi/Feinsinger 2006). While losses of biodiversity are widely recognized, less is known about the threat to the world's linguistic and cultural diversity, and even less understood are the interrelations between biological and cultural diversity (cf. Ericksen/Woodley 2005; Krauss 1991; Maffi 2005; Rozzi et al. 2008).

The idea of the interconnectedness of human habits and the habitats they inhabit has been widespread in the worldviews of many indigenous and traditional societies, and is also substantiated by comparative philosophical critiques, anthropological studies, and the ecological and evolutionary sciences (cf. Brown et al. 2005; Callicott 1997; Harmon 1996, 2002; Hunn 2007; Posey 1999; Prance/Kallunki 1984; Rozzi 2001; Wilcox/Duin 1995). But this notion is only incipiently incorporated in most circles of academic and decision-makers (cf. Maffi 2001). However, recently the United Nations Environmental Programme (UNEP) has highlighted that biodiversity also incorporates human cultural diversity, which can be affected by the same drivers as biodiversity, and which has impacts on the diversity of genes, other species, and ecosystems (cf. UNEP 2007, p. 160). We hope that our focus on the habitat-habit-inhabitant interrelations contributes to better integrating biological, linguistic, and cultural diversity into concepts, policies, and practices that enhance our capacity to

(1) conserve biocultural diversity;
(2) identify responsible agents and victims of losses of biocultural diversity that disrupt environmental, economic, and socio-ecological sustainability;
(3) frame questions about the socio-ecological contexts of sustainability (i.e., sustainability for whom? where? how?).

To introduce our biocultural approach, we begin by offering a concise characterization of the concept of biocultural diversity.

2   Biocultural Diversity: Interrelations of Human Languages, Cultures, and Regional Ecosystems

Human language, culture, and the environment have been interrelated throughout the evolutionary history of *homo sapiens*. During the last two decades, numerous studies have demonstrated correlations between biological and linguistic diversity, derived from processes of co-evolution of human groups with their local ecosystems (cf. Loh/Harmon 2005; Maffi 2005). Over time humans interact with their environment, modifying it and developing specialized knowledge about it (cf. Toledo 2000). In order to convey ecological knowledge and practices, humans have also developed specialized ways of talking about the environment. In some cases, these ecolinguistic relationships have developed through the course of thousands of years. The continued use of these local, co-evolved languages promotes, in turn, the continuity of local ecological knowledges and practices. Relationships between local languages and their socio-ecological environments are particularly apparent in indigenous communities that maintain close material and spiritual ties with their regional ecosystems and biodiversity (cf. Maffi 2005). We highlight that biological and cultural diversity are unavoidably interwoven in all cultures for at least two reasons (cf. Rozzi 2001):

(1) *Homo sapiens*, like other biological species, is a component of ecosystems and biodiversity, and participates in the structure and processes of ecosystems.
(2) Human perceptions and understanding of biodiversity are influenced by language, culture, and technology.

2.1 Humans as Components of Ecosystems and Biodiversity: Cultural Landscapes

According to ecological and evolutionary sciences, *homo sapiens* is an animal species which, like other biological species, participates in the structure, processes, and composition of ecosystems (cf. McDonnell/Pickett 1994). Our species forms part of biodiversity and, with its diverse ethnicities and cultures, humans generate networks of biocultural relations that diversify, and are diversified by, the heterogeneity of ecosystems and landscapes where they unfold. Indeed, novel biocultural approaches in anthropological and ecological research have helped to understand that many landscapes previously depicted as a pure, pristine expression of nature are in fact *cultural landscapes*, either created by humans or modified by human activities.

Some remarkable, recently "discovered" cultural landscapes are found in Amazonia. Since the 1970s scientists have begun to distinguish vegetation patterns in vast tropical forest areas that were the result of extensive plantations of fruit and nut trees, such as the *apêtê* "forest islands" (see Figure 1a). Through indigenous use of fire, forest management, planting and transplanting practices within and between many ecological zones of Amazonia, indigenous people have created a mosaic of forest islands and corridors that also attract useful animals. These discoveries within the world's most extensive forested region have forced scientists to re-evaluate what have erroneously been considered "natural" Amazonian landscapes, and to reinterpret them as "cultural forests", including large agricultural areas, open parklands, hills built with clay, managed wetlands and forests (cf. Heckenberger et al. 2003; Mann 2005).

Cultural landscapes range over a wide variety of ecoregions and historical times. In South America, a great diversity of cultural landscapes is found from the lowlands of Amazonas to the highlands of the Andes, where Inca trails still represent major trade routes that have been used over the past 10,000 years, and today feature visible traces of prehistoric hunter-gatherer communities, the Inca Empire (15th to 16th centuries), the fights with the Spaniard conquerors (17th and 18th centuries), and current use by Aymara, Quechua, and mestizo peasant communities (cf. Moore 2005).

Figure 1:   Two Examples of Cultural Landscapes

(a) In South America, Kayapo Indians create *apêtê* "forest islands" in Amazonian savanna land-scapes. Such "ecological engineering" requires detailed knowledge of soil fertility, microclimate, and plant varieties. *Apêtê* are managed as both agroforestry units and game reserves, and success-ful *apêtê* management depends not just on the cultivators' knowledge of their immediate proper-ties but also about long-term successional processes linked to plants specifically planted to attract useful animals, grow and fruit in the forest islands. Today, Kayapo's knowledge of *apêtê* forma-tion and succession offers valuable insights for designing processes of forestation in savanna and reforestation in denuded areas.

Source: Jose Fragoso, in: Rozzi 2001

(b) In Europe, the Drachenfels hills on the banks of the river Rhine, south of Bonn, represent the first protected area created in Germany. The remains of the quarry that endangered the hill and the castle in the early 19th century can still be seen.

Source: Kurt Jax (early 2001), in: Jax/Rozzi 2004

Cultural landscapes have attracted increasing attention, and the World Heritage Committee of UNESCO has adopted and adapted the concept of cultural landscape as part of an international effort to overcome "one of the most pervasive dualisms in Western thought – that of nature and culture" (UNESCO 2005, p. 84). It is interesting to note, however, that nature and culture have been integrated since the origins of conservation movements in Europe. For instance, the first protected area in Germany, established during the 1830s, was the Drachenfels, a hill with an old castle ruin towering above the banks of the Rhine south of Bonn (Figure 1a). The reason to protect it as a natural monument ("Naturdenkmal") was the danger of a complete destruction of the castle and the mountain side pointing towards the Rhine by a quarry, which had already caused part of the old ruin to collapse. Later the area was greatly extended to include the surrounding hills in the nature protection area ("Naturschutzgebiet") in Siebengebirge. Both the hills of the Siebengebirge and the Drachenfels ruin, however, had a high symbolic value in the context of romanticism and the search for national identity in Germany, which at that time was divided into many small, more or less independent states (cf. Jax/Rozzi 2004). The Drachenfels Naturdenkmal shows how in Germany the conservation movement began not as a movement to protect "wild" landscapes, but as "Heimatschutz" (cf. Dominick 1992; Knaut 1993), which meant the protection of the home country or home landscape (the "Heimat"). This was essentially the protection of cultural landscapes moulded by centuries of extensive use practices (cf. Jax/Rozzi 2004).

The examples of cultural landscapes from South America and Europe illustrate that the biocultural concept of humans as components of ecosystems (modifying and being modified by the habitats they inhabit) can be applied to a wide range of ecosystems subject to different degrees of anthropic influence, from remote areas to the fastest growing metroplexes in the world. This is particularly relevant, given the fact that as of 2007, the world's biocultural diversity encountered a global shift with over 50% of the world's population residing in predominantly urban environments. In response to this shift, the 2008 Erfurt Declaration made a call to apply the Convention on Biological Diversity specifically to urban environments, considering urbanization one of the major drivers for biological and cultural diversity loss (cf. Müller/Werner 2010). Although cities cover only 2% of the world's surface area, they consume 75% of the world's resources. Therefore, it is critical to further incorporate a biocultural approach to examine socio-ecological relations in this major cultural landscape at the beginning of the 21st century, investigating and promoting the cultivation of sustainable biocultural relationships of citizens with both their urban habitats and the neighbouring mosaic of ecosystems.

2.2   Humans' Biocultural Lenses

Humans participate not only in the biophysical, but also in the symbolic, cultural, and linguistic structures and processes of biocultural landscapes. Human perceptions and understanding of biological diversity are embedded in language, culture, and technology. The compound term *biocultural* makes explicit the role that the "cultural lenses" of any human "observer" (including scientists with their research methods, and conceptual taxonomies) have in shaping the construction and interpretation of biodiversity concepts. In turn, the ways humans perceive and understand biodiversity and their environment influence the ways humans inhabit ecosystems, and modify the structure, processes, and composition of living beings, from molecular to global scales. To illustrate this point, it is helpful to look at two contrasting languages, Waorani and English, regarding the way they refer to forest ecosystems.

The indigenous Amazonian Waorani word *ömö* defines forests as worlds inhabited by countless sentient beings, who share with humans the same home, dispositions, values, and culture. This human-forest kinship implicated in the word *ömö* stimulates the performance of rituals, and today it encourages Waorani people to oppose oil extraction in the Amazonian forests (cf. Sawyer 2004). In contrast, the English coinage *woodland* implies that forest ecosystems are a "land of the resource wood". Wood, in turn, refers to an interpretation of trees as a resource, for either fuel or building materials. These contrasting definitions of forest ecosystems illustrate how concepts embedded in language influence both ecological practices, the ways in which humans transform other species and the environment, and ecological knowledge, the ways in which humans perceive other species and their environment (cf. Rozzi 2001). By fostering an understanding of the multiple representations and classifications of biological diversity in various languages, this biocultural method can help to deconstruct the economic-mathematical approach that predominates in European and North American globalized culture, thereby bringing attention to alternative modes of ecological knowledge and practice.

3   Amerindian and Scientific Perspectives of the Inextricable Links of *Habitats, Habits, and Inhabitants*

Both traditional ecological knowledge and contemporary ecological scientific knowledge allows us to understand the vital links between the regional habitats, the inhabitants, and their habits. These habits are essential for the identity and the well-being of both the human and the other-than-human co-inhabitants, thereby generating the sustainability of Amerindian communities. We will succinctly examine the vital links between habitats, habits, and the identity of inhabitants by examining how these bonds are deeply rooted in the life of the largest indigenous group of southern South America, the *Mapuche* people. The Mapuche define themselves as the people (= *che*) of the land (= *mapu*). Their close links to the land are compellingly expressed in their language (= *dungu*), *Mapu-dungun,* that onomatopoeically dialogues with the land (= *mapu*), and the names of the three main Mapuche groups which refer to the habitats they inhabit:

- the *Lafkenche*, people of the *Lafken* or coastal ecosystems (36-40°S),
- the *Williche*, people of the *Willi* or south, inhabiting the evergreen rain forests from the Tolten River (38°S) south to Chiloe Island (42°S), and
- the *Pewenche,* people of the *Pewen* or Monkey-Puzzle tree *(Araucaria araucana)* forests of the volcanic Andean mountain range in southern Chile and Argentina (37-40°S).

The habitat of the *Pewenche* people is the *pewenlemu*, a type of forest *(lemu)* dominated by the *pewen* trees (cf. Rozzi et al. 2010). The social organization and unique ancestral distribution of the *Pewenche* clans is associated with the particular distribution of the *pewenes* (cf. Aagesen 1998). An essential habit of the *Pewenche* is the *pica*, or the gathering of the monkey-puzzle tree cones, whose seeds provide the nutritive foundation of their diet. As illustrated in Figure 2, nowadays the *Pewenche* collect these large cones using ropes, which they throw like lassos in order to bring the cones down from the top of the trees. The seeds contained in these cones posses 0.110 g/100 g and 0.130 g/100 g of cysteine and methionine, respectively (see Figure 2). These are the only two amino acids that contain sulphur in their molecular structure. Additionally, among the fruits and seeds available in the Pewenche territory, the pewen's seeds have the highest levels of methionine (cf. Rozzi/Massardo 2006). This is an *essential amino acid*; i.e., the human body is unable to synthesize methionine, and a lack of it can cause a protein deficiency. Therefore, this amino acid must be obtained through an external nutritive source. An analysis from the medical science perspective provides a functional explanation of this habit, since the tree is fundamental to the diet and health of the *Pewenche*, given that its seeds provide the primary source of methionine available in the volcanic ecosystems in mountain altitudes. This analysis by medical science also allows for a better scientific understanding of the profound meaning of what it is to "be" the people of the *pewen*. By eating its seeds, the *Pewenche* incorporate cysteine and methionine, which become proteins in their bodies. Thus, the *Pewenche* biophysical bodies as well as their cultural identities and welfare arise from this trophic socio-ecological relationships, which can be understood from both the Pewenchen worldview, and through scientific analysis.

The name *Pewenche*, and its people's ancestral worldview, also find a point of convergence with a scientific ecosystemic perspective. An analysis of nutrient flows in high-Andean ecosystems where the *Pewenche* live shows that the entrance of sulphur into the bio-geochemical cycle comes from the volcanoes and their ash, which is transported by wind and water. As illustrated in Figure 2, rivers bring volcanic sulphur to the soil, where molecules of hydrogen sulfide (H_2S) and sulphur dioxide (SO_2) emitted by volcanoes are transformed by bacteria and fungi (through processes of oxidation and reduction) into molecules of sulfate (SO_4), which in turn can be absorbed by the roots of the *pewen*. Once inside the tree, a chain of metabolic reactions begins in the vegetable cells, where enzymes assimilate sulphur from the inorganic molecules of sulfate, incorporating them in a process of synthesis of organic molecules that generate the two amino acids that contain sulphur: methionine and cysteine (cf. Rozzi/ Massardo 2006). Therefore, when the *Pewenche* eat the fruit of the *pewen*, they are also eating sulphur from the volcanic rocks and ashes. Hence, the *Pewenche* are "people of the *pewen*"; and at the same time *Mapuche*, "people of the land". Physical, biotic, and symbolic bodies are interlaced in this profound integration of habitats, habits, and co-inhabitants, and embedded in the *Pewenche* ecosystemic-cultural unity.

Figure 2:   A Scientific Biogeochemical Perspective Concurs with the Integration of *Habitats, Habits, and Inhabitants* Expressed in the *Pewenche* and *Mapuche* Worldviews

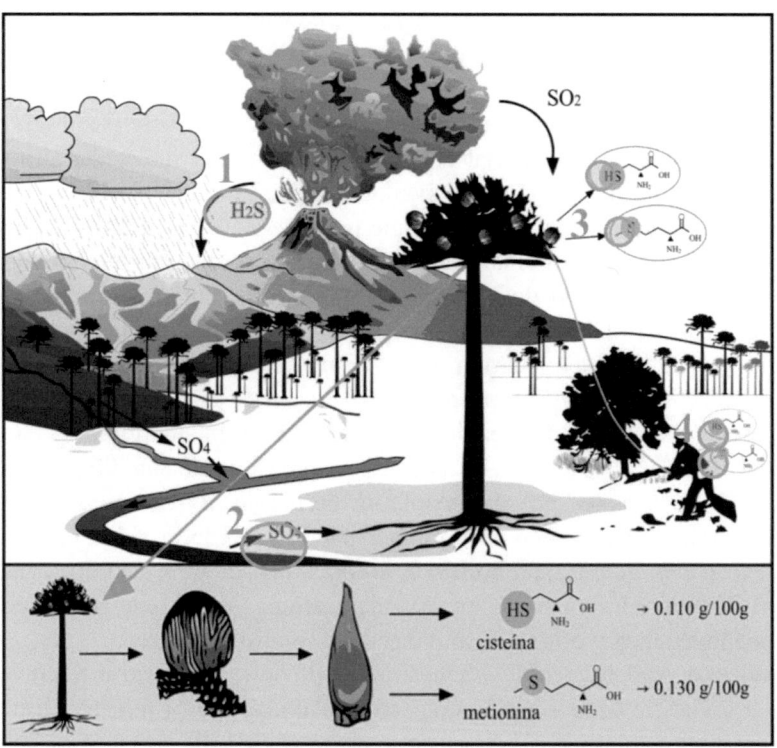

Source: modified from Rozzi/Massardo 2006

4   Loss of the Sustainability of Regional Communities by Disrupting Their Habitats and Habits

A variety of global development projects overlook social and ecological problems derived from the disruption of local habitats and habits that communities have developed within them. A notorious example from Ecuador serves to illustrate this point: the Ecuadorian shrimps, famous in today's international cuisine. Commercial cultivation of two species of shrimps *(Penaeus stylirostris* and *P. vannamei)* began in Ecuador in 1968. Fifteen years later, in 1983, this South American country became the world's principal producer of shrimps (cf. Suarez/Ortiz 2006). This boom involved such a large environmental impact that today the extension of shrimp pools surpasses that of mangroves along the Ecuadorian coast (see Figure 3).

Figure 3:   Shrimp Pools

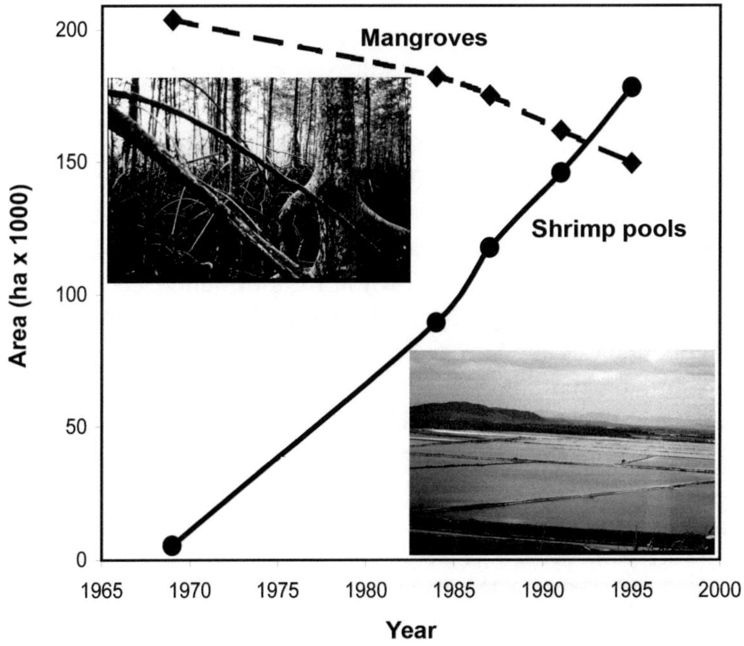

Source: from Suárez/Ortiz 2006, pp. 195-197

In tropical regions of the world, mangroves act as "ecosystem membranes" between terrestrial and marine ecosystems, recycling nutrients and regulating hydrological flows. Their massive conversion to shrimp pools dramatically increases the levels of sedimentation in coastal waters, and the loss of nutrients that are limiting in tropical soils. Shrimp industries also discharge contaminated waters and divert the course of streams and rivers. These processes drastically affect population levels of species of algae, fish, crustaceans, and molluscs that depend on mangroves at some phase of their life cycles (cf. Mera 1999), and the health of humans who consume shrimps and other coastal organisms (cf. Hagler 1997).

In addition, the shrimp industry causes serious social problems by limiting the access of local communities to coastal natural resources and increasing income differences between a few rich people and a growing number of poor people. Coastal areas are public lands and mangroves are protected by several Ecuadorian laws, as well as by international treaties. However, these regulations and the rights of local communities are ignored or easily violated to favour shrimp industries, which limit or forbid access to the traditional users of mangroves by means of government concessions. Furthermore, the conversion of mangroves and the pollution of estuarine ecosystems diminish the quality of life for fisher communities by diminishing the populations and diversity of species of shellfishes, fish, algae, crabs, and oysters that are traditionally gathered in these ecosystems. This illustrates that the export boom of Ecuadorian shrimps has a less known "side effect": it not only has provoked drastic habitat degradation, but it also has brought a reduction in the quality of life of local people inhabiting the coastal region of this country.

Local communities have resisted the invasion of the shrimp industry, and have opposed this type of development since the 1970s. *Concheras*, or women who collect "conchas" or shellfish for selling and for subsistence in the mangroves of the Ecuadorian and Central American coastal communities, have attempted to stop deforestation of Mangroves, risking their lives by lying down in front of bulldozers and excavating equipment that creates the shrimp pools (cf. Hagler 1997). The majority of these women and their communities are African descendents and conscious about how the explosive growth of shrimp exportation entails a contrasting misery for the coastal inhabitants of Ecuador. On March 11, 1999, FUNDECOL (Fundación de Defensa Ecológica) internationally communicated a strong environmental justice demand written by a *conchera*:

> "We have always been ready to cope with everything, and now more than ever, but they want to humiliate us because we are black, because we are poor, but one does not choose the race into which one is born, nor does one choose not to have anything to eat, nor to be ill. But I am proud of my race and of being *conchera* because it is my race which gives me strength to do battle in defence of what my parents were, and my children will inherit; proud of being *conchera* because I have never stolen anything from anyone, I have never taken anybody's bread from his mouth to fill mine, because I have never crawled on my knees asking anybody for money, and I have always lived standing up. Now we are struggling for something which is ours, our ecosystem, but not because we are professional ecologists but because we must remain alive, because if the mangroves disappear, a whole people disappears, we all disappear, we shall no longer be part of the history of Muisne, we shall ourselves exist no longer [...] I do not know what will happen to us if the mangroves disappear, we shall eat garbage in the outskirts of the city of Esmeraldas or in

Guayaquil, we shall become prostitutes, I do not know what will happen to us if the mangroves disappear [...] what I know is that I shall die for my mangroves, even if everything falls down my mangroves will remain, and my children will also stay with me" (in Martinez-Alier 2001, pp. 715f.).

As a result of that local opposition, the government established a biological reserve of mangrove ecosystems in Provincia Esmeraldas in 1995 and, in 1999, created a presidential decree that forbids the cutting of mangroves in Ecuador. These changes to the legislation point to some causes of the rapid environmental degradation occurring in the subcontinent with the highest biodiversity of the planet. At the same time, it provides some hope for a better integration between environmental and social policies by showing that numerous regional populations are aware of the intimate connections between quality of life and the preservation of biodiversity. This awareness is based on the concept of "the good life", "buen vivir" in terms of the Bolivian President Evo Morales, which challenges the concept of the "quality of life" promoted by the market economy that is based almost exclusively on economic indicators (cf. Rozzi/Feinsinger 2006).

The case of Ecuadorian shrimps could apply to innumerable analogous cases throughout South America that affect local cultures that are already living sustainably with their local ecosystem, and whose habits and ways of living are disrupted by development practices that do not take this local connection into account. Based on this, and other cases, which include the expansion of monocultures of exotic tree plantations and salmon farming in southern Chile (cf. Claude et al. 2000; Rozzi et al. 2000), the anchovy fishery in Peru, oil companies in Colombian tropical forests (cf. Sawyer 2004), and dams in Brazil (cf. Fearnside 1999), we identify the following six statements that require urgent critical assessments to transform current prevailing policies in South America:

(1) *Economic growth is presented as helping poor people.* However, mega-projects are frequently opposed by local people whose quality of life is negatively affected. Today, for example, there is a strong opposition against the Pantanal Hidrovia project in which the Paraguay-Parana River would be dredged to let large ships carry cargo from Buenos Aires on the Argentinean coast 3,000 km north to Bolivia, Paraguay, and Brazil. This project could cause the drainage of the world's largest wetland, which is the habitat of endangered jaguars, giant otters, thousands of invertebrates, and tens of Indian tribes, the latter of whom join many nongovernmental organizations (NGOs) and individuals in their protest (cf. Gottgens et al. 2001).

(2) *Macroeconomic indicators* – such as gross domestic product (GDP) or per capita income – can be misleading because of the concentration of income in minorities. For example, in Peru the wealthiest 20% of the population receive more than 60% of the national income, while the poorest 20% of the population receive less than

3% of it (cf. Rozzi/Feinsinger 2006). With black humour, the Argentinean writer Jorge Luis Borges said that: "I do not believe in economic statistics because that figure indicated that in Argentina every person ate a chicken per week, but he knew that some people ate a chicken per day while most Argentineans ate less than half a chicken per month" (in Primack et al. 2006, p. 667).

(3) Large-scale natural resource exploitation models generally satisfy the needs of consumerist societies in distant places, and not of local people. More than 90% of the shrimp produced and exported by companies based in Ecuador are consumed only by people of three regions: USA (51%), Japan (27%), European Union (17%) (cf. Suárez/Ortiz 2006). Similarly, 98% of the king crab cans produced in Cape Horn in southern Chile are exported to USA, Asia, and Europe (cf. Rozzi et al. 2006). In 1978 the Chilean government promulgated the Austral Law that eliminates taxes for large companies to carryout economic activities in the far south in order to promote "development" in the region. Under this economic model, almost all of the money resulting from king crab industry and other fishery exports is deposited in the bank accounts of only a few people, while local people see their daily food taken away, their marine resources becoming extinct, and their marine ecosystems degraded.

(4) *In South American countries there is a marked difference between what is written in the law and what happens in reality.* Today, South American countries and citizens have very little capacity to enforce legal environmental regulations when confronted with corporate economic power. The violation of regulation is facilitated by the fact that economic groups increasingly control the national press and other communication media. Therefore, an informed public discussion of these interwoven environmental and social problems is obstructed by the bias and censorship of the communication media. For example, in 1995 the director of national accounts of the Central Bank in Chile was fired on the spot when he published a report in the official national newspaper about the environmental and social costs of the conversion of native forests into woodchips or substitution by exotic plantations (cf. Claude 1997).

(5) *Agents of losses of biodiversity.* Environmental degradation and losses of biodiversity are frequently caused by a few land owners or companies – national oligarchies or multinational companies (for example, oil, mining, or logging companies) – and not by "the poor" as it is generally presented. For example, the Magellan region of the southern extremity of South America presents one of the lowest population densities in the world (< 1 person/km^2). Nevertheless, more than 33% of the forests of the region (> 2 millions of hectares) have been cleared or burned for large-scale sheep husbandry by the owners of a few haciendas or ranches (cf. CONAF-CONMA-BIRF 1997).

(6) *Short-term economic projects recurrently generate rapid socio-ecological degradation.* Throughout the post-Columbian history of the Americas we find booms of

ephemeral large-scale exploitation as well as monocultures that replace native biota. For example, tropical forests have been replaced by large-scale plantations of sugar cane, banana, and cotton in South, Central, and North America, respectively; large-scale ranching of cattle and sheep also crossed the American continent from Tierra del Fuego to North America; silver and gold fever existed as much in Patagonia, Potosí, Ouro Prêto, Zacatecas, and Chihuahua as in California (cf. Bakewell 1998). These are not mere cases from the past. Today in South America extensive mono-specific plantations of *Eucalyptus* in Colombia, southern Brazil, and Chile are replacing native forests; vast areas of native tropical and temperate forests are cleared and burned for ranching activities; mercury pollution caused by the amalgamation of gold in tropical regions such as the Amazon is affecting the health of aquatic invertebrates, fish, and humans downstream from gold-mining activities (cf. Guimaraes et al. 1999). Historical analyses of these and similar cases throughout South America show repeatedly that they have been associated with ephemeral economic booms that left behind degraded social and ecological environments.

5 Losses of Biocultural Diversity

Biodiversity loss is a well-known phenomenon. During the 21st century, 20% of the world's existing biological species may cease to exist. Less widely known, though attracting increasing attention, is the diversity loss that is affecting the world's languages and cultures. There are an estimated 6,912 languages spoken in the world today (cf. Ethnologue 2005). However, more than half of these languages are spoken by very small communities of less than 1,000 or 10,000 fluent speakers. On the other hand, the top ten languages (Chinese, English, Spanish, Hindi, Arabic, Russian, Bengali, Portuguese, German, and French) comprise more than half of the world's population. This rapidly growing concentration of the world population in a few languages is taking place at expenses of the diversity of human languages that have co-evolved in specific ecological and cultural environments.

This global "language shift" (cf. Harmon 2002) is promoted by growing assimilation pressures that entail collective abandonment of native languages. Today, many threatened languages belong to small language families, and are spoken by less than 100 people. For instance, the Fuegian language family in southern South America includes four languages, two already extinct (Selknam and Haush), and two nearly extinct spoken by less than ten persons (Yahgan and Kaweshkar) (cf. Rozzi et al. 2010). Worldwide more than 10% of the living languages are "nearly extinct", almost 30% are highly threatened (less than 10,000 speakers), and as many as 90% of the languages may vanish during the course of this century (cf. Krauss 1991; Maffi 2005). At the beginning of the 21st century we face three challenging facts regarding biocultural diversity and indigenous people:

(1) More than 70% of the 6,912 languages in the world are indigenous; hence, indigenous peoples constitute most of contemporary cultural diversity (cf. WGPI 2001).
(2) Indigenous people represent a minority; considering its 5,000 ethnic groups, they comprise an estimated population of 300 to 350 millions, i.e. less than 6% of the total world population.
(3) Areas of highest biological diversity on the planet (over a wide biogeographical range from the Polar regions to the deserts, from coastal areas to high altitude zones, from savannas to tropical and temperate rainforests) are inhabited by indigenous people. More than two-thirds of the world's languages are found in the set of 238 ecoregions that were identified by the World Wildlife Fund as having the highest priority for current biological conservation efforts (cf. Oviedo et al. 2000).

These three interrelated facts make evident the current fragility of biocultural diversity. Foreseeing this scenario, in 1988, under the lead of Darrell Posey, the International Society of Ethnobiology was created, and during its First International Congress of Ethnobiology in Belém (Brazil) prepared the Declaration of Belém, which called public attention towards the need to better understand and conserve the "inextricable links" between biological and cultural diversity. Four years later, during another landmark international conference held in Brazil, the Earth Summit, these inextricable biocultural links were widely recognized by the Convention of Biological Diversity (CBD).

The terms traditional ecological knowledge (TEK) and indigenous knowledge (IK) were first used in 1979 and 1980 (cf. Maffi 2001). However, it was only under the influence of the Earth Summit that these terms began to be widely used. Rio 1992 generated global awareness about the complementary nature of biodiversity and the indigenous knowledge of it. The CBD, the Agenda 21 and the Global Biodiversity Strategy included as a principle that "cultural diversity is closely linked to biodiversity. Humanity's collective knowledge of biodiversity and its use and management rests in cultural diversity; conversely conserving biodiversity often helps strengthen cultural integrity and values" (WRI et al. 1992). In turn, the U.S. National Research Council stated in 1992 that development agencies should place greater emphasis on, and assume a stronger role in, systematizing the local knowledge held by indigenous knowledge, gray literature, and anecdotal information. It also emphasized that "a vast heritage about species, ecosystems, and their use exists, but it does not appear in the world literature". Consequently, the declaration mandated that: "If indigenous knowledge has not been documented and compiled, doing so should be a research priority of the highest order. Indigenous knowledge is being lost at an unprecedented rate, and its

preservation, preferably in data base form, must take place as quickly as possible"
(NRC 1992). In terms of sustainability, the effort to maintain not only the knowledge
of these cultures, but also the lifestyle practices or habits inherently tied to this knowledge, must be considered a priority. In order to achieve this, an evaluation of the influence of global development culture and policies upon these diverse cultures and
their habitats must be considered.

6   Formal Education: A Major Driver of Biocultural Homogenization

In spite of the former efforts, patterns of cultural assimilation and homogenization
continue dominate the global scenario. One of the main drivers of linguistic and cultural diversity losses is formal education. Worldwide fewer than 500 languages are
used and taught in formal education, leaving out more than 90% of world's languages.
In addition, more than half of the 193 world's states are officially monolingual. These
educational policies are due not only to the dominance of colonial languages such as
English and Spanish, but also to internal political conflicts, for example, in Africa
many states see minority languages as a threat to national unity. Home to 2,092 languages, Africa harbours more than 30% of the world's linguistic diversity. According
to Herman Batibo, unless "unmarked bilingualism" (in which two or more languages
of unequal social prestige are treated equally) is achieved in Africa's formal education
systems, minority language speakers will continue to face the dilemma of either (cf.
Batibo 2005):

a)   abandoning their native languages (and the eco-cultural knowledge that go with
     them) in order to gain access to wider society or
b)   conserving their languages but remaining marginalized from national affairs.

The temporal rate and biogeographical scale of current global cultural homogenization
is unprecedented. The spread of the dominant culture is proceeding by way of linguistic assimilation as languages of the stronger groups monopolize education, the media,
government, and other avenues of public discourse. Still today, in Africa and South
America it is possible to detect how the use of local languages and forms of knowledge is restricted, and is often denigrated by labelling these vernacular languages as
primitive, even as superstitious, and unfit for the present-day world (cf. Mignolo
2000; Rodney 1982). Analyses about the ongoing linguistic elimination uncover post-
colonial patterns of biocultural homogenization. With the aim of overcoming these
patterns of linguistic discrimination, UNESCO and numerous non-governmental organizations signed "The Universal Declaration of Linguistic Rights" in 1996 in Barcelona, which affirms that "all language communities have equal rights". Linguistic

Human Rights should help halting the overriding effects of the global-uniform educational system, and fostering the continuity of local languages and educational practices.

7   The Inextricable Links of *Habitats, Habits, and Inhabitants* for Sustainable Cultures

The sustainability of the bioculturally diverse communities around the globe requires recovery of the understanding about the inextricable links between the habitats, the habits, and the inhabitants of a region. With this systemic approach, our proposed biocultural units formed by the triad of habitats-habits-inhabitants acquire essential economic, ecological, and ethical dimensions to better support the sustainability of the highly diverse human and non-human communities of life.

Economically, the biocultural triad highlights the importance of sustainability of territorial rights of indigenous and local communities in South America, and elsewhere. As Walter Pengue emphasizes, autonomy and ownership of the territories are the condition of possibility for the subsistence of rural and other local communities in Latin America (cf. Pengue 2008). The victims of the destruction of habitats and their unique biodiversity in the Neotropics are not only biological species other than humans and future generations. Today, in Latin America numerous indigenous, African-American, fishing, and other rural communities resist, protest against their displacements, and the destruction of their regional habitats (cf. Rozzi 2001). As Colombian philosopher Arturo Escobar criticizes in his landmark book "The Invention of the Third World": It "suffices to take a quick look to the biophysical, economic, and cultural landscapes of the Third World to realize that the Development Project is in crisis" (Escobar 1996, p. 9). Against this background Escobar calls for a post-development era, and for its instantiation, the biocultural approach can contribute to assessing and adapting the interrelations of the biophysical, economic, and cultural components of the landscapes by taking into consideration the high diversity of habitats, habits, and inhabitants who inhabit the regions of the Southern and Northern Hemispheres.

The ecological dimension can be illustrated with reference to a key practice of the southernmost ethnic group of the world: the Yahgan people. At the southern end of the Americas, the women of the Yahgan community weave baskets made of rushes. Different types of baskets are used to gather berries and shellfish in the archipelagos of Cape Horn south of Tierra del Fuego (cf. Gusinde 1961; McEwan et al. 1996). These baskets are central for traditional subsistence activities, whose continuity depends on the conservation of the wetlands habitats where the austral rushes *(Marsippospermu grandiflorum)* grow, and provide the necessary vegetal fibres that are gathered by the Yahgan women (cf. Massardo/Rozzi 2006). Today, the preservation of these habits and habitats contribute to the well-being of the Yahgan community, to the preservation of their biocultural identity, and also to the richness of the experience of ecotourists who visit Cape Horn. Visitors appreciate the unique sub-Antarctic plants, the Yahagan weaving culture, and their biocultural interrelationships (see Figure 4).

Figure 4:   Ecotourism

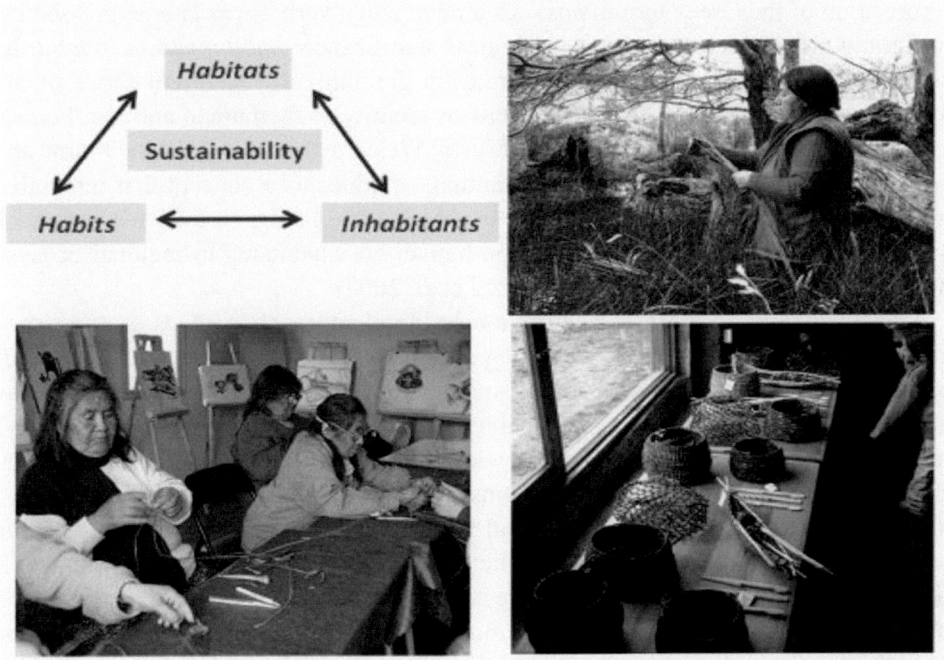

To implement sustainable ecotourism, we propose that we need to conserve and respect the habitats, habits, and inhabitants. For example, in the South American sub-Antarctic region wetland habitats provide the vegetable fibres needed to carry out the habit of weaving baskets by the inhabitants of Cape Horn, the Yahgan people. Today, the basketry by Yahgan women is linked to a programme of sustainable ecotourism, based on biocultural conservation.

Source: Photographs by Sandra Vallejo, Lorena Penaranda, and Ricardo Rozzi; Omora Ethno-botanical Park Photographic Archive

The ethical dimension of the biocultural triad of habitats-habits-inhabitants is essential because during the last four decades the omnipresence of neo-liberal economy in South America has favoured a marked bias towards economic values, which give little attention to regional biocultural contexts (cf. Pengue 2008). This economic bias has added to the Eurocentric bias carried by dominant, colonial ethics that developed with little or no consideration for habitats, non-human as well as non-European human co-inhabitants (cf. Rozzi 2001). It is interesting to note that this omission has moved modern ethics away from the original meaning contained in the Greek term *ethos*. The word *ethics* originated from the Greek term *ethos*, which in its more archaic form meant a *den*: the dwelling of an animal (cf. Liddell/Scott 1996). By an extension of the use of this word, its meaning came to include the dwellings of human beings, and later this noun also became the verb *to dwell* (cf. González 1996, pp. 9-12). This dual interpretation of the Greek term *ethos* – as a noun and a verb – was later expressed by two Latin words, which today gain ecological significance: *habitat* and *to inhabit*. In turn, inhabiting a particular habitat generates in the long-term recurrent forms of in-habiting, i.e., habits that configure the *ethos* or identity of the human and non-human inhabitants. In this way, within the history of Western thought, our biocultural ap-proach allows the recovery of an understanding of ethics as a concept that integrates not only the habits, but also the habitats in which these habits co-evolve as ways of co-habitation with diverse human and non-human co-inhabitants in regional ecosys-tems and the biosphere as a whole (cf. Rozzi et al. 2008).

At the beginning of the 21st century, a biocultural approach to ethics acquires spe-cial relevance to counterbalance prevailing anthropocentric ethical approaches, which frequently overlook regional biocultural singularities, "as if" humans and their identi-ties could exist in isolation from their habitats and non-human co-inhabitants. Today, Amerindian and scientific ecological knowledge as well as Western philosophical tra-ditions provide complementary foundations to better understand the interrelated dy-namics of the inhabitants, their habits and habitats. This understanding redirects our attention towards the heterogeneous mosaic of biocultural landscapes, spanning over a gradient of human influences from remote to rural and urban socio-ecological systems making evident that a singular culture of sustainability fails to fully address, and con-sequently threatens, the great diversity and complexity of these biocultural interrela-tionships. A greater appreciation of this biocultural mosaic within global educational, administrative, and economic systems that prevail today can foster policies that favour the continuity of regional sustainable cultures, with their dynamic, idiosyncratic ways of inhabiting their regional habitats, which could also provide a foundation for a global, heterogeneous meta-culture of sustainability.

References

Aagesen, D. L. (1998): Indigenous Resource Rights and Conservation of the Monkey-puzzle Tree (Araucaria araucana, araucariaceae): A Case Study from Southern Chile. In: Economic Botany, Vol. 52, pp. 146-160

Bakewell, P. (1998): A History of Latin America. Empires and Sequels: 1450–1930. Oxford, UK

Batibo, H. (2005): Language Decline and Death in Africa: Causes, Consequences and Challenges. Clevedon/Somerset, UK

Brown, J.; Mitchell, N.; Betesford, M. (eds.) (2005): The Protected Landscape Approach: Linking Nature, Culture, and Community. Gland, Switzerland/Cambridge, UK

Callicott, J. B. (1997): Earth's Insights: A Multicultural Survey of Ecological Ethics from the Mediterranean Basin to the Australian Outback. Berkeley, CA

Claude, M. (1997): Una Vez Más La Miseria: Es Chile un País Sustentable? [Once Again the Misery: Is Chile a Sustainable Country?]. Santiago, Chile (in Spanish)

Claude, M.; Oporto, J.; Ibáñez, C.; Brieva, L.; Espinosa, C.; Arqueros, M. (2000): La Ineficiencia de la Salmonicultura en Chile [The Inffeciency of Salmon Culture in Chile]. Santiago, Chile (in Spanish)

CONAF-CONMA-BIRF (1997) Catastro y evaluación de los recursos vegetacionales nativos de Chile [Inventory and Assessment of the Native Vegetational Resources in Chile]. CONAF, Santiago, Chile (in Spanish)

Dominick, R. H. I. (1992): The Environmental Movement in Germany. Prophets and Pioneers 1871 - 1971. Bloomington, IN

Ericksen, P.; Woodley, E. (2005): Using Multiple Knowledge Systems: Benefits and Challenges. In: Millennium Ecosystem Assessment, Vol. 4, pp. 85-177

Escobar, A. (1996): Encountering Development: The Making and Unmaking of the Third World. Princeton, NJ

Ethnologue (2005): Languages of the World. Dallas, TX. – URL: http://www.ethnologue.com/ [accessed June 2007]

Fearnside, P. M. (1999): Social Impacts of Brazil's Tucuruí Dam. In: Environmental Management, Vol. 24, pp. 483-495

González, J. (1996): El Ethos, Destino del Hombre [The Ethos, Destiny of Man]. Ciudad de México (Fondo de Cultura Económica) (in Spanish)

Gottgens, J.; Perry, J. E.; Fortney, R. H.; Meyer, J. E.; Benedict, M.; Rood, B. E. (2001): The Paraguay-Paraná Hidrovía: Protecting the Pantanal with Lessons from the Past. In: BioScience, Vol. 51, pp. 301-308

Guimarães, J. R. D.; Fostier, A. H.; Forti, M. C.; Melfi, J. A.; Kehrig, H.; Mauro, J. B. N.; Malm, O.; Krug, J. F. (1999): Mercury in Human and Environmental Samples from Two Lakes in Amapá, Brazilian Amazon. In: Ambio, Vol. 28, pp. 296-301

Gusinde, M. (1961): The Yamana: The Life and Thought of the Water Nomads of Cape Horn. Vol. I - V. New Haven, CT

Hagler, M. (1997): Shrimp – The Devastating Delicacy. Greenpeace Reports

Harmon, D. (1996): Losing Species, Losing Languages: Connections between Biological and Linguistic Diversity. In: Southwest Journal of Linguistics, Vol. 15, pp. 89-108

Harmon, D. (2002): In Light of Our Differences: How Diversity in Nature and Culture Makes Us Human. Washington, D.C. (Smithsonian Institution)

Heckenberger, M. J.; Kuikuro, A.; Kuikuro, U. T.; Russell, Chr.; Schmidt, M.; Fausto, C.; Franchetto, B. (2003): Amazonia 1492: Pristine Forest or Cultural Parkland? In: Science, Vol. 301, pp. 1710-1714

Hunn, E (2007): Ethnobiology in Four Phases. In: Journal of Ethnobiology, Vol. 27, No. 1 (Spring/Summer), pp. 1-10

Jax, K.; Rozzi, R. (2004): Ecological Theory and Values in the Determination of Conservation Goals: Examples from Temperate Regions of Germany, USA and Chile. In: Revista Chilena de Historia Natural, Vol. 77, pp. 349-366

Knaut, A. (1993): Zurück zur Natur! Die Wurzeln der Ökologiebewegung. Jahrbuch für Naturschutz und Landschaftspflege (Supplement). Vol. 1. Bonn (in German)

Krauss, M. E. (1991): The World's Languages in Crisis. In: Language, Vol. 68, pp. 4-10

Liddell, H. G.; Scott, R. (1996): A Greek-English Lexicon. 9th ed. New York

Loh, J.; Harmon, D. (2005): A Global Index of Biocultural Diversity. In: Ecological Indicators, Vol. 5, pp. 231-241

Maffi, L. (ed.) (2001): On Biocultural Diversity. Linking Language, Knowledge, and the Environment. Washington, D.C.

Maffi, L. (2005): Linguistic, Cultural, and Biological Diversity. In: Annual Review of Anthropology, Vol. 34, pp. 599-617

Mann, Ch. (2005): 1491. New Revelations of the Americas Before Columbus. New York

Martinez-Alier, J. (2001): Ecological Conflicts and Valuation: Mangroves versus Shrimps in the Late 1990s. In: Environment and Planning C, Vol. 19, pp. 713-728

Massardo, F.; Rozzi, R. (2006): The World's Southernmost Ethnoecology: Yahgan Craftmanship and Traditional Ecological Knowledge. Bilingual English-Spanish edit. Punta Arenas, Chile

McDonnell, M.; Pickett, St. (1994): Human as Component of Ecosystems. New York a.o.

McEwan, C.;Borrero, L.; Prieto, A. (1997): Patagonia: Natural History, Prehistory and Ethnography at the Uttermost Part of the Earth. Princeton, NJ

Mera, V. (1999): Género, manglar y subsistencia [Gender, Mangrove and Subsistence]. Quito, Ecuador (in Spanish)

Mignolo, W. (2000): Local Histories – Global Designs. Princeton, NJ

Moore, J. (2005): Cultural Landscapes in the Ancient Andes: Archaeologies of Place Gainsville. Gainsville, FL

Müller, N.; Werner, P. (2010): Urban Biodiversity and the Case for Implementing the Convention on Biological Diversity in Towns and Cities. In: Müller, N.; Werner, P.; Kelcey, J. G. (eds.): Urban Biodiversity and Design. Hoboken, NJ, pp. 3-34

NRC – National Research Council (1992): Conserving Biodiversity: A Research Agenda for Development Agencies. Washington, D.C.

Oviedo, G.; Maffi, L.; Laren, P. B. (2000): Indigenous and Traditional Peoples of the World and Ecoregion Conservation: An Integrated Approach to Conserving the World's Biological and Cultural Diversity. Gland, Switzerland

Pengue, W. (2008): La Apropiación y el Saqueo de la Naturaleza [The Appropriation and Plundering of Nature]. Buenos Aires, Argentina (in Spanish)

Posey, D. (ed.) (1999): Cultural and Spiritual Values of Biodiversity. London/Nairobi (Intermediate Technology Publications and UNEP)

Prance, G. T.; Kalunki, J. A. (eds.) (1984): Ethnobotany in the Neotropics. Advances in Economic Botany. Vol. 1. Bronx, New York

Primack, R.; Rozzi, R.; Feinsinger, P.; Dirzo, R.; Massardo, F. (eds.) (2006): Fundamentos de conservación biológica: perspectivas Latinoamericanas [Essentials of Conservation Biology: Latin American Perspectives]. 2nd ed. México City, México (Fondo de Cultura Económica) (in Spanish)

Rodney, W. (1982): How Europe Underdeveloped Africa. Washington, D.C.

Rozzi, R. (2001): Éticas ambientales latinoamericanas: raíces y ramas [Latin American Environmental Ethics: Roots and Branches]. In: Primack, R.; Rozzi, R.; Feinsinger, P.; Dirzo, R.; Massardo, F. (eds.): Fundamentos de conservación biológica: perspectivas Latinoamericanas [Essentials of Conservation Biology: Latin American Perspectives]. 2nd ed. México City, México (Fondo de Cultura Económica), pp. 311-362 (in Spanish)

Rozzi, R.; Arango, X.; Massardo, F.; Anderson, C. B.; Heidinger, K.; Moses, K. (2008): Field Environmental Philosophy and Biocultural Conservation: The Omora Ethnobotanical Park Educational Program. In: Environmental Ethics, Vol. 30, No. 3, pp. 325-336

Rozzi, R.; Feinsinger, P. (2006): Desafíos para la conservación biológica en Latinoamérica [Challenges for Conservation Biology in Latin America]. In: Primack, R.; Rozzi, R.; Feinsinger, P.; Dirzo, R.; Massardo, F. (eds.): Fundamentos de conservación biológica: perspectivas Latinoamericanas [Essentials of Conservation Biology: Latin American Perspectives]. 2nd ed. México City, México (Fondo de Cultura Económica), pp. 661-688 (in Spanish)

Rozzi, R.; Massardo, F. (2006): Similitudes y diferencias interculturales en las éticas ambientales [Intercultural Similarities and Differences in Environmental Ethics]. In: Primack, R.; Rozzi, R.; Feinsinger, P.; Dirzo, R.; Massardo, F. (eds.): Fundamentos de conservación biológica: perspectivas Latinoamericanas [Essentials of Conservation Biology: Latin American Perspectives]. 2nd ed. México City, México (Fondo de Cultura Económica), pp. 319-321 (in Spanish)

Rozzi, R.; Massardo, F.; Anderson, C.; Heidinger, K.; Silander jr., J. (2006): Ten Principles for Biocultural Conservation at the Southern Tip of the Americas: The Approach of the Omora Ethnobotanical Park. In: Ecology & Society, Vol. 11, No. 1, p. 43. – URL: http://www.ecologyandsociety.org/vol11/iss1/art43/

Rozzi, R.; Massardo, F.; Anderson, C.; McGehee, S.; Clark, G.; Egli, G.; Ramilo, E.; Calderón, U.; Calderón, C.; Aillapan, L.; Zárraga, C. (2010): Multi-Ethnic Bird Guide of the Sub-Antarctic Forests of South America. Denton, TX/Punta Arenas, Chile

Rozzi, R.; Silander, J.; Armesto, J. J.; Feinsinger, P.; Massardo, F. (2000): Three Levels of Integrating Ecology with the Conservation of South American Temperate Forests. The Initiative of the Institute of Ecological Research Chiloé, Chile. In: Biodiversity and Conservation, Vol. 9, pp. 1199-1217

Sawyer, S. (2004): Crude Chronicles: Indigenous Politics, Multinational Oil, and Neoliberalism in Ecuador. Durham, UK (American Encounters/Global Interactions Series)

Suárez, L.; Ortiz, D. (2006): Producción de camarones y destrucción de manglares en Ecuador [Shrimp Production and Destruction of Mangroves in Ecuador]. In: Primack, R.; Rozzi, R.; Feinsinger, P.; Dirzo, R.; Massardo, F. (eds.): Fundamentos de conservación biológica: perspectivas Latinoamericanas [Essentials of Conservation Biology: Latin American Perspectives]. 2nd ed. México City, México (Fondo de Cultura Económica), pp. 195-197 (in Spanish)

UNEP – United Nations Environmental Programme (2007): Global Environment Outlook: Environment for Development. Nairobi (UNEP)

UNESCO – United Nations Educational, Scientific and Cultural Organization (2005): Operational Guidelines for the Implementation of the World Heritage Convention. Paris (UNESCO World Heritage Centre)

Toledo, V. M. (2000): Ethnoecology: A Conceptual Framework for the Study of Indigenous Knowledge of Nature. Lecture at the 7th International Congress of Ethnobiology, Athens, Georgia, USA, October

WGIP – UN Working Group on Indigenous Populations (2001): Indigenous Peoples and the United
    Nations System. Geneva (WGIP, Office of the High Commissioner for Human Rights, United
    Nations Office)

Wilcox, B. A.; Duin, K. N. (1995): Indigenous Cultural and Biological Diversity: Overlapping Values
    of Latin American Ecoregions. In: Cultural Survival Quarterly, Winter, pp. 49-53

WRI – World Resources Institute; WCU – World Conservation Union; UNEP – United Nations Envi-
    ronment Programme (1992): Global Biodiversity Strategy: Policy-maker's Guide. Baltimore, MD
    (WRI Publications)

Three Steps towards a Culture of Sustainability

Oliver Parodi

This contribution was written to draw attention to elements which, in my mind, must be taken into account and put into effect on the way towards a culture of sustainability. I would like to take three steps in different directions, but all of them leading to a culture of sustainability.

This first requires some basic thoughts to be spent on start and finish, on "culture" and "sustainability" and a "culture of sustainability". A first step will then show the way out of an existing gap between the spheres of "culture" and "nature", and point to culture-based misconceptions of our 'environment' which need to be corrected. Another step demands cultivation of technology and tries to incorporate this in the language of "functioning technology." The third step then points in a clearly different direction, making reference to the individual, personal sides of sustainability and their relevance to achieving sustainable development.

1 Start and Finish: Culture and Sustainability

First of all, the concepts of "culture" and "sustainability" as used here will be explained so that the distant finish of a *"culture of sustainability"* can be described at least in a vague outline.

1.1 On the Concept of Culture

The concept of "culture" is used here in the sense of a contemporary understanding of culture in which culture is no longer defined as the opposite of nature, but the simultaneous existence of the basic cultural elements of *collectivity, communication,* and *convention* (cf. Hansen 2001). The size of, and the features connecting, these collectives can differ widely: Cultures can be seen in nations, companies, clubs, small families, etc.

The term "culture" as used below is not primarily meant to refer to any distinction from other collectives, not to the culture of Americans, Chinese, Germans, etc., nor does it refer to that realm of "high culture" which comprises the arts, theatre, film,

etc., but refers in a much more general and basic sense to culture as something characteristic of any (permanent) collective in conventions and communication, keeping that
collective together, also relating to us and continuously permeating our everyday existence.[1]

1.2   On the Concept of Sustainability

"Sustainability" will be used here in a narrow sense of the term as explained in detail
by Jürgen Kopfmüller (cf. Kopfmüller, this publication) basing on the interpretation
written down in the UN Brundtland report (cf. Hauff 1987), dealing with an intergenerational global justice linked with the care for and concern about our environment
(not only) as our common natural livelihood. It should be emphasized at this point that
this is not about differences in specific concepts of sustainability (such as strong or
weak sustainability; one, three, or five pillars) but rather about the idea of sustainability underlying all these concepts, or the *pool of ideas* of sustainability (such as the
permanence of mankind, globality, intergenerational justice interdisciplinary perspective), which became established in the wake of the Brundtland report (cf. Hauff 1987,
Kopfmüller et al. 2001).

1.3   Culture and Sustainability – Some Links

In a functionalist interpretation, culture can be seen as a program for permanent maintenance of a collective. "'Culture' is a common regulatory mechanism creating community [...], established to secure permanence in time and space: This is the productive as well as conservative moment of 'culture'" (Böhme 2001, p. 3).

As a consequence, sustainability (in the original narrow sense of the term) would
be the implicit nucleus and objective of any culture. Or, to put it differently, sustainability would be the explication and rational design of both a cultural programme and
core cause *per se* formulated for the "collective" "mankind".

Realizing that our (global) way of life is not sustainable implies that our (modern
Western) culture is – unable to sustain itself – a non-sustainable culture because it
attacks its ecological, economic and social foundations.

This association of culture and sustainability impressively shows how perverted,
respectively wrong, our present way of life and our situation in life are. Sustainable
development is not the basis of our culture; today, it is moreover its counterdesign.
"Permanent existence", the conservative, preserving moment of sustainability, has

---

1   When reference is made below to "our culture", this does not imply a homogeneous collective
     but, vaguely, fundamental cultural characteristics, conventions of thought, and basic attitudes of
     the occidental Western modern cultural complex.

meanwhile become the new, irritating, even revolutionary element of our culture and our way of life. At this point, it becomes evident that the sustainability idea incorporates a fundamental criticism of culture.

In that functionalist interpretation, this simply means: Our modern culture does not work; it is a non-culture or no culture at all.[2] And even from a humanistic point of view our modern culture is often a non-culture, failing in basic claims like freedom, solidarity, sympathy, generational and intergenerational justice. Moreover Klaus Töpfer (former head of UNEP) once said: "We are basing our entire Western way of life on three grand delusions: By living at the expense of our environment, the developing countries and the following generations." This is neither permanent nor viable nor sustainable.

Where cultures do not develop sustainably (which is likely to be the case almost on a global scale), they are in a crisis of existence – or (as many presume) perhaps even dissolving. And what next? Perhaps a culture of sustainability.

1.4   Culture of Sustainability

What can be said about such a future culture of sustainability? Not much – and only in speculative terms. In my view, a culture of sustainability theoretically would be the result of the sustainability concepts and, in practice, the implementation of sustainable development: a collectively supported, jointly agreed, and understandable sustainability which is institutionalized and internalized and is handed down through conventions, patterns, habits and even feelings.

In the same way in which one swallow does not make a summer, concepts of sustainability do not produce a culture of sustainability. The current rational, scientifically based and political sustainability concepts (cf., e.g., Bundesregierung 2002; Kopfmüller et al. 2001; Ott/Döring 2004; UN-DSD 2009) are important milestones on the road to a culture of sustainability. However, that culture must go far beyond these concepts and political measures. Even the "cultural sustainability" discussed in some places (cf. Krainer/Trattnigg 2004; cf. also Kowalski/Schaffer 2010) should be superseded by a culture of sustainability because a "cultural sustainability" remains partial (like "ecological" or "institutional" sustainability) and limited in scope.

---

2   Two views can be distinguished here: (1) With a view to the modern Western cultural area it can be said: This does not work, at least it no longer works today. It bears fundamental (functional) features of a non-culture. (2) With a global view to the totality of mankind, the "functional" crisis could also be interpreted as a crisis of origin: Culture does not yet function because there is no such global culture as yet. We have been living in a world society for some time already, but we are far from living in a world culture. "Mankind" so far has remained a concept and, to all extents and purposes, an a-culture.

In a culture of sustainability, this sustainability is lived every day. In the same way in which the former grand cultural achievements of democracy, liberty, autonomy, education, etc., nowadays are effective in the cultural background and only appear on the scene when endangered, sustainability in the future should withdraw into the cultural background as an idea and an achievement once fought for, and steer the collective from that background.

In a first approximation, a culture of sustainability would be a translation and realization of the basic values and ideas of existing sustainability concepts into a lived culture. A culture of sustainability thus is not primarily a definition and implementation of the sophisticated rules, indicators, etc. of existing sustainability concepts but, in a more comprehensive and softer sense, the collective institutionalization of the continuation of those humanistic normative basic ideas underlying the concepts (such as globality, intergenerational justice, extended anthropocentrism, etc.).

Looking at the concepts of sustainability and taking their claims (global, integrative, at least anthropocentric, intergenerational) seriously reveals their full scope. Among other things, it is about nothing less than mankind, the community of all human beings, achieving the "all mankind become brothers" ideal or, expanded in an ecocentric sense, "all life becomes brothers".[3] It is quite possible to see sustainability as the (almost only) major design of the future which, at least in part, is being touted in societal debates and implemented. A culture of sustainability thus would constitute a link to the Western cultural area, while its implementation would show major differences from today's modern way of life and everyday practice.[4]

2   Readjusting Basic Cultural Attitudes

After this brief outline of the start and finish of a culture of sustainability, the following sections will focus on some elements of content on the way to such a culture of sustainability. This first step is to overcome an idea which is nearly constitutive of our (Western) cultural image and also of our concept of technology, namely: the polarizing division of nature and culture as well as of nature and technology. The instrumental relation of man and his "environment" based on this concept must be corrected and modified.

---

3   A culture of sustainability could overcome modern and post-modern times through synthesis, institute and fulfill humanism, cause today's culture to decline and, perhaps, mark the departure into a new, trans-anthropocentric age.

4   This applies irrespective of influences which must be expected to act on a global culture of sustainability from forces outside Western cultural areas and concepts.

2.1   Prevailing Separation of Culture and Nature

The basic concept of culture as *counter-nature* (cf. Großklaus/Oldemeyer 1983; Parodi 2008) underlies the modern concept of culture, is valid even today in broad areas of our cultural practice (and theory) and is effective largely without being queried. This can be briefly illustrated as follows:

- Nature is considered the counter-*concept* of culture (dichotomic world formula): "The concepts of nature and culture are sufficient to describe this world" (Marschall 1993, p. 17).
- The theory and philosophy of culture are often based on the separation of nature and culture (cf. Hansen 2000).
- A common concept implies: "Culture is the transformation of nature by work."
- Another common concept is this: "Culture is what makes us different from nature."
- Even the sustainability debate is influenced by this separation; the ecological pillar is based on the natural sphere, while the economic and social pillars are rooted in the sphere of culture.[3]

2.2   Present Separation of Technology and Nature

In an analogous way, *technology* can be regarded as *counter-nature*. This is associated with the concept of incompatibility of technology and nature. Throughout Western cultural history the concept of technology, with a few exceptions, has constituted the counter-concept of "nature". When modern times began, technology closely associated with the natural sciences (and later on with the economic system) became the central cultural program. Its content is man's greatest possible *independence* of nature, *domination* of nature, and *exploitation* of nature.

Even modern common "definitions of technology" clearly reveal this dichotomy of technology and nature and the exploitation of nature based on it. Indications of the prevailing technology/nature divide can be found, e.g., in philosophical definitions:

- "Technology, after all, is nothing but overcoming nature by human consciousness. […] Technology being counter to nature is a principal characteristic" (Günter Ropohl, quoted from Huber 1989, p. 35).
- "Technology [is considered] the opposite of nature" (Prechtl/Burkhard 1996, p. 512).
- Technology "means exploiting natural resources and the forces of nature in the interest of satisfying human needs" (Brugger 1998, p. 393).
- More proof (of a de-facto opposition to nature) can be found in prevailing technical practice:

- The way in which mankind handles the world by technical means is the main cause of the disappearance of nature and living space.
- Nature conservation and technology are diametrical opposites.
- There is no such thing as "nature technologies" or "conservation technologies" – the very concepts give rise to linguistic uneasiness (at least in German).

2.3   Outdated Separation

This polarized, exploiting relationship to nature via *technology as counter-nature* is no longer modern but outdated and dangerous. It is important to correct this relation between nature and technology, which is perceived as a wrong, dangerous attitude. This approach is supported by two things (among others):

- First, the disappearance of nature in our world of life as a consequence of the ubiquitous introduction of technology into our natural living environment. Nature is cultivated, turned technical, disappears as such, merges with technical artefacts and culture. What remains are ecological connections. Technology and nature are merged into "ecofacts" (Parodi 2008, p. 194, after Karafyllis 2003). Where, "in an ecological context, technology and nature are blended inseparably and unforesee-ably, it no longer makes sense to arrange phenomena by the distinction between technology and nature" (Luhmann 1997, p. 522).
- Secondly, the ecological crisis which impressively shows that the current concept of technology as a practiced program of dominating and exploiting nature is now producing consequences which threaten the very existence of mankind. The ecological crisis, however, is the expression of a cultural practice based mainly on the man-culture-technology versus nature split.

2.4   Correcting Misconceptions

History shows that sustainability designs were sparked off by ecological problems. In a cultural perspective, this means that they are ignited by the ecological deficits of the long-term, complete cultural practice of modern nature management. This, in turn, indicates that sustainability, if it is to go beyond the mere control of symptoms and beyond increasing efficiency, can be installed and implemented permanently only if the underlying cultural misconceptions are corrected. These misconceptions are fixed in the counter-natural position of culture and technology, are expressed in the ecological problem situation, but are not limited by dealing with nature. They even exist in the relation to our social, individual, and "generational" environment as well as to our living environment. The following misconceptions or outdated attitudes of men or a collective to their ecological, social, individual and generative "environment" have to be corrected:

- Overemphasis on separation and being separate – neglecting connectedness with the environment.
- Overemphasis on autonomy and independence – neglecting inclusion and dependence.
- Overvaluation of individuality and difference – undervaluation of collectivity and what is similar.

Separation, autonomy, and individuality expose human beings, take them out of their natural environment. They generate and suggest power. Overemphasizing this can be considered a misconception in two ways: on the one hand, in an ethical sense, because overvaluation and emphasis take value out of any environment, open the door to violence and exploitation; on the other hand, epistemologically, because emphasis, if it is only a theoretical suggestion without any reality, gives rise to wrong conclusions and failing actions. Irrespective of which aspect applies: Wrong actions also harm the whole and, in this way, directly or indirectly also those who (think they) are powerful and ruling – us as human beings. In this connection, it is irrelevant whether these misconceptions are adopted towards nature, the environment, or other persons. "It is the same misconception of persons relative to the whole which, on the one hand, exploits and destroys the natural environment and, on the other hand, impairs social order and development" (Meyer-Abich 1984, p. 264).

The same culturally deep-rooted, wrong attitudes can be found behind today's ecological and social misconceptions.

Recognizing these misconceptions is mostly painful. In cultural history, this can be seen as the scientific "humiliation of people" mentioned by Johannes Rohbeck referring to Sigmund Freud (cf. Rohbeck 1993, p. 10).[5] However, mere recognition is not sufficient to correct cultural practices.

It should be emphasized at this point that I am not interested in relinquishing entirely the instrumental attitude of human beings vis-à-vis their environment, especially in technology, "cultivated" in an extreme sense up to the present time. I am more interested in diminishing the importance of that approach and supplementing and correcting it. The distant user's attitude of man relative to his environment as an object of use must be reduced, and the instrumental attitude must be balanced more and more by an attitude of valuation and association. If one wants to follow Martin Buber and Ernst Oldemeyer, (technical) use of the co-world would have to be in the "humility of

---

5   After cosmological injury, Copernican removal from the center of the world, biological injury as per theory of evolution, and psychological injury in psychoanalysis, human beings in the industrial age experience technological injury (cf. Rohbeck 1993, p. 10). The active proponents of technology must recognize that they are not (any more) "masters of their creation, but are ruled by the products they themselves created" (Rohbeck 1993, p. 10).

being part" of a larger, e.g. eco-natural, entity (cf. Buber 1960; Oldemeyer 2005; Parodi 2008). "This is no attempt to do away with technology but rather to release it from its opposition to nature, into which it has run" (Meyer-Abich 1984, p. 265).

3 Cultivation of Technology

In this next step, the *integrative idea* of sustainability is to be strengthened and focused on one area which plays a key role in our present-day world of life and also with respect to sustainable development: technology. Let us then refer to another separation that needs to be overcome: that of technology and "culture". "Overcoming" in this case is not meant to level out all differences and deny the possibility of analytical distinction, but rather functions as a link between the two areas and means the implementation of technology as a cultural enterprise.

First and foremost, it is safe to say that our world of life has to a large extent become a technical or technically dominated one (see Section 2.3). The world is increasingly turning into a technotope (cf. Erlach 2000). Also our way of handling the world and our environment, irrespective of whether this is natural, ecological, cultural, or social, in most cases is mediated technically. Technology more and more acts as a medium, linking man to his environment. Human beings nowadays grasp and understand[6] this environment indirectly, by technology. In the dual sense of Jakob J. von Uexküll, human beings perceive and modify[7] their environment increasingly by means of technology.

3.1 From Making Culture Technical to Making Technology Cultural

Also cultures and cultural practices are not unaffected by technology. On the contrary: Culture is seen to become more and more technological, first of all, purely in the manner of an object: Our culture, our collectives, communication, and conventions more and more rely on technical equipment and processes. More and more technical artefacts permeate our everyday existence, connect us with the environment, or constitute it.

Also mentally, our culture (again and again) is subject to technology. This is not about technical artefacts but rather about things technical (also transported in those artefacts) in the form of technical fitness and rationality for a purpose. Today our culture is permanently threatened by being reduced to that instrumental attitude explained in the previous chapter.

---

6   In German "begreifen".
7   In German "wahrnehmen".

Reducing culture to technology can be counteracted by introducing culture into technology. This is to imply the full programmatic incorporation of technology into (the respective) culture, which is the complete permeation of technology by culture.

In this program, technology must not be considered, evaluated, and designed as a sphere autonomous and separate from culture. On this side, there is technology (cars, TV, telephone), on the other side, there is our culture, there are movies, communication. On this side, there is the purpose of our technical activities, our work, and detached from this, on the other side, there is the sense of our life. (This is commonly referred to as "alienation".) Instead of making the purpose sense, as is the case when culture is made technological, which also reduces human beings and their culture to *homo faber* or *homo oeconomicus*, the purposes would be embedded in the relationships of the respective culture, thus providing sense and meaning.

In a concrete way, making technology part of culture means the pro-active inclusion of culture in the development and use of technology. Technology development is to be pursued with culture in mind, i.e. many more and, above all, cultural aspects should be included in designing technology.

3.2 Functioning Technology

The omnipresence of technology, its power, and its role in our everyday world make it important that culture and, with it, sustainability also infuse technology – not only in theoretical ideas, but in a very specific sense, in technical systems, structures, and equipment. In the interest of this development, a soundly based, profound linguistic rearrangement will be proposed here first.

Where only manufacturing and using very specific technical artefacts is referred to (cars, mobile phones, dams, power plants), first of all a catalogue of requirements can be compiled which such technical products ideally should meet (see Table 1).

The question from what point in time on technology or a piece of equipment is said to *function*, will barely extend to the second point of the catalogue of requirements to be mastered for that purpose. A car functions when it runs, can be steered and, perhaps, also braked. A power plant functions when it produces electricity, a genetically modified plant functions when it produces the desired chemical substance, etc. "Functioning" can now be used to draw a line between points 2 and 3 exactly marking the well-known, criticized split between nature and culture.

So, in common usage and, consequently, in culturally accepted convention, technology simply functions when it meets the purpose of dominating nature and controlling situations in accordance with the laws of nature. This can also be supported theoretically.

Table 1:   Catalogue of Requirements

Technology should be …		
(0)	conceivable, generally imaginable	
(1)	scientifically possible (in terms of physics, chemistry, biology, …)	- NATURE -
(2)	feasible in engineering terms	
(3)	economically meaningful	
(4)	legally arguable	
(5)	politically desired	- CULTURE -
(6)	socially wanted	
(7)	ethically tenable	
(8)	aesthetically adequate	

Author's archive

3.3   Luhmann's Effective Isolation

According to Niklas Luhmann, technology can also be understood as "functioning simplification". Accordingly, technology arises in a "process of effective isolation", in "excluding the rest of the world". "Functioning can be ascertained when the world excluded can be kept from impacting the intended result." "The major distinction determining the 'technology' form is that between controllable and uncontrollable situations" (Luhmann 1997, pp. 524f.).

This "process of effective isolation" of technology, this "exclusion of the rest of the world" occurs in the development of technology mainly along the line dividing nature and culture. This initially leaves out the entire "cultural" hemisphere of the world. Technology is designed with respect to nature and the control of it. Technology *functions* when it is able to correctly model and control natural conditions.

This concept of technology may have been adequate and acceptable at the time of incipient agriculture, may be even at the time when railroads were built in the Wild West. However, in our present cultivated life full of technology, in which more and more people, ecology, technology and culture, and less and less nature, are encountered as technology becomes increasingly more powerful, this concept is outdated and, as explained above, in summary even very dangerous.

One question comes to mind: Does technology really function if it is realised in accordance with the laws of nature but, at the same time destroys the eco-natural foundation of existence of mankind and human society? Does technology really function if it violates fundamental cultural achievements (such as democracy, human rights, private sphere, dignity) while observing the laws of nature? Does the three-gorge dam function if it makes millions of people homeless and dooms hundreds of thousands to poverty? Does gene food function if consumers do not want it? Does "developed" technology function in the "developing" third world if this technology is not used in that part of the world because of cultural peculiarities?

According to Luhmann, the "'successful' reduction" occurring with functioning technology "boils down to harmless ignoring" (Luhmann 1997, p. 525). Ignoring cultural aspects in technology here and now is seen no longer as harmless. Effective isolation, "exclusion of the rest of the world", must no longer (at the latest as of today) occur along the dividing line of nature vs. culture. A successful reduction of complexity is no longer possible by leaving out the cultural side and, in this way, the main human aspect. In this regard, the interpretation of technology must be expanded in the same way as the concept of functioning technology.

The term *functioning technology* should henceforth be used only when that technology is able to model correctly, and control, not only natural situations (or those obeying the laws of nature), but also cultural aspects (social, economic, culture-specific ones, etc.). Technology functions only when it meets the societal functions it is expected to fulfil and, ultimately, makes sense within the framework of that respective culture.

According to the catalogue of requirements above, this would mean: Functioning technology is the correct term only when this technology *also* meets at least basic requirements under points (3) to (8). Technology does not function, thus the necessary agreement, if it is not desired, creates social unrest, causes intra- or inter-generational injustice, violates the law or human rights, fails to meet sustainability requirements, or has major aesthetic deficits. Such comprehensive view should be addressed already in the design phase of technology. Specifications could be complemented with these categories (items (3) to (8)) in the very design of technical products, thus further institutionalizing cultured technology.

3.4   Implications of Functioning Cultured Technology

Implementing this kind of technology functioning also in the cultural sense would have far reaching practical implications. Here is one example: A large hydroelectric dam accordingly would function in Central Europe, while a plant with the same (physical and engineering) units would not function in a developing country where dams are often associated with displacement, corruption, dependency, and hunger, thus violating human rights.

An expanded catalogue of requirements of this kind certainly would not make it any easier to design functioning technology for the world. However, would this not point to the very challenges today associated with technology on a large as well as on a small scale? Enhanced requirements would not lead to a (further) acceleration of technical innovation, but perhaps it is this decelerating element which could work as a module in a culture of sustainability.

Moreover, the often suggested or assumed "contextual independence" of technology would be finished once and for all. Technology is dependent on a context: Its conditions, impacts, secondary consequences begin and end (not solely) in the natural sphere but, above all, in the cultural sphere.

Cultured and culturally functioning technology would make this technology more comprehensive and thus more human, also in a humanistic sense. Technology as a powerful means of redesigning the human environment would be an expression not only of its dominating and useful capabilities but, comprehensively, also of its humanity taking into account as many facets as possible. Technology would contribute towards implementing the human aspect in human environment, would allow human beings to come to the fore in their handling the world. However, this would result in a more human design of our sphere of living.

4   The Individual Side of Sustainability

In a third step, the "sustainability" concept will now be put into a direct relation with man and the individual, respectively, thus focusing on sustainability outside the *societal* concept.

4.1   Two Faces of a Culture of Sustainability: The Collective and the Individual

In accordance with the discussions of the concept of culture (see Section 1.1), and in the sense of Klaus P. Hansen, culture always encompasses two poles: the collective and the individual (cf. Hansen 2000); the two together support or create culture.

For the individual, culture can be regarded as a collective canon of standardized patterns of action and meaning, reaching the individual in the process of socialization. Individuals make up the collective. That collective, in turn, "forms" those individuals who derive their identities from responses to collective criteria which, unlike those criteria, fill the collective arsenal of interpretations (cf. Hansen 2000, chap. 3.2). Where the individual steps into the background, culture emerges, and vice versa. It can be said that culture, especially cultural development, occurs between these two poles, in exchanges between the collective and the individual.

Sustainability as an idea and as a concept, however, is mostly considered and discussed as a collective matter (of politics, society, etc.). Sustainability is something which society, politics, companies seek, or should seek, to achieve, implement, or attain. However, the individual and personal side of sustainability are hardly noticed; it is not part of the sustainability discourse. This focus of sustainability on the societal sphere is at least one-sided, from the point of view of cultural theory, and is also unsatisfactory in the light of its objective, namely the implementation of sustainability.

As a cultural enterprise sustainable development, if it is to continue, ultimately must also be accepted by people. It must be internalized and lived. Failing this, sustainability is a mere concept, a political strategy or, at best, a collective shell superimposed without any content, bound to collapse sooner or later.[8]

Sustainability, ultimately, must also be something subjective, personal, an internal affair of people. Sustainable *development* of a collective must be reflected also in an internal development of individuals. Consequently, some personal elements of sustainability will be discussed below.

4.2   The Impact and the Attractiveness of the Idea of Sustainability

It should be stated from the outset that sustainability is something potentially affecting anybody or, sooner or later, making him or her concerned in one way or the other. This concern shows either actively and prospectively in the idea and implementation of a sustainable development or, failing this, sooner or later in a reactive way, in the downsides of a previous, non-sustainable development: Scarce resources, social unrest, damage to the environment, mass migration, rising sea levels, etc. invade our world of living, thus making us suffer.

Over the long term, there is almost no alternative to sustainable development.[9] The question remains of the magnitude of social, ecological, and economic distortion, restrictions in the freedom to act, suffering and violence associated with a change to a culture of sustainability. David W. Orr, in this connection, refers to "more or less grace" in people turning towards sustainable development (Orr as quoted in McDaniel 2002, p. 1461).

In addition, sustainability is no particular theory, at least not in its capability to make people concerned; this is reflected in its claim to globality, among other things. It is not just certain groups (the poor, Catholics, car makers, whites, or farmers) who are affected by sustainability, but simply all people – and not only they.

If "affected" is given a positive connotation, the result is "attractiveness" – which is also to be found in the pool of ideas about sustainability. It has to be kept in mind that the concepts of sustainability arose from the anticipation of possible distortions.

---

8   A cultural sustainability shell imposed top down would probably suffer a fate similar to that of the "Lipsi" – a dance created by the sovereign in the GDR around 1960: it would decline.

9   This applies at least in the light of Hans Jonas' primacy of mankind's absolute duty to exist (cf. Jonas 1986).

And concepts of sustainability, by criticizing existing (socio-ecological) shortcomings, show points of departure for improving things. Consequently, sustainability clearly is also a vague to concrete counterdesign of the present situation.

The features potentially attractive to individuals (or collectives) as a counterdesign in this real Utopia called "sustainability" will be listed summarily and incompletely below. In the sense of this chapter, the list shows no objective truths but rather subjective proposals for interpretation. At least in this sense, sustainability as an idea and as a concept provides answers to present widespread points of concern in our living environment.

Counterarguments of sustainability:

- In a fundamental sense, justice is opposed to the prevailing (economic) injustice.
- Life at the expense of "those with fewer assets" (the poor, animals, ecosystems, coming generations) is compared to life in respect and in favour of those.
- Fast moving life, progress – durability, sustainability.
- Post-modern fragmentation – the whole.
- Shortsightedness – broadening of the horizon.
- Plurality of values and arbitrariness – binding nature of the normative.
- Unlimited possibilities – limited possibilities of existence.
- Individualism creating loneliness – mankind.
- Social isolation – community.
- Alienated human beings – the co-world and the (ecological) web of life.
- Human hubris – being part of ecological networks.
- Pure Civilization – the value of nature.
- The primacy of economy – ecology and social matters.
- Striving for things material – dematerialization of the economy and turning to the intellectual/spiritual (immaterial) values.
- Liberation from nature – liberation from manmade scourges of mankind.
- Arbitrariness – freedom within limits.
- Separation and dominance of analysis – integration and synthesis.
- Lack of orientation – concept.
- Experience of the complex – (rational) management of complexity.

The list of attractive potential counterarguments to be used against frequent concerns could be continued.

4.3   Existential Questions and Life Plans

Above and beyond these answers of sustainability to concerns about the world of life, the concepts of sustainability also affect (other) profound problems of personal existence, and can thus strongly influence individuals, especially in today's secular societies with their insufficient availability of interpretations. Thus, questions about the future, the position of man, existence after death, and the like are touched upon and even explained. The sustainability concept by Konrad Ott, for instance, uses the idea of intergenerationality to make "the living transitory links in a chain of generations" (Ott/Döring 2004, p. 343).

Strength and purpose in this continuous chain of transience is offered, in an anthropocentric sense, by "mankind's absolute duty to exist" (Jonas 1986, p. 80) or, in an ecologically broadened biocentric interpretation of sustainability, the preservation and maintenance of the web of life. At any rate, it can be said that: "A theory of sustainability leaves many people […] not as unaffected in their existence as we are left unaffected by many other good theories" (Ott/Döring 2004, p. 343).

Against the background of the existential depth of theory and the immense range of the sustainability idea (in a spatial sense: global, in a social sense: all of mankind; in a sense of time: intergenerational), concepts of sustainability (such as the integrative concept), without intending or claiming to be, can be seen as experiments towards an ethical theory of everything (cf. Parodi 2008, p. 216). These experiments, when interpreted individualistically, can quite well be regarded in the tradition of classical ethics as far as their comprehensive striving for the good life is concerned. In this way, the sustainability concepts (at least implicitly) contain moments of a life plan, a "life philosophy".

Even if the "good life" sought in sustainability is turned into a post-modern soft and pluralistic format of "life which is not bad", and sustainability designs appeal first to collectives and institutions, and normative postulates must be restricted to "guide rails" or "safe minimum standards," they do offer the possibility of comprehensive individual orientation and a (moderate and open, but existing) comprehensive life plan (in a way which, nowadays, perhaps can only be offered by the religions).

The cultural counterdesign of sustainability (cf. Parodi 2009) makes people concerned, can affect them (in their existence), offers perspective and orientation. Thus, sustainability, though unintended, incorporates a comprehensive ethical power which has become rare.

4.4   Changing Awareness

In addition to ideas of conceptual sustainability, demands are being heard that there should also be an individual *change of mind* towards sustainability. "By whatever name, something akin to spiritual renewal is the sine qua non of the transition to sustainability" (Orr 2002, p. 1459). Also on grounds of theories of culture in which, on the one hand, the individual is seen as a factor of cultural change and, on the other hand, the mental/spiritual dimension is considered a powerful agent, it can be presumed that, in the absence of any "change of mind" and awareness of individuals, there will hardly be anything like sustainable development. Individual concern, attractiveness, depth, and orientation to the concepts of sustainability offer reasons and points of departure for this idea. "If we want to make the transition [to sustainability] gracefully [...], we need enhanced spiritual awareness" (McDaniel 2002, p. 1461). This challenge on the road to sustainability, according to Orr, is by far the biggest challenge, not least because it may be most difficult to approach (politically) and is right in the hands of the individuals.

Another open point is the meaning of "change of mind", and how far this has to go. Orr considers that the transition to sustainable development cannot be achieved merely by rational means. Moreover, "a transformation of mind and heart, desire and intention" (McDaniel, 2002, p. 1461) is needed. So, do we have to become new persons right away? Those who want may do so. In the long run, the implementation of sustainable development and the achievement of a culture of sustainability will (have to) establish a new world view and a fundamentally new way of dealing with the world. We will have to address the world in a different way. If one looks at the misconceptions described in Section 2, one recognizes the need for a major individual change in perception of the world and in self-perception (in Uexküll's dual sense).

Such approaches towards a change of mind can already be recognized in many cases, and small steps are being taken in this direction towards a culture of sustainability. Innumerable projects, initiatives, groups, events, and new patterns of consumption now pointing in the direction of sustainability make this an obvious conclusion.[10] Often, these steps have little theoretical and rational backing,[11] nor do they meet the requirements of those comprehensive concepts of sustainability. How could they? Yet, in a lived experiment, they all make contributions on the way to a culture of sustainability, irrespective of whether these contributions are of an ecological, economic, spiritual or other nature.

One last and important point is this: As long as a culture of sustainability has not yet been achieved, and sustainability merely exists as a draft, a (vague) idea, one must deliberately and expressly *decide* for sustainability. "*Decision* means literally a cut [...] a cut between past and future, an introduction of an essentially new strand into the emerging pattern of history" (Shackle 1969, p. 3).

Sustainability lived indeed would be such a cut, and a culture of sustainability would represent precisely such a new and important strand to be incorporated into the

---

10   Here are a few arbitrary examples just for illustration:
     −   School of Sustainability: http://www.hoc.kit.edu/schule-der-nachhaltigkeit;
     −   "Sustainability as an art of living": http://www.nachhaltigkeit-als-lebenskunst.de/LOHAS: http://www.lohas.de/;
     −   CITTA – Forum für neues Bewusstsein: http://www.citta-forum.de/;
     −   Global Community "Wombat": http://www.globalcommunity.org/flash/wombat.shtml.
11   In the same way in which really new developments often suffer from a lack of (possibilities of) explanation (cf. Parodi 2004).

history of mankind. However, this also implies that old traditions of a non-sustainable culture must be abandoned.

[This article has already been published in German in Parodi, O.; Banse, G.; Schaffer, A. (eds.): Wechselspiele: Kultur und Nachhaltigkeit. Annäherungen an ein Spannungsfeld. Berlin 2010, pp. 97-115.]

References

Böhme, H. (2001): Was ist Kulturwissenschaft? – URL: http://www.culture.hu-berlin.de/lehre/kulturwissenschaft.pdf [25.05.2010] (in German)

Brugger, W. (1998): Technik. In: Brugger, W. (ed.): Philosophisches Wörterbuch. Freiburg i. Br., pp. 393-394 (in German)

Buber, M. (1960): Urdistanz und Beziehung. Heidelberg (in German)

Bundesregierung (2002): Perspektiven für Deutschland. Unsere Strategie für eine nachhaltige Entwicklung. Berlin. – URL: http://www.bundesregierung.de/nsc_true/Content/DE/__Anlagen/2006-2007/perspektiven-fuer-deutschland-langfassung,templateId=raw,property=publicationFile.pdf/perspektiven-fuer-deutschland-langfassung [15.03.2011] (in German)

Erlach, K. (2000): Das Technotop. Die technologische Konstruktion der Wirklichkeit. Münster (in German)

Großklaus, G.; Oldemeyer, E. (eds.) (1983): Natur als Gegenwelt. Beiträge zur Kulturgeschichte der Natur. Karlsruhe (in German)

Hansen, K. P. (2000): Kultur und Kulturwissenschaft. 2nd rev. ed. Tübingen (in German)

Hauff, V. (ed.) (1987): Unsere gemeinsame Zukunft. Der Brundtland-Bericht der Weltkommission für Umwelt und Entwicklung. Greven (in Ferman)

Huber, J. (1989): Technikbilder. Weltanschauliche Weichenstellungen der Technologie- und Umweltpolitik. Opladen (in German)

Jonas, H. (1986): Das Prinzip Verantwortung. Versuch einer Ethik für die technologische Zivilisation. Nördlingen (in German)

Karafyllis, N. C. (ed.) (2003): Biofakte. Versuch über den Menschen zwischen Artefakt und Lebewesen. Paderborn (in German)

Kopfmüller, J.; Brandl, V.; Jörissen, J.; Paetau, M.; Banse, G.; Coenen, R.; Grunwald, A. (2001): Nachhaltige Entwicklung integrativ betrachtet. Konstitutive Elemente, Regeln, Indikatoren. Berlin (in German)

Kowalski, J. S.; Schaffer, A. J.: Im Spannungsfeld von internationaler ökonomischer Verflechtung und sozio-kultureller Globalisierung. In: Parodi, O.; Banse, G.; Schaffer, A. (eds.): Wechselspiele: Kultur und Nachhaltigkeit. Annäherungen an ein Spannungsfeld. Berlin 2010, pp. 189-202 (in German)

Krainer, L.; Trattnigg, R. (eds.) (2007): Kulturelle Nachhaltigkeit. Konzepte, Perspektiven, Positionen. Munich (in German)

Luhmann, N. (1997): Die Gesellschaft der Gesellschaft. Vol. I. Frankfurt am Main (in German)

Marschall, W. (1993): Die zweite Natur des Menschen. Kulturtheoretische Positionen in der Ethnologie. In: Hansen, K. P. (ed.): Kulturbegriff und Methode. Der stille Paradigmenwechsel in den Geisteswissenschaften. Tübingen, pp. 17-26 (in German)

McDaniel, J. (2002): Spirituality and Sustainability. In: Conservation Biology, Vol. 16, No. 6, pp. 1461-1464

Meyer-Abich, K. M. (1984): Wege zum Frieden mit der Natur. Praktische Naturphilosophie für die Umweltpolitik. Munich (in German)

Oldemeyer, E. (2005): Die Ich-Es-Einstellung als Voraussetzung technischer Kreativität. Bewusstseinsgeschichtliche Bemerkungen im Anschluss an Martin Buber. In: Dürr, R.; Gebauer, G.; Maring, M.; Schütt, H.-P. (eds.): Pragmatisches Philosophieren. Festschrift für Hans Lenk. Münster, pp. 302-314 (in German)

Orr, D. W. (2002): Four Challenges of Sustainability. In: Conservation Biology, Vol. 16, No. 6, pp. 1457-1460

Ott, K.; Döring, R. (2004): Theorie und Praxis starker Nachhaltigkeit. Marburg (in German)

Parodi, O. (2008): Technik am Fluss. Philosophische und kulturwissenschaftliche Betrachtungen zum Wasserbau als kulturelle Unternehmung. Munich (in German)

Parodi, O. (2004): Rationalität unter ökologischem Vorzeichen. In: Fobel, P.; Banse, G.; Kiepas, A.; Zecha, G. (eds.): Rationalität in der Angewandten Ethik. Banská Bystrica, pp. 159-170 (in German)

Prechtl, P.; Burkhard, F.-P. (eds.) (1996): Metzler-Philosophie-Lexikon. Begriffe und Definitionen. Stuttgart (in German)

Rohbeck, J. (1993): Technologische Urteilskraft. Zu einer Ethik technischen Handelns. Frankfurt am Main (in German)

Shackle, G. L. S. (1969): Decision, Order and Time in Human Affairs. Cambridge

United Nations – Division for Sustainable Development [UN-DSD] (2009): – URL: http://www.un.org/esa/dsd/index.shtml [15.03.2011]

From the Cultural Dimension of Sustainable Development to the Culture of Sustainable Development

Jürgen Kopfmüller

1   Introduction

Before the concepts of "sustainable development" and "culture" can be treated in depth, their definition and meaning must be clarified. It soon becomes apparent that this effort is as complex, difficult and, consequently, often controversial for the concept of culture as for that of sustainability. As this issue is covered in greater detail in other contributions to this volume, I would like to limit myself first to distinguishing two definitions: On the one hand, the definition of culture in the narrower sense of the term as the intellectual-artistic realm of a society, i.e. music, literature, theatre, painting, but also education and knowledge. In the other, broader definition, which will underlie this contribution, culture encompasses everything created by human beings and comprises all processes of the way in which people interact with other people and with the natural environment. Consequently, this implies also basic attitudes and values, traditions, lifestyles, ethics, religion, but also the legal, economic, social and political systems of a society.

"Culture" thus would mean the way in which we live or want to live and how we shape social development. To find the proper place for this concept of culture, let me use an example based on an item well known to all of us: "Civilization" means owning a toothbrush, "cultural technique" means being able to use it, while "culture" means actually using it, i.e. the ability and willingness, respectively, to implement things found to be correct.

In the debate about the definition and implementation of the guiding principle of sustainability, which has been going on for more than twenty years, some outstanding milestones can be identified:

(1) The 1987 report by the Brundtland Commission of the United Nations (cf. Hauff 1987) with its widely quoted central definition according to which sustainable development has been achieved when it meets the needs of present generations without compromising the ability of future generations to meet their own needs.

(2) The UN Conference on Environment and Development held in Rio in 1992 with the Declaration of Rio and the Agenda 21 adopted there.
(3) The World Summit on Sustainable Development organized in Johannesburg in 2002 with the "Plan of Implementation" it adopted.

On the basis of these documents and the sustainability debate so far some key challenges can be highlighted in the way the guiding principle of sustainability is implemented:

- What is at stake is nothing less than the development of a "new ethics of human survival" and a "worldwide programme of change" based on it – concepts representing the motivation and guiding orientation of the Brundtland Report (cf. Hauff 1987).
- Guidance is provided mainly by the implementation of the postulate of justice taking into account both inter- and intra-generational perspectives. In other words: The application of the principle of responsibility to persons living in the future and those living today is in the focus of this debate.
- This mainly implies reflecting on and, in particular, solving problems of distribution with respect to a variety of environmental resources, income, and assets, but also benefits and burdens resulting from political measures.
- The focus on the postulate of justice implies that the guiding principle be put into concrete terms and operationalized in a holistic way adequately reflecting the ecological, economic, social, institutional, and also cultural aspects of social development.
- From all this result the claim as well as the task to shape social development in the direction of sustainability. In view of the multitude and intensity of existing problems, this will require some far reaching changes in the existing patterns of production and consumption as well as different political and institutional framework conditions.

2 "Culture" in the Key Documents of the Sustainability Debate

One glance at the milestones of the sustainability debate referred to above shows that the concept and the subject area of culture do not rank prominently in those milestones. The concept practically does not occur at all in the Brundtland Report and only occasionally in the other documents. In the Declaration of Rio[1] with its 27 development principles for a "new and equitable global partnership", the focus is on the right

---

1   Cf. http://www.un.org/documents/ga/conf151/aconf15126-1annex1.htm.

of development for all people worldwide, and on such subjects as reducing poverty, enhancing participation, a new world economic system, or the role of women. Only Principle 22 contains a specific reference to the subject of culture in demanding recognition of the identity, culture, and interests of indigenous ethnic groups. The Agenda 21 as the global action programme implementing the guidelines of the Declaration[2] comprises 40 chapters about various topics, none of which specifically refers to culture (cf. e.g. Jerman 2001). However, culture as a concept is mentioned in various places, mainly in such terms as agriculture, aquaculture, or marine culture; sometimes it refers to the cultural multifunctionality of forests, and various chapters contain the requirement to take into account cultural factors and features in achieving the respective goals. In the Johannesburg Plan of Implementation, which is focused especially on the subjects of combating poverty, protecting resources, financing development, and good governance, the concept of culture is used primarily to underline the importance of maintaining cultural diversity and the cultural heritage in the interest of sustainable development, especially with a view to indigenous groups of populations.

On the whole, it can be stated that the references to cultural aspects, limited as they are, in the documents referred to above mainly serve functional, instrumental purposes, i.e. primarily with a view to other objectives without giving these an independent perspective of implementation. Only rarely is the meaning of "culture" and cultural aspects, respectively, expressed in precise terms. It is also striking to see that the few specific references are mainly given to the preservation of cultural diversity, mostly in countries in the "south", and their indigenous populations. No specific players in the cultural sector are addressed.

3   Culture in the Concepts of Sustainability

A similar picture is seen for the existing (scientific) sustainability concepts. In the debate in Germany and, in principle, also in many other countries, the so-called "one-pillar concepts", mostly focused on the ecological dimension of sustainable development, the "three-" and "four-pillar concepts," and transdimensional integrative concepts can be distinguished.

Three documents about the "one-pillar concepts" will be referred to below: In the "Zukunftsfähiges Deutschland" ("Sustainable Germany") study by the Wuppertal Institute (cf. BUND/Misereor 1996), the first study about sustainability in Germany to meet with relatively broad public response, the subject of global ecological justice in the "global environmental space" is in the focus of interest, with far reaching target values for ecological key indicators being derived for Germany. Various guiding prin-

---

2   Cf. http://www.un.org/esa/dsd/agenda21/res_agenda21_00.shtml.

ciples about ways of meeting those targets are formulated ("The Right Measure of Time and Space" or "Living Well Instead of Owning Much"), while the concept of culture is not used explicitly. In the quasi-follow-up study published recently, these key principles are supplemented and modified. Reference is made, among other things, to the so-called Social Pact of the United Nations which supplements political and civil human rights (Civilian Pact) by defining economic, social, and *cultural* human rights (cf. Brot für die Welt et al. 2008a). In addition, the authors of the study refer to the "cultural helplessness" in society which blocks necessary processes of change, referring, for example, to the inflexible patterns of our way of meeting our needs – for instance those based on fossil fuels (cf. Brot für die Welt et al. 2008b). Also in the two studies by the German Federal Office for the Environment of 1997 and 2002, which show ways towards permanently ecological development, the concept of culture found little explicit reference. On the other hand, they did cover, in a comparatively comprehensive way, the role our consumption behaviour plays in meeting environmental objectives, and the meaningful changes which could be made.

As concerns the "three-" and "four-pillar concepts", the two concepts best known in Germany will be discussed first. While the concept of culture played hardly any role in the "Arbeit und Ökologie" ("Work and Ecology") study commissioned by the Hans Böckler Foundation, an organization close to the trade unions (cf. DIW et al. 2000), the final report by the Committee of Inquiry of the 13th German Federal Parliament, "Protecting Man and the Environment" (cf. DBT 1998), was characterized by a slightly broader reflection on the concept of culture. First of all, in addition to the core dimensions of ecology, economy, and social matters, the areas of culture and education were considered quasi-accompanying aspects to which great importance was attached within the framework of strategies implementing goals in the three dimensions. Besides this instrumental view of cultural aspects, cultural problems requiring corrective action were addressed above and beyond the ecological or social problem areas, and topics such as social stability or solidarity were characterized as important cultural factors.

Mention should also be made of the United Nations Commission on Sustainable Development, whose widely quoted process of developing a sustainability indicator system including various test countries for the first time also had achieved an expansion of the three classical dimensions by a fourth, institutional dimension (cf. BMU 2000). Nevertheless, no explicit reference to cultural topics was made, no independent indicators for those topics were mentioned, and cultural aspects again were covered only in their potential supporting function in the implementation of strategies related to the other indicators.

Within the framework of this "pillar"-oriented pattern of thought, the question of how "culture" could be integrated into this structure was discussed mainly in three options: in the format of an attachment to one of the "classical" pillars, as an additional, independent fourth or fifth pillar (cf. e.g. Wehrspaun/Schoemps 2002), or as a cross-sectional subject. However, no specific and specifying activities to that end have so far been initiated.

Criticism of the approaches designed along the single dimensions finally gave rise to the "transdimensional", integrative approaches. Here reference must be made to the integrative sustainability concept of the Helmholtz Association (HGF; cf. Kopfmüller et al. 2001) and the sustainability strategy of the German federal government (cf. Bundesregierung 2002). The point of departure in development of the integrative concept, which has been applied so far in a multitude of research projects within and outside the HGF (cf. Kopfmüller 2006), were not the single developmental dimensions but the elements considered constitutive of sustainable development: The requirement of intra- and intergenerational justice, the global perspective, and the anthropocentric approach. These three elements, especially the justice requirement, then give rise to a holistic integrative concept of sustainable development in which the economic, ecological, social, institutional, and cultural aspects of societal development are adequately taken into account.

These constitutive elements were "translated" first into three general sustainability goals extending beyond single dimensions:

(1) securing human existence;
(2) maintaining society's productive potential;
(3) preserving society's options for development and action.

These goals were put into concrete terms in a next step defining guidelines and rules for action representing the core of the concept (see Table 1). On the one hand, they comprise substantial rules as minimum requirements for achieving the general objectives and, on the other hand, instrumental rules describing how to put these minimum requirements into effect.

Two of the substantial rules in this concept explicitly refer to culture. One of them is the rule about "preserving the cultural heritage and cultural diversity". Based on the principles of the 1991 "World Report of Culture and Development" by a committee appointed by UNESCO (cf. WCCD 1991), two equivalent functions are ascribed to culture: on the one hand, the instrumental function referred to above in the sense that cultural capabilities and capacities can be important tools for socio-economic development of societies; on the other hand, culture is also attributed a value of its own. It not only serves to allow other objectives to be reached, but is the very social basis of these objectives. Among other things, culture determines how people live or work together and how they manage their natural environment. In this concept, culture is the most important source of creativity – undoubtedly an important factor in sustainable development – and therefore must be preserved, and its diversity must be protected from the many threats in the form of globalization and international cultural uniformity. In this respect, culture is regarded not as a static concept but as a dynamic process: What is considered worth preserving must be defined in societal communication and negotiation processes.

Table 1:   System of Sustainability Rules

Substantive Rules		
Securing Human Existence	*Preserving Societal Productivity Potential*	*Preserving Possibilities of Development and Action*
1.1 Protecting human health	2.1 Sustainable use of re newable resources	3.1 Equal opportunities in education, work, information
1.2 Ensuring basic provisions (food, education, …)	2.2 Sustainable use of non-renewable resources	3.2 Participation in societal decision-making pro-cesses
1.3 Ensuring independent existence	2.3 Sustainable use of the environment as a sink	3.3 Preserving cultural heri-tage and cultural diversity
1.4 Equitable distribution of possibilities to use the environment	2.4 Avoiding untenable technical risks	3.4 Preserving the cultural function of nature
1.5 Balancing extreme differences in income and assets	2.5 Sustainable development of capital assets, human and knowledge capital	3.5 Preserving social resources
Instrumental Rules		
– Internalization of external ecological and social costs – Adequate discounting – Limiting national debt – Fair world economic boundary conditions – International co-operation – Capability of social institutions to elicit response – Reflectivity of social institutions – Controllability – Capability of self-organization – Balance of power		

Source: Compiled after Kopfmüller et al. 2001, pp. 172, 174

The other rule referring to culture is that of "preserving the cultural function of nature". This is mainly about considering not only the life-preserving function of nature as a source of raw materials and a sink of pollutants, but also the function of enriching human life as an object of sensory, contemplative, or aesthetic experiences. Despite all cultural differences, there are some value categories for nature of almost general validity: nature's value as a place of experience and recovery, respectively; its mere existence (which arises from the knowledge that special natural assets exist); the symbolic value; the reminder value (which is strongly connected with individual or group identities); and the scarcity value as a criterion of the need for protection. The concepts applying, for instance, to natural or cultural landscapes worth preserving or protecting are widely regulated by international agreements, if possible, involving the population affected and important groups of civil society.

With these two rules, the logic of the integrative concept of HGF attributes to cultural aspects of sustainable development an independent function equivalent to the other aspects.

4   The Politico-societal Level

In the sustainability strategy of the German federal government (cf. Bundesregierung 2002), which can also be classified as an integrative approach, it is not the individual dimensions which constitute the point of departure and the structural framework, but four cross-cutting principles:

(1) Intergenerational justice
(2) Quality of life
(3) Social cohesion
(4) International responsibility

These are then put into concrete terms in thematic fields and indicators. Compared to other national sustainability strategies and other documents, this strategy deals with the subject of culture and sustainability in a relatively reflected way. Mention is made of the fact that the implementation of sustainable development challenged creative potentials in a society which were decisively based on cultural capabilities. Hence, a "culture of sustainability"[3] should be developed in which imagination and creativity had to be employed to arrive at visions going beyond conventional technical and efficiency-oriented approaches. Culture is seen as an important part of quality of life, and cultural diversity is regarded as just as important as biodiversity. Reference is made to a "culture of mutual co-operation" necessary to implement sustainable development, and contributions by contemporary art are attributed an important function in the process leading to sustainable development. This makes the German strategy one of the very few documents assigning to this sector of culture an explicit role in creating wider awareness in this realm.

---

3   In the author's opinion, this is the first time this concept appears in an official document in such clear words.

However, if one considers the actual way in which the four guiding principles were put into effect in the 21 thematic fields and 25 indicators, i.e. the real core of the strategy (see Table 2), one finds already at this point that the "philosophy" referred to in the introductory parts was not properly put into effect. Also the different key topics emphasized (climate protection, mobility, or land consumption), which were partly modified and amended in the biannual progress reports about the strategy and the strategic approaches outlined and taken up in the progress reports show hardly any reference to these aspects. This again reveals a persistent phenomenon diagnosed in the debate about sustainability policy, namely the discrepancy between announcements and implementation, between theory and the daily practice of real politics.

Table 2:   Structure of the German Sustainability Strategy

Four Guiding Principles			
Intergenerational Justice	**Quality of Life**	**Social Cohesion**	**International Responsibility**
21 Thematic Fields, 25 Indicators			
– Resource conservation – Climate protection – Renewable energies – Land consumption – Diversity of species – National debt – Economic provisions for the future (investments) – Innovation – Education	– Economic prosperity (GDP) – Mobility – Nutrition – Quality of air – Health – Crime	– Employment – Perspectives for families – Equal rights – Integration of foreign citizens	– Co-operation for development – Open markets
Key topics: Energy efficiency/climate protection; mobility; nutrition/health; shaping demographic change; education campaign; innovation in industries; land consumption			

Source: Bundesregierung 2002

In the same connection, the level of local Agenda-21 initiatives must be mentioned which, for a long time, played a pioneering role in putting the guiding principle into effect from the beginning of the so-called Rio follow-up process in the early 1990s. This function has lost much of its significance over the past few years, at the latest with the publication of a national sustainability strategy. While Germany and other countries were still in a growth phase up until the end of the 1990s, as far as the number of local initiatives is concerned, there has since been a phase of settling and consolidation. This is due to the gradual disappearance of numerous initiatives but, at the same time, associated with an increase in quality of those remaining. This is expressed especially in a paradigm shift away from focusing mainly on the environment and classical economics in favour of local sustainability strategies. This clearly expands the system of targets and criteria, frequently guided by existing "overarching strategies" at the levels of federal states or the national level. In some very rare exceptions, a systematic system of municipal sustainability management is being built up, based, among other things, on more systematically qualified processes of participation, the "citizen municipality" model, "good governance" approaches, and clear roadmaps of specific strategies of implementation.

At the same time, two emerging trends and perspectives, respectively, on a local level can be recognized: On the one hand, there is a tendency favoring so-called metropolitan regions as one possible approach towards improved positioning of regions in global development and competition processes and, on the other hand, more attention is devoted to small towns and their roles and potentials for sustainable development. The focus here is on the importance of these towns in regional economic systems and their potential to act as "substantive niches" in globalized processes. At the same time, an opportunity is seen in this way to put more emphasis on the importance of local traditions, identities and cultures, to preserve their diversity and, in this way, to develop small towns into potential "nuclei" of sustainability.

Still, it must be said quite generally that regions and municipalities at an early stage were seen as suitable places of cultural development, and thus also of sustainable development, but to this day cultural aspects have not achieved any central importance on that level. Issues of culture more likely are attributed to a different dimension (mostly to the "social" dimension) and not considered an independent area. The criteria used, and the topics treated, rather revolve around the numbers of theatres or cinemas available, or the number of visitors to museums, and only in very rare cases there is a search for, or strengthening of, regional identities, ways of adequate societal coexistence, or the like. Finally, only a small number of examples of successful political implementations of these declarations of intent can be found today.

In addition to those referred to above, there are various other documents and activities showing that the subject of sustainable development and culture has already been addressed in a reflected way. Here reference is made to three of those documents: on the one hand, the 1996 report by the UN World Commission on "Culture and Development", entitled "Our Creative Diversity" (cf. WCCD 1996), which is based on the world report of 1991. It considers the search for, and formulation of, a "global ethics" as an important step and a result of global cultural development. Such ethics is to incorporate values, for instance human rights, democracy, or transparency, as well as tolerance and solidarity. It also asks for better implementation at a political level, especially for more weight to be attached to cultural aspects in development politics, stronger emphasis put on diversity and balance instead of according peculiarities, and for the establishment of an action plan to that effect. That plan was published by UNESCO in 1998 under the title of "The Power of Culture" in an effort to link cultural policy more closely to matters and politics of development (cf. UNESCO 1998). This action plan refers to the establishment of development strategies more sensitive to culture as a core duty based on the fundamental understanding that sustainable development and cultural creativity, diversity, and development are interdependent. This incorporates a clearer definition of cultural rights as human rights, but also of topics such as equal access of people to the different media. Consequently, key duties of cultural policy are found to be the need to establish targets (where possible also quantitative in nature), and create the structural preconditions of, and the means for, generating human creativity and corresponding self-development.

In Germany, this area was covered in 2001 by the "Tutzinger Manifest für die Stärkung der kulturell-ästhetischen Dimension von Nachhaltigkeit" ("Tutzing Manifesto for Strengthening the Cultural-aesthetic Dimension of Sustainability").[4] The origin of that initiative was the meeting on "The Aesthetics of Sustainability," organized by the Evangelische Akademie Tutzing, among others. The meeting and the Manifesto were to create greater public awareness of the fact that sustainable development must be considered a cultural challenge, and that sustainability policy and cultural policy must be interlinked more closely. Major challenges are seen in the fact that implementation of the demanding principle of sustainability will require substantial changes in societal norms, values, and action patterns, and that culture must successfully be considered and used as a means of reflecting value orientations and of balancing various criteria and interests. For this purpose, the approaches used in the different Agenda-21 processes and in cultural policy must be intertwined more closely, and culture must be seen as a cross-cutting dimension relative to other dimensions. The Manifesto also makes a special point of the need to look for specific patterns, forms, and aesthetics of sustainability and use them to enhance the fascination and attractiveness of the guiding principle to people. The importance of the interaction between natural and social scientific strategies and the cultural-aesthetic competence to share the "sustainability project" must be emphasized and made more evident to people by including competent players.

Finally, in 2006, the "Culture and Arts for Sustainable Development" manifesto was written by, among others, the Kulturpolitische Gesellschaft, Bonn, the Evangelische Akademie, Iserlohn, and Pan y Arte e. V., Münster[5]. The document was to stress the need for closer co-operation between foreign cultural policy and development policy, and to make proposals of practical implementation. It is based on the

---

4   Cf. http://www.kupoge.de/ifk/tutzinger-manifest/.
5   Cf. http://www.kulturbewegt.org.

reasoning that intercultural co-operation and the perception of, and dealing with, the world views of other cultures constitute important preconditions of a common perception of global responsibility and common global sustainable development. This is the basis on which principles were formulated for an enlarged cultural foreign policy of Germany. They refer to the importance of culture as a fifth dimension added to the quadrangle of development politics, the necessary co-operation of the government with civil society, the role of federal states and municipalities in this process, the enhanced co-operation of non-governmental organizations in Germany and developing countries, up to the demand to include cultural objectives in the list of millennium development goals of the United Nations.

5   Conclusion and Perspectives

All these examples show that we suffer from a twofold deficit in sustainable development and culture (cf. Kurt/Wagner 2002; RNE 2002): on the one hand, a persistent clear deficit in taking into account cultural aspects in the sustainability debate at all levels. This has many reasons, one of which certainly is that in a modern society characterized by functional differentiation, pluralization of ways of life, and individualization of lifestyles, a guiding concept as complex as that of sustainable development, or the complicated cause-effect relations of environmental problems, are difficult to illustrate by clear pictures and hard to make people aware of. Moreover, exhortations to change individual behaviour clash with elementary ingrained patterns of behaviour, and the possibilities to solve problems by individual behaviour are perceived as a mere drop in the bucket. There is another deficit in the sustainability debate, namely that many cases still are narrowed down to environmental aspects, technical approaches to problem solving or orientation by the efficiency principle.

On the other hand, there is also a deficit in reflecting on sustainability among players and politicians in the cultural sector. Where this principle is treated at all in culture and the arts, the outcome frequently is a restricted view of its environmental aspects.

These examples also show at least that there are approaches towards a more reflected, more extensive way of handling the cultural dimension as well as proposals of specific steps in implementation, and a debate to this effect seems to have been started. However, what is still missing in many ways are appropriate steps in political implementation as well as effective activities in civil society at a national and local as well as international level.

It is safe to say that the concept of sustainability is still reflected and anchored in society to an insufficient degree and that there are major deficits in what may be called sustainability policy. In many cases, there are no clear targets, and where they exist, there is frequently a lack of political measures to be taken. In many problem areas, this is associated with the same inadequacy of results. These problem areas, after all, did not arise out of the blue but, as a rule, were caused by specific – cultural – patterns of behaviour.

Consequently, a "culture of sustainable development" or a cultural shift towards sustainability would be necessary in the sense of the guiding principle becoming an integral part of patterns of thought and behaviour as well as of political decisions. In analogy with the "toothbrush example" mentioned above, it could be said that we "possess" such a "culture of sustainable development" (after all, some approaches are already in existence), that we are also able to apply it (for we know at least theoretically what ought to be done), but – unlike the toothbrush case – we do not do so, at least not to the necessary extent.

This is not the place to discuss why this is the case. However, some major elements will be outlined which ought to give rise to such a "culture of sustainable development". First of all, reference should be made to the need for "changed cultures" in the groups of societal players. In science as one of the major providers of orientation and advice to society, one very central element would be for interdisciplinary and transdisciplinary handling of questions to constitute the rule rather than the exception, for which, of course, the necessary institutional, structural, administrative, and also financial preconditions would have to be established. In the economy, especially more awareness and suitable incentives would have to be created for responsible action in business in the interest of sustainability, which could be gauged by standardized criteria, where possible, and whose outcome could be made transparent and published. Finally, it ought to be possible to create conditions for closer integration of sustainability criteria in the personal criteria for decision-making of people.

All this requires an adequate "code" being created in the form of politico-institutional framework conditions. These would have to comprise the definition of targets, the execution of target-oriented measures, and the appropriate control mechanisms, but also an element as important as systematic monitoring of laws and draft legislation for their potential impact on sustainability. This would have to be associated with a changed culture of societal decision-making processes, for instance, with respect to adequate participation of stakeholders or the question of the competent geographic-political level in the sense of the subsidiarity principle.

Moreover, also some of the "big issues" should be raised again, or in a modified way and, if possible, should be answered as well. This refers especially to the role quantitative economic growth will be able to play in a future resource-related finite world, and what societies and economic systems, respectively, could be like which would have to function with less or no growth. In this connection, there is also need for a redefinition of what we mean by "progress", "prosperity", or "quality of life", and how we want to measure them. The debate in the 1970s about the need for, and shape of, a new world economic order is another issue to be clarified, as is the question of a feasible global governance architecture for adequate management of the globalization processes in industry, politics, and society.

This would have to be associated with the dissemination and popularization of relatively new concepts and ideas associated with them. Examples proving this point, for instance, are the "culture of moderate economic activity", which bears in mind the different limiting factors as well as the consequences of economic activities, or the "culture of the market" in the sense of "adding ethics to the markets", which means that, above and beyond the classical criteria of market control by supply and demand, the socio-economic distribution of goods and services traded via markets would be assigned adequate importance.

The real challenge is posed not so much by the individual elements of such a culture of sustainable development, some of which have been addressed here and which, *per se*, are rarely absolutely new, but rather the need to put this into effect jointly, where possible, and create the necessary preconditions, respectively.

When dealing with the conditions and possibilities of implementing this cultural shift within the broad concept of culture as defined above, it is necessary to find a meaningful measure of objectifiability in order to assess the compatibility of economic or social developments with these goals of cultural shift and, where necessary, take controlling action. On the other hand, beyond all objectifiability, it is also necessary in a society to keep working towards integrating this principle of sustainability into the different action systems. The "culture of sustainable development" would then mean incorporation of the principle into our everyday life and our functional systems (see Wehrspaun/Schoembs 2002). Support by players from the arts and culture in the narrower sense of the term is of considerable importance also for this to work. Consequently, increased initiation and better promotion of good practical examples are urgently required in order to show that it has been, or is, possible to work for better perception and suitability for everyday use, of the principle of sustainability to achieve the desired improved broad impact.

[This article has already been published in German in Parodi, O.; Banse, G.; Schaffer, A. (eds.): Wechselspiele: Kultur und Nachhaltigkeit. Annäherungen an ein Spannungsfeld. Berlin: edition sigma 2010, pp. 43-57.]

References

BMU – Bundesministerium für Umwelt, Naturschutz und Reaktorsicherheit (2000): Bericht zur internationalen Testphase des CSD-Indikatorensystems. Berlin (in German)

Brot für die Welt; BUND – Bund für Umwelt und Naturschutz Deutschland; EED – Evangelischer Entwicklungsdienst (eds.) (2008a): Wegmarken für einen Kurswechsel. Zusammenfassung der Studie "Zukunftsfähiges Deutschland in einer globalisierten Welt". Stuttgart a.o. (in German)

Brot für die Welt; BUND – Bund für Umwelt und Naturschutz Deutschland; EED – Evangelischer Entwicklungsdienst (eds.) (2008b): Zukunftsfähiges Deutschland in einer globalisierten Welt. Einblicke in die Studie des Wuppertal-Instituts für Klima, Umwelt, Energie. Stuttgart a.o. (in German)

BUND – Bund für Umwelt und Naturschutz Deutschland; Misereor (eds.) (1996): Zukunftsfähiges Deutschland. Ein Beitrag zu einer global nachhaltigen Entwicklung. Basel (in German)

Bundesregierung (2002): Perspektiven für Deutschland. Unsere Strategie für eine nachhaltige Entwicklung. Berlin (in German)

DBT (1998): Abschlußbericht der Enquete-Kommission "Schutz des Menschen und der Umwelt – Ziele und Rahmenbedingungen einer nachhaltig zukunftsverträglichen Entwicklung". Konzept Nachhaltigkeit – Vom Leitbild zur Umsetzung. Bundestagsdrucksache 13/11200. Bonn (in German)

DIW – Deutsches Institut für Wirtschaftsforschung; Wuppertal-Institut; WZB – Wissenschaftszentrum Berlin (ed.) (2000): Arbeit und Ökologie. Projektabschlussbericht. Düsseldorf (in German)

DUK – Deutsche UNESCO-Kommission (1997): Unsere kreative Vielfalt. Kurzfassung des Berichts der Weltkommission Kultur und Entwicklung. Bonn (in German)

Hauff, V. (ed.) (1987): Unsere gemeinsame Zukunft. Der Brundtland-Bericht der Weltkommission für Umwelt und Entwicklung. Greven (in German)

Jerman, T. (ed.) (2001): ZukunftsFormen. Kultur und Agenda 21. Essen (in German)

Kopfmüller, J.; Brandl, V.; Jörissen, J.; Paetau, M.; Banse, G.; Coenen, R.; Grunwald, A. (2001): Nachhaltige Entwicklung integrativ betrachtet. Konstitutive Elemente, Regeln, Indikatoren. Berlin (in German)

Kopfmüller, J. (ed.) (2006): Ein Konzept auf dem Prüfstand. Das integrative Konzept nachhaltiger Entwicklung in der Forschungspraxis. Berlin (in German)

Kurt, H.; Wagner, B. (2002): Einführung. In: Kurt, H.; Wagner, B. (eds.): Kultur – Kunst – Nachhaltigkeit. Die Bedeutung von Kultur für das Leitbild nachhaltige Entwicklung. Essen, pp. 13-30 (in German)

RNE – Rat für Nachhaltige Entwicklung (2002): Kultur und Nachhaltigkeit. Thesen und Ergebnisse aus einem Ideenworkshop. Berlin (in German)

UBA – Umweltbundesamt (1997): Nachhaltiges Deutschland. Wege zu einer dauerhaft umweltgerechten Entwicklung, Berlin (in German)

UBA – Umweltbundesamt (2002): Nachhaltige Entwicklung in Deutschland. Die Zukunft dauerhaft umweltgerecht gestalten. Berlin (in German)

UNESCO – United Nations Educational, Scientific and Cultural Organizsation (1998): The Power of Culture. Aktionsplan Kulturpolitik für Entwicklung. Verabschiedet auf der UNESCO-Konferenz „Kulturpolitik für Entwicklung" in Stockholm. Paris/Bonn (in German)

WCCD – World Commission on Culture and Development (1991): World Report of Culture and Development. Paris

WCCD – World Commission on Culture and Development (1996): Our Creative Diversity. Report of the World Commission on Culture and Development. Paris

Wehrspaun, M.; Schoemps, H. (2002): Schwierigkeiten bei der Kommunikation von Nachhaltigkeit. Ein Problemaufriss. In: Kurt, H.; Wagner, B. (eds.): Kultur – Kunst – Nachhaltigkeit. Die Bedeutung von Kultur für das Leitbild nachhaltige Entwicklung. Essen, pp. 43-57 (in German)

Culture and Sustainability in the Web of Everyday Life

Karl Heinz Hörning

Modern age, with its ways of life consuming resources and ruining the climate, has had great difficulties so far in coping with the problem of ecological sustainability.[1] For far too long, it has carelessly exploited nature and, in doing so, neglected the problem of sustainability this raised, which had existed all the time.[2] The re-"discovery" of sustainability dates from the energy crisis in the early 1970s. That crisis became history because it violently shook the cultural foundations of modern times. Awareness of the finite nature of resources, as a kind of bad conscience, has since become part of a culture wasting energy here and there. However, the normative principle of sustainability taken literally means much more, in fact, initiates a profound cultural change occasionally even referred to as a cultural revolution. It not only raises uncertainty about many things we are taking for granted, it not only causes doubt and concern. It demands cuts: It fundamentally attacks our ideas of a good life, demanding from us new different techniques of survival and patterns of life.

However, our ingrained ways of life cannot be changed that easily. Most of us guess, or know, what is not sustainable, indeed damaging, about our way of life. But a lifestyle based on sacrifice stands little chance with most members of our present societies. This makes many people impatiently call for the state and its tools, be they political regulations and laws or economic incentives and burdens (such as ecotaxes, subsidies, "scrapping" bonuses). However, seen from a distance, the results so far of these interventions have been rather disappointing, especially so when measured against the great hopes and promises. So, more and more doubt is being expressed about the ability of politics to contribute in such a comprehensive way to the protection of the environment and climate.

It is for this reason that I am going to plead for a change of perspective in the sustainability debate. Instead of staring at climate summits and climate pacts and com-

---

1   This essay is based on lectures the author gave at the Evangelische Akademie Loccum, the University of Klagenfurt, and the Berlin Academy of Arts in 2008 and 2009.

2   Ulrich Grober, in his cultural history of the sustainability concept, finds the question of the right of man to exploit nature raised first in an allegorical narrative of the Saxonian humanist Paulus Niavis in 1429 (cf. Grober 2010).

plaining about their missed opportunities, instead of propagating new political, economic, or technical goals, which remain unattainable, I will start with the *influence of culture on everyday life*, which is to, or can, become sustainable. It is the practice of our everyday life, it is the culturally ingrained habits and the smoothly working social practices which offer excellent starting points for changing our behaviour also towards sustainability. From this vantage point, I think, bottom-up processes can be started or initiated to an extent not so far considered sufficiently in sociological studies. A helpful corollary is the principle of sustainability's recent influential ally: the discussion of "global climate change", which considerably intensifies and dramatizes the pressure on sustainable action. It is especially this greater pressure which gives us a much clearer view of the scope and the possibilities of, and also the hurdles on the way, to change, which open or block the way to sustainability in everyday life.

To advance the question of the opportunities and obstacles of ecologically sustainable action, I would like to assume a *practical perspective* below, finding everyday people in their different areas of life. On this level, even the most gradual changes away from indifferently damaging to carefully resource protecting actions must be taken seriously and analyzed carefully. In this effort, one line of theory is helpful which attracted more and more attention in sociology in the past decade: the "theories of social practice" (cf. Hörning 2001, pp. 157-243; Reckwitz 2003). That bundle of theories, however different its individual strands,[3] starts from basic assumptions:

- *Firstly*: Most things we do in everyday life are not the result of well-thought-out intentional decisions, but are based on knowledge arising from practical experience and ability in interpretation, which we practiced in frequently repeated trains of action, and which allows us to do many things, if not most things, without prolonged pondering.
- *Secondly*: It is only in the context of situations in practical life that existing knowledge becomes relevant and effective, finding its use and its modification. Only when we face, and are upset by, major problems, when we look for concrete solutions and have to, or want to, change our practices, all these large inventories of knowledge become subject-related which we, as members of a knowledge society, can use, but which mostly rest within us passively. In this way, knowledge follows practice and not, as is usually assumed, practice follows knowledge.[4] From this point of view the question, impatiently raised again and again, why all

---

3   In sociology, this relation to practice is evident especially in the work by Pierre Bourdieu and Anthony Giddens, who are influenced by the later work of Ludwig Wittgenstein and the ethnomethodology, all of whom directly or indirectly learned from pragmatism (see Reckwitz 2000, especially pp. 542-643).
4   This is based on the fundamental assumption of the primacy of practice elaborated particularly clearly in the pragmatism of John Dewey and others in their anti-Cartesian action model; for transfer into the debate about the theory of practice, see Hörning 2004b.

this knowledge about climate change does not result in appropriate action, is posed the wrong way or is due to a biased discourse among intellectuals with not too much confidence in everyday "people".

The centre of this theoretical approach is constituted by *"social practices"*. They are continuous, they are well trained; as everyday trains of action and customs, they are mainly influenced socially and culturally. They are generated in life with others, in the family, at school, in education, at work, during sports, in everyday life. This is where they are trained, become taken for granted, and yet carry a wealth of important cultural significances and values without our communicating about them. In this way, a multitude of social practices unfold in modern differentiated societies. I would like to select below practices of living, nutrition, consumption, communication, and time. We participate in them, we engage in them, and we play them mostly by implicit "rules of the game".[5] Unlike individual intentional actions, they do not have to be started by a player by whatever motivating force. From the outset, a practice is embedded interactively in situations of life and cultural contexts, in which also material things, technologies, artefacts play an important role. As a rule, social practices are practices *with* and *in* things, *with* technologies *in* buildings, *with* cars *in* cities. In this way, artefacts are seen as integral components of social practices, influencing these, characterizing them together with other features, becoming "players" without determining them.[6]

These concrete examples can show how social and cultural changes may occur in a sustainable sense, but also the profound obstacles in their way. The cultural aspect of it, the aspect we call *"culture"*, from a point of view of the theory of practice is expressed only in actual practice. This is where the cultural web of patterns of purpose and interpretation develops its effect. Our action then turns it into something important and valuable for us and our co-players. Theories about practice emphasize culture in a specific use: "Culture as practice" – "doing culture" (cf. Hörning 2004a; Hörning/ Reuter 2004). In this usage, the concept of practice in a way acts as the link between the cultural schemes of interpretation and knowledge, cultural coding on the one hand, and jointly acting subjects on the other hand. In continuing practices, the cultural schemes act less as external norms and interpretations, but more as cultural presumptions and knowledge in store, which become the unspecific substrates to the actions of the players, suggesting to them specific trains of action as being obvious and excluding others as unsuitable, in this way stabilizing collective patterns of action and habits. For this to occur, specific interpretive competences of the players are required which

---

5   "Practices" are built up in analogy with what Wittgenstein circumscribes as "language games": "The essential feature of a language game is a practical method (a kind of action)", a practice in accordance with open, though not random, rules (cf. Wittgenstein 1988, pp. 241-345).
6   The influence of artifacts is a subject of debate. To Bruno Latour, the non-human "players" are constitutive of the social side of things, prerequisites of social action routines, stabilizing social orders ("technology as a society designed for permanence"; cf. Latour 1991, 2001).

unfold existing pools of cultural knowledge and interpretation in practice by making them part of their knowledge for action.

When seen from this perspective, the stability of cultural forms lies less in the continuity of cultural systems or schemes and more so in specific conditions of development under which people grow up in social and cultural worlds and, in this process, are able to acquire and train their abilities, skills, and also cultural competences. Just think of the potentials for learning and training, the far-ranging changes in working and communication practice as a result of computers, mobile phones, and the Internet. Using the new technical equipment not only provides us with new skills and experience, but also changes our ideas and our judgment of what we have to think of them, and also provides us with new cultural competences about how to best fit them into our life.

However, the starting conditions for the strict, demanding principle of sustainability are much more difficult than those associated with the spread of new communication technologies, which opened far ranging spaces of possibility often forcing cultural traditions and conventions to capitulate very quickly. I would like to demonstrate this problem of sustainability in two large practical areas. On the one hand, the social practices associated with *dwelling* and, on the other hand, the social practices of *nutrition*. Both are not only key practices in everyday life, but also play a particularly dangerous role in *climate*.

Dwelling is a central part of our routine practice of life: If we want to change it so as to achieve more sustainability, especially by clearly reducing energy consumption, we hit upon a complex of particularly compact trains of action which cross-link large areas of social life and cannot be changed easily without fundamentally reshaping collectively established conventions and cultural presumptions of what is the good life. The apartment, the house is the place where we preferably stay, cultivate our habits, and are familiar with everything in such a way that we can feel "at home". In his "Poetry of Space", Gaston Bachelard says that a large share of our memories and imaginations are associated with the house (cf. Bachelard 2003, pp. 30-59). This is the place, above all, where many things occur with a certain continuity, such as sleeping, reading, cooking, working, relaxing, talking, establishing privacy.

Small wonder, then, that energy consumption in private households is not easily changed in view of the many significant roles. This change is even more unlikely to be achieved by merely technical systems, such as the electronically networked "smart home" or the fully insulated "low-energy house" (also referred to "zero-emission house" or "passive house") with its strict heat control and sophisticated ventilation technology. These houses are still closely associated with the Bauhaus idea of a rationalistically perfect building. The *Bauhaus* claimed for its products a maximum of objectivity achieved by sober aesthetics and strict functionalism. Its original opposite was seen to be the ornament, but what was at stake from the beginning was a new *logic of dwelling*, expressed in buildings, room layouts, furniture, and objects of daily use, supported by explanations and theories and, above all, by drill, rules, and alphabets which had to be learned by the students (cf. Galison 1990; Wünsche 1989).

Eighty to ninety years later, these maxims still have a strong impact on today's architects. However, ecologically sensitized architects now increasingly translate the Bauhaus principle of "form follows function" into "form follows sustainability" or "form follows energy". Yet, everything is still subordinated to one single principle. But: *There is no longer just one logic of dwelling.* From the point of view of the inhabitants, there are a great many criteria and yardsticks to apply to a building, a house, an apartment. Several studies of the low-energy house, for instance, show that its extremely low acceptance is in no way only due to the lack of knowledge or the "wrong" preferences of the inhabitants, but mainly to the difficult integration of the sophisticated technology into the established practices of living. Inhabitants have major problems especially with the disturbing noises produced by the ventilation systems, the new windows to be kept closed at all times ("living like in a thermos"), and the heat generated inside which should be sufficient, if possible, to do without additional space heating (see also the excellent empirical study by Rohracher 2006).

The problem lies in the absence of solutions fit for everyday use. The architects and all the other experts involved must say goodbye to the either-or approach and adopt a both-and patchwork geared more towards finding flexible, open solutions and taking into account different cultural local customs. Success then is more likely to be achieved by mixes of new and conventional elements which not only strive for absolutely new solutions but also pick the new features out of established ones. In my view, the gist of ecological building and living lies in *common social learning processes*, in which all participating players, the inhabitants first of all, the design engineers, architects, ventilation companies, craftsmen and all the others, establish permanent feedback. The outcome could be a comprehensive design including the inhabitant not as a willing or unwilling end user but as a player learning and strengthened through participation. It is only in these exchange processes that experts realize what ideas of adequate dwelling practice underlie decisions by users, and how much room is available for sustainable changes. After all, objects, rooms, apartments, buildings do not exist as independent entities, but are profoundly involved in everyday practice. They find their specific places in the practice of a "form of living," as Wittgenstein emphasizes in his "Gebrauchstheorie der Bedeutung" on the basis of language philosophy: "Allow meaning to be *taught* you by use" (Wittgenstein 1988, p. 550). Martin Heidegger puts it even more fundamentally: "Dwelling is the *essence of being. Only when we are able to dwell, we are able to build*." For this reason, we "must build out of dwelling and think for dwelling" (Heidegger 2004, pp. 155f.).

As long as there are no participative exchange processes in which the boundaries between experts and users become transparent, we have to do with *"imagined lay persons"*, i.e. concepts, images of lay persons underlying the actions of experts mostly unrelated to any specific topic and with previous awareness,[7] which are continuously reinforced by a onesided flow of communication in which experts again and again try to remedy the alleged knowledge deficit of users by supplying even more information, pamphlets, and advice. They still cling to onesided transmitter-receiver model and reject the cycle model with its continuous flow of communication with no beginning and no end. In that flow, many are involved in knowledge generation, advancing the ecologically important processes of joint will formation and decision-making by their reference to specific problems.

This becomes relevant in particular when considering that it is not so much a matter of what is called "new building", which is so dear to the hearts of architects, but rather the ecological rehabilitation of a vast number of energy-devouring old buildings. However, progress in this respect is very slow for many reasons. Actually, people in the upwardly mobile middle classes, who are so fond of moving into apartments in old buildings in large cities, would have to advance rehabilitation (cf., e.g., Dangschat 2002). Although most of them are associated with the ecological idea and represent it verbally, their everyday actions are hardly conducive to saving energy. Saving energy is not really part of the urban way of living, given its lavish use of energy, light, and movement. People in small and medium-sized cities are more advanced in these respects. This is evident from the success of the municipal movement called "100 Percent Renewable". Many municipalities, cities, and regions in Germany have switched their energy supplies completely to renewables for electricity and heat.[8] Obviously, the "scale effect" plays an important role in overcoming the associated acceptance problems. The fact that we are fraught with a global problem seems to make the conclusion obvious

> "that we can solve that problem only globally. [...] However, it could be just the other way around. Large problems require small solutions, complex problems require simple solutions. For example, smaller groups (are) very much more effective than large ones in finding and implementing solutions [...]" (Welzer 2009, p. 107).

Transparent municipal contexts are helpful, more inclusive, and they are not easily bypassed. They create specific common units for co-operation and, on top of this, socially shared yardsticks and interpretations. Taking into account public interests in our everyday affairs, i.e. acting as responsible citizens willing to contribute to resource

---

7 "Imagined lay persons" as referred to by science sociologists, such as Helga Nowotny and others, mean implicit models of addressees, users, who are supposed by the experts to have specific capabilities and take specific actions. The expert imagines something which he/she does not know precisely, or which he/she imagines or wishes in the light of his/her perspective (cf. Nowotny 2004).

8 Thus, the "100 Percent Renewable" municipal movement reported in early 2010 that Neckarsulm was building a solar district, Föhrensbach had restored a decommissioned hydroelectric plant, Husum, Emden, and others successfully operated wind power plants, and the town of Prenzlau, Uckermark, produced more electricity from renewable energies than it consumed, thanks to a sophisticated storage of biogas (cf. www.kommunal-erneuerbar.de [14.01.2010]).

conservation, is easier when we can be confident that others will act in a similar way. To strengthen that confidence, especially citizen initiatives and neighbourhood initiatives as well as other social networks can be very helpful. There is much to say in favour of "municipalization on a small scale" and the buildup of We-groups (as Claus Leggewie and Harald Welzer state concisely) in which the "yardsticks for good or bad actions, for shame, success, pride and the like [...] develop and remain in place" (Leggewie/Welzer 2009, p. 233). At any rate, ecological shifts of this type involve a lot of social learning and experiencing potential, but also much communication and many processes of mutual understanding on a local level which, for example, could be able to override the otherwise powerful interests of house owners. What we refer to as civil society develops mainly on the local and regional levels of action. This is where public space assumes new contours.

And now for the *practice of nutrition*. Also nutrition is a key social practice, any change in which, as in dwelling, profoundly goes against collectively established habits and cultural presumptions of a good life. And yet, we have recently been able to observe a fast ecological change in nutritional habits. There are many explanations for this development, as complex processes of this kind cannot be reduced to one single reason.

If established routines are to be given up in order to achieve sustainable action, a lot of irritating, provocative events must accumulate to make us inspect, reflect, and search. In low-cost situations, we are very ready to shift to organic products; we do not have to considerably change our routine consumption practices. However, if it is a matter of switching from a nutritional practice firmly established since childhood, this takes a lot of knowledge about health and disease and a number of scandals associated with animals and meat and the resultant public discourse. On the other hand, there must be an urban middle class movement able to make the increase in time and cost required for ecological nutrition plausible by investing a lot into social communication. In this connection, we should not misunderstand the concept of "movement". It does not refer to associations, groups or organizations expecting similar action from their members, but draws attention to large open associations of individuals acting in a similar way on their own and finding it reasonable to consume organic food. In addition, they communicate, permanently balance their actions against those of others, try to make their actions clear to others, and find social connection and recognition from what they do. In this respect, they continuously refer to patterns of argumentation found in public and media discourses.

Why does the switch to ecological practice in nutrition proceed so quickly? In terms of cultural sociology, I attribute this to a specific *subject model* which propagated fast over the past few decades. It is based on the cultural revolutionary movements of the 1960s in Western Europe and North America directed against rationalist modern times and against the bourgeois standards of normality, which established a *counterculture* of boundless, playful searching for intense, authentic experiences of their selves. They propagated a subject culture with specific aesthetic-expressive characteristics closely coupled to new forms of music, art, sexuality, and consumption (cf. Reckwitz 2006, pp. 441-630). However, the subject model as a generalized life-style became more widespread only after the 1980s. It quickly penetrated into urban centres and became a

> "model of a subject self-fashioning himself or herself experimentally via objects and services of consumption, finding satisfaction there [and] transforming this into physical experience" (Reckwitz 2006, p. 555).

From that point on, the *guiding semantics of experience* stepped into the foreground not only in the meaning of event consumption, but mainly by upgrading the body as the place of manifold experiences and practices (cf., empirically, Schulze 1992). It is interesting to see how consumption for purposes of self-fashioning is guided more and more by *immaterial* objects and events, by information, advice and communication, entertainment and experience, shopping and, above all, body care and health care.

Against this cultural background, my question can be answered more easily. The ecological switch in nutritional practice is so successful because it is not counteracted by cultural coding; on the contrary, organic is fun, supporting the increasing care for the body and for health, thus becoming the element of subjective self-fashioning. It also furnishes the matching framework of cultural justification. After all, organic nutritional practice is associated not only with health and wellness, but it also furnishes arguments against the ecologically disastrous agricultural industry: Ecologically oriented consumer decisions can influence food production.[9] This success is also due to the fact that the new practice of nutrition is linked to many traditional cooking and eating habits handed down by the grandparent generation, i.e. it is in no way a practice to be started from scratch. This lowers cultural barriers.

The two examples of dwelling and nutrition show very well the *close interrelations of culturally and ecologically sustainable change.* In this process, sustainability loses its character of an abstract principle, emerging instead as an *open process of searching, learning, and experience,* which does not necessarily intend to achieve completely new results but can also link to old models. In that case, it is more important to investigate scope, find solutions for our convictions which are practicable and achievable, and which allow us and all those coming after us to enjoy a good life also tomorrow and the day after tomorrow. Only in this way can we ward off subjective overstraining by the august imperative of sustainability. How else could I, as an addressee of that imperative, succeed in extrapolating the consequences of my action to the ecology of the world society at any moment in time, as is demanded by many environmental ethicists. Only in this way can we turn an abstract topic, like the present

---

9   For the "food chain" (production – trade – consumption) and the possibilities and difficulties of action by those participating in the food chain and the players relevant to sustainable consumption, cf. the research findings in Brand 2006; Brunner/Schönberger 2005; Eberle et al. 2006.

"climate change," which will quickly turn out to be a killer argument when used against individuals, into a cultural subject, something that affects us, something which can also be handled socially. It is then no longer a matter of "committing individuals," as is often said, or accusing them of denying reality in the absence of appropriate action. Instead, we must not demand *too little* in social and cultural terms and thus overlook the great opportunities inherent in processes of social and cultural change.

"Climate change" undoubtedly is a big cultural challenge showing the main deficits in sustainability in a particularly drastic and dramatic way. In this role, it can *enlighten* us about our bad habits and negative value orientations, but can also *provoke* us by drawing attention to, and scandalizing, our careless social and cultural practices, and may play the role of a *conflict generator* making us argue, with "sustainability" as the yardstick, about what is so damaging about our everyday practices, what needs to be better, what has to be avoided at all cost, and also what has to happen at all cost, and what can be assigned second priority (cf. Hulme 2009, pp. 326-365). This broadens the horizon, allows us to handle criteria and norms and make judgments about bad, wrong, energy-wasting habits, clearly differentiating them from desirable, right, sustainable practices.

In this way, a *normative concept of culture* takes priority which is directed against the seeming equivalence of all forms of life and culture by emphasizing the better practices, worth studying, of common survival, and by establishing a distance relative to the other squandering, ecologically "uncultivated" habits. Not everything is right, not everything is permitted. This normative nature of culture develops within the concrete action process; it is not applied externally. Although, in a crisis (the present "climate change"),[10] it establishes a close network of relations with external norms and principles, our findings of what is fitting or not fitting in a specific case, good or bad, advantageous or detrimental, is due to practical knowledge and judgment based on cultural criteria and normative frameworks, but undergoes specific shaping and change in the continuation of the respective practices.

This reveals a *new freedom of modern man* not only to shed something – for instance outdated traditions – or fight for his right for something – for instance equal treatment –, but also a new freedom *for* something (for this distinction, cf. Berlin 2002). So far, we have understood this modern freedom for something mainly as a freedom to educate ourselves, inform ourselves, consume, achieve self-realization and participate in the world's progress and prosperity. From now on, we will have to learn and practice new freedoms in addition: the freedom to restrict ourselves, address waste, avoid damaging patterns of behaviour, encourage ourselves and others to improve, handle objects with more care, save energy, drive smaller cars, decelerate

---

10 About the historical dimension of societal crises and their perception, cf. Scholten 2007; for the sociological analysis of such crises, cf. Friedrichs 2007.

things, practice new ways of time management.[11] Above all, this refers to the freedom to change one's lifestyle, be more relaxed and circumspect or, in a more general sense or most importantly, the freedom to interpret prosperity in a new and different *cultural* sense. None of this will be completely new, because we never start from scratch. Social practice of life is always both things: repetition *and* change, iteration *and* innovation, persistence *and* new development.

[This article has already been published in German in Parodi, O.; Banse, G.; Schaffer, A. (eds.): Wechselspiele: Kultur und Nachhaltigkeit. Annäherungen an ein Spannungsfeld. Berlin: edition sigma 2010, pp. 333-345.]

References

Bachelard, G. (2003): Poetik des Raums. 7th ed. Frankfurt am Main (in German)

Berlin, I. (2000): Two Concepts of Liberty. In: Berlin, I.: Liberty. Oxford/New York, pp. 166-217

Brand, K. W. (ed.) (2006): Von der Agrarwende zur Konsumwende? Die Kettenperspektive. Ergebnisband 2. Munich (in German)

Brunner, K. M.; Schönberger, G. U. (eds.) (2005): Nachhaltigkeit und Ernährung. Produktion – Handel – Konsum. Frankfurt am Main/New York (in German)

Dangschat, J. S. (2002): Soziale Aspekte der nachhaltigen Stadtentwicklung. In: Klotz, A.; Frey, O.; Rosinak, W. (eds.): Stadt und Nachhaltigkeit. Ein Diskurs. Wien/New York, pp. 43-62 (in German)

Eberle, U.; Hayn, D.; Rehaag, R.; Simshäuser, U. (eds.) (2006): Ernährungswende. Eine Herausforderung für Politik, Unternehmen und Gesellschaft. Munich (in German)

Friedrichs, J. (2007): Gesellschaftliche Krisen. Eine soziologische Analyse. In: Scholten, H. (ed.): Die Wahrnehmung von Krisenphänomenen. Fallbeispiele von der Antike bis zur Neuzeit. Cologne, pp. 13-26 (in German)

Galison, P. (1990): Aufbau/Bauhaus: Logical Positivism and Architectural Modernism. In: Critical Inquiry, Vol. 16, pp. 709-727

Grober, U. (2010): Die Entdeckung der Nachhaltigkeit. Kulturgeschichte eines Begriffs. Munich (in German)

Heidegger, M. (2004): Bauen Wohnen Denken. In: Heidegger, M.: Vorträge und Aufsätze. 10th ed. Stuttgart, pp. 139-156 (in German)

Hörning, K. H. (2001): Experten des Alltags. Die Wiederentdeckung des praktischen Wissens. Weilerswist

Hörning, K. H. (2004a): Kultur als Praxis. In: Jaeger, F.; Liebsch, B. (ed.): Handbuch der Kulturwissenschaften. Vol. 1. Stuttgart, pp. 139-151 (in German)

---

11   The "player juggling with time" is a good example showing how this new style of time management could be organized. We, i.e. my colleagues from Aachen and I, conducted an empirical study of ways of time management when using new communication technologies, in this way emphasizing this type in great detail (cf. Hörning et al. 1997).

Hörning, K. H. (2004b): Lob der Praxis. Praktisches Wissen im Spannungsfeld technischer und sozialer Uneindeutigkeiten. In: Gamm, G.; Hetzel, A. (eds.): Unbestimmtheitssignaturen der Technik. Eine neue Deutung der technisierten Welt. Bielefeld, pp. 297-310 (in German)

Hörning, K. H.; Ahrens, D.; Gerhard, A. (1997): Zeitpraktiken. Experimentierfelder der Spätmoderne. Frankfurt am Main (in German)

Hörning, K. H.; Reuter, J. (eds.) (2004): Doing Culture. Neue Positionen zum Verhältnis von Kultur und sozialer Praxis. Bielefeld (in German)

Hulme, M. (2009): Why We Disagree About Climate Change. Understanding Controversy, Inaction and Opportunity. Cambridge/New York

Latour, B. (1991): Technology Is Society Made Durable. In: Law, J. (ed.): A Sociology of Monsters? Essays on Power, Technology, and Domination. London/New York, pp. 101-131

Latour, B. (2001): Eine Soziologie ohne Objekt. Anmerkungen zur Interobjektivität. In: Berliner Journal für Soziologie, Vol. 11, pp. 237-252 (in German)

Leggewie, C.; Welzer, H. (2009): Das Ende der Welt, wie wir sie kannten. Klima, Zukunft und die Chancen der Demokratie. Frankfurt am Main (in German)

Nowotny, H. (2004): Der imaginierte Dialog zwischen Wissenschaft und Öffentlichkeit. Von imaginierten Laien zur sozialen Robustheit des Wissens. In: Gisler, P.; Guggenheim, M.; Maranta, A.; Pohl, Chr.; Nowotny, H. (eds.): Imaginierte Laien. Die Macht der Vorstellung in wissenschaftlichen Expertisen. Weilerswist, pp. 171-195 (in German)

Reckwitz, A. (2000): Die Transformation der Kulturtheorien. Zur Entwicklung eines Theorieprogramms. Weilerswist (in German)

Reckwitz, A. (2003): Grundelemente einer Theorie sozialer Praktiken. In: Zeitschrift für Soziologie, Vol. 32, pp. 282-301 (in German)

Reckwitz, A. (2006): Das hybride Subjekt. Eine Theorie der Subjektkulturen von der bürgerlichen Moderne zur Postmoderne. Weilerswist (in German)

Rohracher, H. (2006): The Mutual Shaping of Design and Use. Innovations for Sustainable Buildings as a Process of Social Learning. Munich/Vienna

Scholten, H. (Hg.) (2007): Die Wahrnehmung von Krisenphänomenen. Fallbeispiele von der Antike bis zur Neuzeit. Cologne (in German)

Schulze, G. (1992): Die Erlebnisgesellschaft. Kultursoziologie der Gegenwart. Frankfurt am Main/New York (in German)

Welzer, H. (2009): Vom Wissen zum Handeln – vom Handeln zum Wissen. Harald Welzer im Gespräch mit Sebastian Gießmann. In: Gießmann, S.; Brunotte, U.; Mauelshagen, F.; Böhme, H.; Wulf, Chr. (eds.): Politische Ökologie. Bielefeld, pp. 103-110 (Zeitschrift für Kulturwissenschaft, No. 2) (in German)

Wünsche, K. (1989): Bauhaus: Versuche, das Leben zu ordnen. Berlin (in German)

Wittgenstein, L. (1988): Philosophische Untersuchungen [1935/45 & 1947/49]. In: Wittgenstein, L.: Werkausgabe. Vol. 1. 4th ed. Frankfurt am Main, pp. 225-580 (in German)

Part 2

Epistemic Topics,
Knowledge and Ethical Dilemmas

Material Goods and Individuation Processes

The Ethics of Consumerism between Mankind's Potential for Transcendence and the Forces of Culture

Renate Hübner

1 Introduction and Structure of the Article

Since 1996 the slogan "Using not owning"[1] has been valid in Germany as one guiding principle for the development and advancement of strategies for the sustainable use of products. Even if the slogan is legally not completely accurate (the relation of possession to ownership), it reminds us that the use of objects – and not their purchase – constitutes the true benefit of a good. That means that in order to use goods it is not really necessary to buy them. Renting, lending, sharing, upgrading, repairing, etc. goods are not new but very effective strategies for conserving resources.[2] The common aim of these strategies is to substitute the purchase (and with that the production) of new goods, either by services that accompany ownership (life extending) or that substitute ownership (intensifying use). In the first case ownership by the user of a product is a prerequisite; in the latter the owner has to forgo ownership of the good (and only pay for its function).

Many successful examples have led to the increasing dissemination of these strategies, most of all in the commercial-industrial domain (cf. Fleig 2000; Hübner et al. 2007; Reisinger/Krammer 2007; Stahel 2004). In the area of private consumption, however, the economic (and with this also the ecological) success largely lags behind the expectations. Why is that so? How can one explain the relative disinterest of consumers in long-lasting goods and services like repairing, upgrading, and maintaining (*"caring* strategies") and likewise in lending/borrowing, renting, sharing (*"sharing* strategies"), even if these offers provide many advantages to the user, as they are mostly more cost-effective, more reliable, and save on the effort of maintenance and disposal?

---

1   In German: nutzen statt besitzen.
2   Verbraucherzentrale Baden-Württemberg e. V.: Nutzen statt Besitzen, Vol. 1 & 2, December 1996.

Before new concepts and further product-service systems are developed, it must first be acknowledged that many of the offers of product services which up till now have been understood as sustainable are not suitable for the masses – at least not under the given conditions in rich, westernized, industrial countries. This statement again leads to the basic question of why is that so? Motives that go beyond standard economic thinking, together with findings from various disciplines must be included in such an analysis, with different approaches being conceivable. On the basis that objects in general use and objects of everyday life serve the ongoing genesis and design of identity in a manner so far underestimated by research in general, the present text examines the connection between everyday objects and the process of individuation.

This article is thus based on two hypotheses: first, material goods fundamentally influence human processes of individuation; second, ownership and individuation are so closely co-dependent that concepts which facilitate usage without acquisition of ownership have less effect the more social importance is given to individual personal development. This is shown when a colleague from the business administration sciences supposes that "ownership cannot be cracked by us" ("Eigentum ist für uns nicht zu knacken"; Paech 2007, oral presentation). Based on specific research results he concludes that "even highly efficient, ownership-substituting services lack cultural compatibility". Different qualities of use seem to exist, depending on whether one is the owner or not. But how is that to be understood? Is in our Western civilizations *having* (following Erich Fromm) more important than *using*? Or is *buying/purchasing* even more important than having and using combined?

Therefore the aim of this article is to consider how, i.e. with which strategies or concepts, the development of personality is dependent on or is made dependent on goods. In this four key strategies are discerned: Individuation through production, individuation through use or usage, individuation through purchase (shopping/consumerism), and individuation through ownership. Why is it important to consider such basic ideas? If, with regard to sustainable development, it is necessary to reduce the use of resources absolutely, the way in which goods are handled must be changed drastically. To do so the roots of all activity with goods must be uncovered: What is the role of goods for the self, for the identity of a person, and what are the contexts? What causes the magic of objects or commodities (cf. Hübner 2010), this magic attraction towards goods? Finally, these four strategies are considered in connection with the present economic system which in order to show why the very buying is becoming increasingly important for the maintenance of the system.

2 Individuation – Prerequisites and Processes in the Development of Identity

It is clear that many goods can be used without being "owned", without the user being the owner. It is also clear that goods will need to be repaired if, as the owner, you hope to be able to use them for longer. Here two central concepts which govern our use of goods are addressed: possession (in the sense of rightful occupancy) and ownership, whereby the institution of ownership goes far beyond the right to use something. The logical consequence of this is that material goods have a meaning which also goes far beyond the "pure" functions of their purpose and use. The present text, however, is not intended as a treatise of these legal differences (for more on this see Hübner et al. 2005, p. 67; Hübner et al. 2007, p. 65). Rather the central linguistic element, namely the term *ownership* is of interest, containing as it does the word "own", pointing to something of one's own, a self, to acquisition, to something special (e.g. idiosyncratic). What has it to do with this "one's own", this property, with a self and with one's identity, and what contribution does our use of goods and of objects make to this self, to its perception, to its development? How can this need, which transcends our use of goods, be captured or grasped? And how – vice versa – can that meaning of goods be explained that goes beyond the practical function of how they are used? Why is it important for more and more individuals to acquire as many goods as possible, to "have" them for oneself in Fromm's sense? Which role does ownership of goods play; especially when there is less and less time to use these goods? Or is it the other way round? Do we have to "have" everything ourselves, because time is increasingly scarce?

In the wealthy societies of the so-called Western world, i.e. in societies in which a reasonably large number of their members manage to satisfy their basic needs with relatively little effort, goods are certainly endowed with a meaning or function that goes beyond basic provision. Instead of the welfare of society in general that of the individual and its free development comes increasingly to the fore. What meaning do goods have and what role do they play in this context? In order to understand the present, demonstrably unsustainable patterns in which material goods are (being) used, and also to be able to change these, we have to analyze how goods, as material objects, have contributed or (can) contribute to individuation, to the development of people's personalities.

2.1 The Right to Free Development of the Personality

The term individuation can be traced from Latin (individuus = not dividable) and simply means "to make oneself indivisible/undividable". The psychoanalyst Carl Gustav Jung introduced this term to psychology with the meaning "become a single being,

and, insofar as under individuality we understand our innermost, last and incompara-
ble singularity, become our own self" (Jung 1933, p. 65). Therefore one could translate "individuation" also as "the genesis and realization of the self", a path to one's
own whole, a process of becoming a singular being, an individual. One's own whole
again presupposes a self, a self that recognizes itself as an individual and as such is
also recognized by others. This process can be conscious or unconscious, controlled or
by chance, directed or without direction. The human being is a creature that can think
and that has consciousness. One can assume that the genesis, this becoming of the
self, happens more or less consciously, not completely by chance and not without
direction. For the human being that means that it can influence this process or even
actively shape it. But to what extent these processes are set in motion or how they take
their course depends not only on the respective individual, but also on the individual's
circumstances or environment. This process is overshadowed by a continual oscilla-
tion between necessities and possibilities, the two "forms of despair", as Søren
Kierkegaard describes it in 1849 in his book "The Sickness unto Death".

The individual, and with it the becoming of the self, did not have the same meaning in the history of mankind as they have today. There were times, and there are still
cultures, in which the collective, and not the individual, was or is the centre of consideration (e.g. Asian cultures, tribal cultures). In European cultures today free personal
development is valued most highly. In Germany this is stated explicitly. Article 2,
paragraph 1 of the German Constitution guarantees the free development of the personality. This comprehensive right to free development of the personality accords a
special role not only to the individual but also to the development of identity within
modern society. In a time or culture in which the circumstances not only allow the
free development of individuals but also encourage, almost demand it, one becomes
so to speak "a task for oneself" (Gross 1999, p. 9). What is special about the human
being, what predispositions make it possible for an individual to even think about
changing and developing him- or herself?

Predispositions: The Potential for Transcendence – Differentiation towards Oneself

The prerequisite for the free development of the human being is that the human being
is not fixed once and for all, but is able to define him- or herself anew over and over
and again. As a being with shortcomings, the human being is by nature neither purely
instinctive, nor capable of creating a second nature which solves all problems. Presumably developments of artificial or virtual worlds, like artificial cities (e.g. Las Ve-
gas), artificial worlds (e.g. Disneyworld, Legoland) or virtual parallel worlds (Second

Life) do not change anything.[3] These missing instincts are seen as natural deficiencies, whereby the human energy (impetus) remains essentially undirected, which makes the human being open, unfinished, and unfinishable – prerequisites for its freedom. Nevertheless, for all their shortcomings, human beings are still part of nature. But the human can interfere with nature, can adapt or resist, even his or her own nature; he or she can set him- or herself apart from nature and their own self. This ability of the human being is a prerequisite for a free development of the personality which he or she owes to a freedom – previously undefined – "a difference of the human being to itself" (Heintel 2007, p. 37). By this Peter Heintel means that predetermined element of the human being which is not nature: the human being can interfere in its processes, influence and change them, strive to make something new. This includes, effectively, interfering again and again in its own being as an object. As such a *being of differentiation* (cf. Gross 1994; Heintel 2007, p. 37) the human being oscillates repeatedly between reality and potential. Its identity not only *is*, but continually *comes into being*, as a process of setting itself apart from, on the one hand, his or her own ego, and on the other, from the other, from that outside him- or herself.

This potential for transcendency, this capacity of the human being to transcend its being (with its ego), that is to go beyond the limits of its behaviour, its experience and its consciousness, thereby realizing the state beyond these limits, thus becomes the second prerequisite for developing its self. Religion, dreams, desires, visions, identification, and projection are typical phenomena of the potential for transcendence, which therefore play an essential role in the course of the process of individuation.

Challenges: Exploiting the Potential for Transcendence

Identity as "the one indispensable pole of human thinking and acting" (Stross 1991, pp. 1f.) poses new challenges for the individual, which should be faced knowingly in order that the individual can protect him- or herself from manipulation and projection. The exploitation of the potential for transcendence firstly requires the human being to have the necessary abilities to recognize its own self (e.g. reflection) and secondly the ability to develop this self, i.e. to achieve growth in the maturity of one's personality (cf. Erikson 1966, p. 123). At the same time reference images or options must be present which point beyond the present being (cf. Fischer et al. 2008, p. 11). These options are to be found, for instance, in:

- role models of social institutions (e.g. gender, hierarchy, family, work, neighborhood, politics, community, clubs, educational systems etc.);

---

3   To what extent these attempts to satisfy human needs as far as possible synthetically, that is with a substitute for nature, develop into a culture would have to be discussed separately – "Artificiality as a World Culture?".

- wishes, visions, dreams based on external influences (e.g. education/training, advertising, peer group, partner, parents, books, idols etc.);
- prevalent qualities of the human being which differentiate it from nature, from animals, i.e. 'cultural' qualities (e.g. homo faber, homo ludens, homo oeconomicus, homo sapiens, homo consumens, ...);
- transcendental concepts of individual shaping of one's existence and future (e.g. having or being in Fromm's terms, or religious notions of the "Beyond").

According to Erik H. Erikson, identity would therefore be characterized by the self's feeling of reality, which has to a large extent been achieved, then needing to be revised repeatedly. The world of images created by the ideal self would, in contrast, be the number of ideal aims to which the self (cf. Erikson 1980, pp. 199f.) aspired but were never fully achievable. Idealized images in the form of the options listed above are radically increasing in comparison to former epochs of human history, as is the imagined probability of their realization.

We have to thank so-called progress for this increase in the options available and also in the hoped-for likelihood of their realization. How is this to be understood? Thanks to economic and technical progress more and more products can be bought by ever increasing sections of the population. Thanks to social progress, social barriers (e.g. barriers of class or gender, or assignment to a certain social strata) have been overcome. Likewise, notions that one's role is determined for life have decreased, work and family situations are increasingly rarely once-and-for-all decisions, while ways of life and the opportunities for shaping them are becoming more and more varied. Flexibility in all areas of daily life has become almost a norm. In addition, there is the phenomenon of having more time at one's disposal: in the so-called affluent or prosperous societies less and less time has to be spent on satisfying basic physical needs than in poor societies. So there is more time in the former for the non-physical, for the transcendental – which, however, can manifest itself in the physical, in so far as it is reflected in mobile, consumerist behaviour. Therefore it is only logical that to the major questions mankind asks itself about its existence (Where from? Where to? Why?), other philosophical questions have been added, which – today – have perhaps greater relevance: Who am I? Who/what do I want to be? Questions then that revolve not around mankind as a species, as a collective, but around the single individual.

2.2   Processes of Individuation

The conscious search for the self, this process of developing one's own identity while still remaining identical to oneself is an ambitious challenge which Erikson describes as follows: "In the course of one's life the ego as an organizing central authority is faced by a changing self, which demands that it be made congruent with all former and future selves" (Erikson 1980, p. 191). The process of individuation, consisting of processes of self-observation, of choosing from options, and of changing the self (cf. Fischer et al. 2008, p. 11) can happen once, several times, or continuously. Under the present circumstances, the human being can answer the questions of "Who am I?" and "Who do I want to be?" for itself once or several times, and answer differently every time. Individuation comprises the development of one's own abilities, talents, and opportunities within the context of changing environments. On the one hand, that sounds wonderful. It does, however, constitute an increasing stress factor for many people. The more options for choice there are, the more contradictions make themselves felt between model images, one's own desires or imaginations, external expectations, between keeping and changing. Thus the process of individuation is affected by balancing contradictions resulting from the following challenges: dissociation from the external world, inner conflict between freedom and security and – as instrument and result – the extent of the physical-material part in the process of individuation.

Frame or Reference: The Tension between the Inner and the Outer

The human being is part of one or several social systems. Thus the process of individuation always occurs in the field of tension between the two poles of the *individual* and the *collective*. Being observed by others *and* the self's realization of that fact influence the perception and assessment of one's own self, and thereby of the process of individuation. As social systems are not static but changing all the time, the collective as a pole of both differentiation and of belonging exists as a constant stimulus/irritant in the course of a person's individuation. And it is this very pole of the collective which almost logically requires a further question: "How do I want to affect my environment?" (see Figure 1).

Figure 1:   The Self in Tension between Internal and External

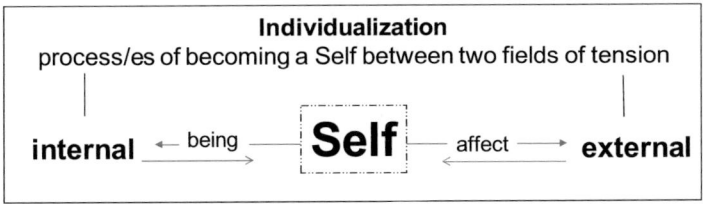

Author's archive

Perhaps this question offers even more scope for development than the previous ones, and is probably of greater relevance in the management of day-to-day living. Alfred Schütz explicitly differentiates between taking action (a term which includes the inner attitude) and "affecting" (having an effect on the external), "the intervention of the self in the universe and in universal time" (Schütz 2003, p. 11). The question of what the effect can be therefore surpasses the question of what is being. In this case the effect on others, on one's surroundings, on the environment in the broadest sense (the external effect) is more important for an individual than the being (the internal effect). This development of the "social person in the lonely self" (Schütz) is an interplay between the internal and the external, both always existing. The answer to the two questions "What/who do I want to be?" and "How do I want to affect (others)?" thus swings back and forth between the internal and the external, between desires (= wanting, internal) and duties (= obligation, external), and between abilities (= being able to, internal) and basic conditions (= being allowed to, external).

Process: The Tension between Security and Freedom

The two questions of wanting to be and wanting to affect contain the core notion of wanting. They can only be asked in this way in a society of free individuals which has sufficient physical-material security (welfare). This means it must be possible for the wanting to become reality beyond dreams and wishes. In order to confront the questions of being and affecting the human being must be free of shackles and constraints, and the human being must have overcome the state of being not free (slavery, dictatorships, norms).[4] Only then is he or she free for something, free to determine, to develop his or her life and identity themselves. Wanting postulates a need, more even: a free will, freedom. Freedom is therefore not only the human being's disposition to be able to develop freely, freedom requires a wanting, the will to determine this "vague difference of the human being to itself" (cf. Heintel 2007, p. 37), to develop it, to set parameters itself. Effect depends on having the potential to be seen and grasped, and so comes into being only through the physical-material manifestation of the wanting. Decisions only manifest themselves as physical in their realization, thereby becoming stipulations. This, however, leads to the inner contradiction of freedom: Every realization, every decision (e.g. a decision for academic studies, for a partner, for a career, or for a household appliance) offers a form of security, but at the same time imposes a limitation on one's freedom. On the other hand, each decision opens up new possibilities, and with these new realizations of freedom, which would not have existed without this decision.

Thus the process of individuation is strictly speaking a balancing of the freedom paradox,[5] the frame of reference being the individual him- or herself.[6] The second big field of tension arises through the frame of reference outside the individual, the eter-

---

4   Private, personal ownership is to be seen as an essential instrument to overcome heteronomy.
5   "You can't have your cake and eat it too" (an English proverb).
6   "Who is stronger: Me or me?" (as Johann Nestroy, an Austrian poet, expressed it in 1850).

nally recurrent decision relating to the collective – where do I want to belong, which groups do I want to differentiate myself from (see Figure 2)?

Figure 2:   Tensions in the Process of Individuation

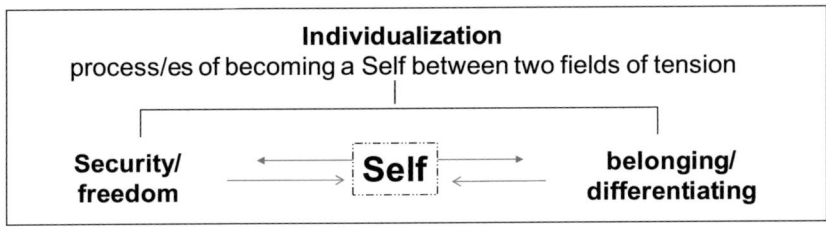

Author's archive

Finally, it is not only the differentiating oneself (from one's own self and from nature) and the answers to the questions of wanting to be and wanting to have an effect which belong to the exploitation of the potential for transcendence. A third process is necessary: the transformation process – how do I become what I want to become? How can I achieve that I appear the way I want to appear? The transformation process does not only depend on one's own, inherent (to one's self) potential, but – even more than the other two processes – upon the external circumstances and the physical-material possibilities.

The Dimension of Materiality: Tension between the Physical and the Non-physical

Parallel to the physical and non-physical dimensions of the human identity, material and immaterial goods open up the range of possibilities that exists between the physical, material pole, and the non-physical, or metaphysical pole. In the course of the practical realization of the self's formation and development, another dimension is added to this internal-external frame of reference: the dimension of physical materiality. Effect is achieved only through the inclusion of the body, that is, through visible doing, as the process happens. Schütz describes this as the "enforcement of the pragma in the body movement" (Schütz 2003, p. 11). Thus, the process of individuation always happens in the field of tension between the physical-material pole and the non-physical, immaterial one. Both being and affecting can always be considered as the relative share of the physical-material and the non-physical, immaterial parts (see Figure 3).

Figure 3:   Tension in the Material Dimension

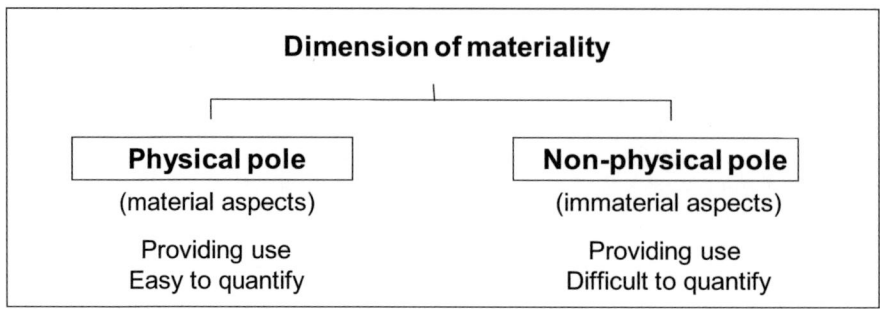

Author's archive

The physical-material pole

In order to satisfy its basic needs, that is simply for its "naked" survival, the human being needs material goods – food, and tools to produce it, to transport it, etc. He needs goods to protect himself, to move and to survive in his environment. Through technical and economic progress the ever-increasing and efficient production of more and more complex goods has come about. These do not only serve to satisfy physical needs. To that is added the phenomenon of relief (cf. Hübner 1991, p. 29): The use of many consumer goods makes everyday chores easier and so adds to the physical relief of the human being, thereby in turn releasing further resources, which, admittedly among other things, too, can be used to satisfy non-physical needs.

The non-physical, immaterial pole, also the metaphysical pole

It is difficult today to believe that the human being is only Physis and thus only "a kind of biochemical soup" (cf. Howanietz/Spohn 1990, p. 11). The mind and the soul of a human being cannot be verified with scientific means, and remain a phantom for many for the present. Yet, a self makes decisions, perceives feelings, and sets goals which go beyond material things and which cannot materially be sufficiently explained and achieved. And thus it seems as if this metaphysical pole of being leads to needs which cannot – or only to a limited extent – be satisfied by physical or consumer goods.

As will now be explained, material goods, objects, consumer goods, objects of everyday use, all these are not to be assigned solely to the physical pole. Goods thus play an essential, and probably in certain respects underestimated role in how humans' wanting to be and to affect is expressed.

3 The Dialectics of Objects: The Potential for Identification and Self-expression

The way we use goods, particularly material goods with a physical presence, is therefore a phenomenon which goes beyond the thing itself, and is thus a socio-cultural phenomenon. It includes more than the simple using of the good, because the good's potential extends beyond the needs which can be satisfied through using it – and yet it never fulfils all the expectations. As a result, the significance of goods goes far beyond their physical-functional characteristics. This combination of technical (objective) characteristics with the non-physical (subjective) potential – inherent to all goods – for identification and projection is the contribution that goods can make to the process of individuation.

If one sees humans, as Karl Marx did, as a species which is active in a world of objects, then humans develop in their "active interaction with nature", this being the principle of dialectic materialism. Consequently goods are the objectification of ideas, which happens not only in the production process but also when the goods are being used and possibly also at the moment of their purchase. These externalizations of the human being, in which the individual can recognize, confirm, and realize him- or herself, will now be analyzed with respect to their contribution to the individuation process.

3.1 Producing Things – Individuation through Production

Marx regards the productive ability as the basic characteristic of all humans – men and women as productive beings (cf. Liessmann 1999). Realizing one's own potential in production can however presumably only be achieved if the person producing can experience and control all phases of the production process, up to and including the finished product. Thus production can probably only be relevant for one's identity if all the production processes take place in one location, require human – perhaps even manual – labor, and can be controlled by the human producer. This, however, is only possible in the case of hand-made goods, which renders it virtually impossible to produce completely identical goods. Hand-made articles are consequently unique, which probably contributes to the identity-generating effect of goods – for the user, too. Manually produced goods usually aim to be long-lasting and repairable, thereby often accompanying the user over many years, and thus often determining his or her everyday life in an unobtrusive fashion, but the more sustainably for that. Certain watchmakers still advertise their products using these characteristics, emphasizing their power of identification on account of their stable, long-lasting values.

Industrial production looks very different. Increasingly, division of labour leads to the de-centralization of production locations, sometimes across the whole world. Each location specializes in one component or one part of the process, with many of the processes at least partially automated. This allows (and also demands) the production of absolutely identical, standardized goods on a large scale. This leads to prices which make even complex goods affordable for nearly everyone, at least in industrial countries. This has also many ecological and social consequences. Many of the effects of industrial production of goods are known, because they are highly visible or obvious (cf. Hübner 2010, p. 128): traditional social structures are changed, new social groups are added, such as those of the industrial worker, or of the so-called brain worker (e.g. managers, programmers, product developers, designers); resource consumption rises over or out of proportion, making whole regions dependent on one technology, on the production of one good. This becomes particularly evident in times of crisis.

However, many consequences are less obvious and do not show themselves so openly, creeping in (too slowly to be perceived), or remaining hidden (in the background and therefore hardly noticeable). Among these is the estrangement from goods, which according to Marx is a result of production conditions under capitalism. Mass production by machines offers the self, the individual, hardly any possibility to recognize and realize him- or herself in their entirety in the production of goods, since in reality the good is produced to a large part by another material good (the machine). Work in production increasingly comes to mean operating (in German "serving") the machines, in place of producing goods. Furthermore, the large numbers of items produced, and the impressive reduction in the time taken to produce an item, hardly gives the individual time to identify with what is produced. Moreover, under these conditions, the individual has hardly any opportunity within the production process to influence the product's success on the market, while income and wages are largely uncoupled from product type and quality, and, instead of the single product, what counts is large numbers and faultless batches. In contrast to the manual production of goods, which required suitable, product-specific skills, industrial qualifications are largely independent of the type of product: unskilled workers for basic manual tasks, skilled workers to use machinery, management expertise for the most efficient organization of (wo)men and machines and finally marketing experts and designers for the constant development of new products. Sales are left to the traders; again a completely distinct layer in an economic system which practices extreme division of labour and which increasingly demands ever greater marketing and sales expertise than product expertise. In the face of ever shorter innovative cycles, knowing a product well is hardly of practical relevance. Industrial production thus hardly seems to offer – except perhaps for designers and developers – much potential for the self-fulfillment of the individual through producing goods.

3.2   Using Objects – Individuation through Usage

In usage, in the act of using, "the function of goods realizes itself, where previously, as the result of production, only the potential function was attributed to it" (Ropohl 1999, p. 308). Here we can distinguish between two functional potentials: the substitution and the complementation potentials. Goods can perform certain actions instead of humans (substitution), relieving humans physically and making processes more efficient. Other goods, however, provide new functions which otherwise could not be performed by humans (complementation), thereby enlarging their potential to act.

Products, goods, and objects serve to satisfy needs, a phenomenon which is purely subjective and therefore highly elusive. An initial approach can be made via the term "provision of gain" (subjective, realising effect) or via the function of goods (objective, intended effect). The gain from goods arises from both functions of goods, the use function and the symbolic function.[7] While the usage function signifies the exploitation of the physical-technical potential (substitution or complementation), the symbolic function aims to exploit its non-physical characteristics. The symbolic function is not necessarily connected to the technical functions of a good, arising instead from the knowledge that the consumer has about the product's characteristics, based on existing (or imagined) knowledge. This real (or artificial) knowledge is produced by companies through information and advertising (cf. Bömmel 2003, p. 94).

Thanks to technical and economic progress there is a product answer (cf. Heintel 1999, p. 52) for every human need – and also for every contradiction of our needs. The product answers to the five global values – which went global long ago, when globalization became possible – of mobility, flexibility, convenience, security, and hygiene and the needs logically connected with them lead to more and more similar goods worldwide. Similar goods and similar demands on humans also lead to increasingly similar lifestyles, to a monotonizing of the world, as Stefan Zweig already noted in an essay in 1925 (cf. Zweig 1976, p. 7). In order to prevent this monotonizing, this unifying of lifestyles, ever more and newer goods and styles must be produced and distributed. In the face of a vast variety of goods, ever-changing fashions and trends contribute to compensating for the lowering of the basic usefulness of the usage function, by increasing the symbolic value in order to communicate variety and diversity. Those goods are successful which skillfully connect usage and symbolic functions, i.e. goods with high flexibility, mobility, and convenience potential (usage function), but equally high identification and differentiation potential (symbolic function).

To sum up, in the course of industrialized mass production decreasing opportunities for self-realization in the course of the production of goods have led to consumption (in the original sense of the Latin word *consumere*, meaning use up or use, not in

---

7   How far aesthetics is part of usage or of symbol and if it must be seen as a function in its own right and be included in explanations for now remains open to myself after some discussions.

the present sense of buy) offering itself as an alternative field, as presented in the newer theories of household production: the consumer as an active designer of his or her living circumstances (cf. Bömmel 2003, p. 106).

3.3   Acquiring Things – Individualization through Retail Activity

Shopping is a form of acquisition. However, the reason for the acquisition of goods seems to have changed: in former times goods were acquired to be used, to be made use of in order to satisfy a need. The use, the application, and the gain were in the foreground. Today, however, in affluent societies shaped by industry "purchasing new articles is necessary in order to guarantee production" (Scherhorn 1997, pp. 29f.). Scherhorn's formulation is perhaps a little exaggerated, and the individual presumably does not act with that intention in mind. The economic system, in the weave of which almost everybody is involved in some way, ensures, so to speak anonymously and collectively, that retail activity is upheld and "private consumption does not collapse". Shopping has top priority and works in the interest of sustaining the (established) system of production. Even Austrian advertising slogans like "Stinginess is cool"[8] do not call for people to save more or to refuse to go shopping, but overtake the current development in so far as hunting for bargains becomes fashionable, the absolute trend: one does not buy because one needs a good, but because it is so cheap that one would be a "stupid man"[9] not to buy at that price!

The concept behind all this is that of a society dominated by production, one dependent on the selling of goods. Where markets are saturated this can only work if the goods are short-lived, i.e. they go out of date technologically or fashion-wise as fast as possible. New versions of goods supplant former versions which still work, are perhaps better, and usually cheaper than employing upgrade or repair strategies. Disposal and fresh purchase are the logical result. The throw-away good is the ideal good from the point of view of this economic system. In this industrial "Rapid Replacement System" (Giarini/Stahel 2000, p. 100), offering long-lasting products which can be repaired or upgraded has little chance of success. Even long-lasting products are used significantly less or for shorter periods than their technological life would actually allow (e.g. mobile phones, personal computers). "Single products with a short life which can neither be fitted into the system nor be repaired cheaply nor adapted to changes have led to an increasing part of our income being spent firstly on the replacement of (already existing) products – which does not increase our prosperity

---

8   Advertising slogan ("Geiz ist geil") of the chain store Saturn in Germany and Austria. It was first used in 2003 within a longer running advertising campaign in the print media, on the radio, and on television.

9   "Ich bin doch nicht blöd, Mann!" advertising slogan of "Mediamarkt", an electronic goods chain in German speaking countries.

but only sustains or maintains it – and secondly on the disposal of rapidly growing mountains of refuse, containing ever more complex and poisonous material" in the words of Orio Giarini and Walter R. Stahel (Giarini/Stahel 2000, p. 100). In an age of saturated markets and needs whole sectors of industry are seeking new needs in the interest of their own growth. The attempt is being made to maintain the old pattern of an industrial, social, and economic system "which is dependent on the continuous production of unimportant and quickly obsolete products, and which therefore has no interest in people seeking a new source of satisfaction other than the material" (Philip Cushman in Nuber 1995, p. 22). To that end, they try to blur the distinction between material and immaterial goods, since "if people were […] really aware of this distinction it would endanger the consumer society. […] Therefore they try – e.g. through advertising – to establish a connection between material products and a feeling of individual well-being" (Gerhard Scherhorn in Nuber 1995, p. 25).

In this economic system the consumer is degraded to the role of buyer. Not the goods but the process of buying is central and great efforts are made to stage this as an adventure. Even though appeals are made to consumers, given their responsibility towards nature and their fellow beings, to think and act regionally, ecologically, and socially, it is virtually impossible under the current framework conditions to avoid being sucked in by the pressure to buy, however subtly it is exerted. Renouncing consumption in the sense of not going to buy things is also politically not desirable, since politicians actively and massively woo the consumers as a key factor in the upkeep and stability of whole sectors of the economy, persuading them to go out and buy real assets or articles. This buying thus becomes an activity, an adventure, an economically significant occupation.

3.4   Having things – Individuation through Ownership

Being able to acquire something can also be seen as the active realization of freedom (cf. Georg Wilhelm Friedrich Hegel's Philosophy of Law). It is part of the character of a physical good that it lets itself be acquired and is then at one's disposal. This is achieved through the buying process, the result of which is ownership of the good. With the purchase the buyer acquires full rights of usage and command over it (rights of ownership and mastery). The having, that is the owning of a good, opens up new, in my opinion, key dimensions in relation to the individuation process, which derive from the following options:

(1) to acquire something as an act of freedom;
(2) to have complete command over something as a boundary to the external;
(3) to have the choice between being able to use one's own possession oneself at any time or of allowing it to be used for a fee;
(4) to have the choice of doing nothing with it.

Goods which are used but are not in the ownership of the user tap into these dimensions only in a restricted way, if at all. Once goods have left production they initially
have no social form or subjective significance, insofar as they are separated from their
social context. For the consumer the industrially produced product is nothing special
or individual, it is – for a start – arbitrarily exchangeable. However, goods are not
only the materialized ideas of a designer or manufacturer, and in that sense complete;
they also provide a surface onto which future owners can project their desires, visions,
and needs. The original technical-functional use intended and inherent in the product
does not suffice to grasp the possibilities that an object offers. Only through acquisition are goods embedded into definite relationships with human beings. Into which
ones remains open, for as long as they are on the market (cf. Sorgo 2006).

The potential of an object extending far beyond the function attributed by the
manufacturer/seller thus really only arises firstly through its relation to the individual
human being, and secondly through its integration into an individual context, into specific life worlds. Thereby a multitude of highly subjective, possible interpretations
open up as to how material goods can have an effect on identity. This effect depends
on the one hand on the importance attributed to the goods for that purpose, and on the
other to their resulting power in the shaping of identity.

Due to the importance attributed to an object because of various attendant circumstances, such as it being a present, or a souvenir, or through the conscious development and fostering of its symbolic value (e.g. branding), a good becomes individual,
or personalized in Jean Baudrillard's terms (cf. Baudrillard 1991, p. 175). The individual meaning of an object arises from its projection potential offering an opportunity for the individual to identify with the object (internal effect) or differentiate him-
or herself from others (external effect). The potential for identification and differentiation is connected directly with the institution of ownership (renting a Mercedes is not
the same as owning one).

In addition to the potential for identification and differentiation, ownership offers
possibilities which are only indirectly related to the good per se. The extension of an
individual's scope and freedom of action comes about through the goods' potential for
substitution and complementation: on the one hand goods make daily chores easier,
thus providing advantages of scale *(extending the scope of action via relief from work,
and substitution)* and on the other hand they repeatedly offer new possibilities of action *(extending the scope of action with new opportunities, by complementation)*. Under the given circumstances the realization of these two functions depends on the
availability of such goods. At the moment only the institution of ownership seems to
grant relevant advantages like saving of time, flexibility, and spontaneity. The major
expectation placed on products or material goods is thus to be able to do anything at
any time. In this case material goods are effectively reduced to their technical functionality, this being, however, a functionality which firstly only exists within the context of the individual's life world, including his or her goods, and secondly clearly

depends on their full availability, which currently can hardly be realized in any other form than through the institution of ownership.

4 Summary: Sustainable Consumption between *Buying*, *Having*, and *Using*

In societies composed of free individuals, the motto "Who am I – and if yes, how many?"[10] (cf. Precht 2007) as the core mantra of self design is becoming the central challenge. Goods can play a more or less significant role in responding to it. Thus an individual can always be effectively motivated to purchase an unsustainably large number and variety of goods if this supports his or her individuation process. Not only advertising, but also other developments like "lifelong learning", technical and medical progress, or science and research in general contribute to the fact that humans increasingly see their identity as something that is permanently "designable", "changeable" and "improvable" – and rightly so – (re)designing one's self has become an ethically respectable task. The concomitant need and desire to be able to shape, change, and adapt one's respective identity at any time is the essential prerequisite for the success of the "buy and dispose of" logic of the current industrial economic system.

4.1 Buying and Throwing away – the Logic of Industrial Mass Production

Industrial mass production is based on the law of economy of scale, whereby the costs per item decrease the more items the plant produces. Competition on price leads to a self-accelerating spiral. Under the present circumstances (low-cost resources and transport, increasing costs for human labour) it makes economic sense to build bigger and bigger plants. Automation levels in the plants increase, making them more complex and more expensive, and furthermore they cannot be made redundant (unlike humans). Stopping production therefore costs a lot of money. That means, measures must be taken to ensure that plants work to full capacity. This leads necessarily to demand at least remaining constant, or perhaps even needing to be increased. In unsaturated markets this is not a problem, whereas in saturated, mature markets demand sinks to the level required for replacing products – meaning many plants would not be working to full capacity (cf. Giarini/Stahel 2000, pp. 48f.). The costs per item would grow again, and competition would decline. As costs cannot be reduced ad infinitum, production facilities cannot be moved to cheaper regions infinitely, the market must

---

10 Translation from the German book title "Wer bin ich – und wenn ja wie viele?".

take the initiative. In saturated markets the demand for goods must be maintained so to speak artificially, or even increased, using both technical and non-technical strategies. Technical strategies are for instance shorter and shorter innovation cycles, reducing product lifetime, or increasing product variety.

In non-technical strategies goods are presented in connection with desires, visions, and dreams and thus are symbolically loaded. Thereby a lot of effort is put into imbuing goods with a significance, something that in former times possibly occurred in another fashion or even by itself, over longer periods of production or usage. The estrangement of humans from their objectified ideas caused by industrial production and the thereby lost opportunity of identification with the production of material goods should be able to find itself again and to develop, if not in the production then at least in the consuming (in the further sense of buying, having, and using). However, the shorter the lifetime of products, the less identification potential they provide, and the less their having and using is relevant. All that remains is purchasing, and those – relatively soon – no longer wanted, used, or usable goods should not be a burden on the individual or on society, and so the efficient waste disposal sector gets rid of any worries about the "after-life" (in German "ent-sorgen" = "remove worries").

This linear, one-way industrial system has no interest in a sustainable use of goods with a correspondingly lower use of resources. According to industrial logic, economic systems in prosperous countries (in saturated markets) have less and less interest in providing society with important goods of high quality. Instead, ever more money is being invested in the production of meaning for goods, so that the existing system can be maintained, based on the paradigm of perpetual growth. Consequently, the real challenge in saturated markets is to develop products, paths, and ways to give essentially meaningless goods meaning – and hence enable buyers to identify with them.

4.2   Meaning – Coming and Going: The Problem of Sustainable Use of Goods

But what is meaning, and how does it come about? Meaning is not inherent to goods "like a cookie in a box" (documenta, school of visitors d7/d6, Kassel, Germany, 1982). Perhaps it is useful to consider the example of modern or abstract art, i.e. that type of art where you cannot guess from the outside what its meaning is. One then seeks the meaning of the piece of art – what does it express? What does the artist want to say with it? On the basis of descriptions or explanations, if available, an understanding can be gained of the meaning the artist "shoves into" his or her object. The same is true for objects in daily use. Their functionality, look, feel, and information (e.g instructions for use, advertisement, image) create an infinite variety of possible meanings, which only when included in the concrete world of an individual become meaningful and specific in practice, i.e. unique. However, in order for the existing industrial economic system to be maintained, it is now not enough for objects to be given sufficient potential significance to support the individuation process, as will be explained below.

It is of at least equal importance within industry's "quick replacement system" (see above) that objects of everyday use lose their meaning again in a relatively short space of time, since meaning is of course to be realized by other, newer goods. Whenever shorter innovation cycles and a growing variety of products should lead to shorter and shorter purchasing intervals, high quality, repairable, long lasting goods, ("teddy bear goods" which can be "personified", and with which one can identify for a longer period) – in short, goods which change everyday life into a specific, individual one – contradict this system. The ideal good from the system's viewpoint is – as explained above – the disposable good. This means not only that it can only be used once, but also that it must lose its meaning relatively quickly; a good, therefore, that you can part with easily ("chewing-gum good"). Ideally, this separation from the good, the discarding process, will have been given a special meaning as a result of environment protection measures being taken which support and promote recycling. There is no need for the buyer/user/disposer to have an unpleasant feeling when throwing something away, as they are doing something "good" for the environment. This meaning is also one that the individual does not produce him- or herself, but one which has been externally developed and created in the last few years in the course of environmental protection efforts.

In fact, therefore, meaning is not dependent on the goods alone, but on the context in which they can be purchased, used, or shown. Thus meaning arises through every individual's life world – free according to Wittgenstein through "everything that is the case". According to this an individual life environment is "the totality of facts, not of things" (Wittgenstein 1984, § 1.1).

Alongside the possible meanings and contexts created by business, the individual's own interpretation also adds to the creation of meaning. The fact that meaning can develop at all needs something which somehow connects the happenings, the experiences, the past, present, and future, in some way, which gives the single facts something in common, and perhaps allows them to become a single, unified whole. For this to happen, and perhaps also as the basis for the development of meaning, some form of "common thread" (in German "der rote Faden") is required which turns the contexts, facts, and circumstances into something continuous, something specific that belongs to the individual and which the individual identifies with. This thread relates to the transcendental, to that immaterial, meta-physical dimension which in turn attributes meaning to the concrete case, the concrete thing, fact, and context. Whereas Fromm makes a distinction in this context between being and having, the two basic forms of existence (cf. Fromm 1976), a further form of existence seems to have been added in the course of the technical and social development of the last

30 years, namely the doing, the making, the being busy (not in the sense of Hannah Arendt's vita activa, but in the sense of a demonstrative activism). In this context having is admittedly necessary, is instrumental, but no longer a form of existence. The having of goods is no longer in the foreground for the sake of having, but in the service of "being able to do anything at any time". In order to judge a person, it is less and less important what the person owns (in the wealthy societies everybody has almost everything anyway), and increasingly important what he or she makes or does with it. Although it continues to be important to have as many goods and as great a variety as possible, it is no longer a question of materialism. In this context material goods are attributed a different form of meaning: one has to have everything possible in order to be able to do everything all the time.

Seen in this way the meaning of ownership is to be reappraised. The questions of whether ownership can be "cracked", and whether sustainable user systems after all have a chance of being successful on the markets will finally depend on whether it will be possible to succeed through a service economy in fulfilling customers' demand "to be able to do anything at any time", at a competitive price. That is to say the question must be asked of how the framework conditions/basic parameters need to be changed and to be adapted in order to guarantee the competitiveness of such offers. Can *access* (cf. Rifkin 2000), i.e. entry, access, and connection, replace ownership and – understood as a new principle of sustainable economic activity – be developed further? Or does "disappearance of ownership" remain an unrealistic vision?

References

Baudrillard, J. (1991): Das System der Dinge. Über unser Verhältnis zu den alltäglichen Gegenständen [1968]. Frankfurt am Main a.o. (in German)

Bömmel, H. van (2003): Konsumentensouveränität. Neue Gestaltungsoptionen des Konsumenten in der postindustriellen Wirtschaft. Marburg (in German)

Erikson, E. H. (1980): Identität und Lebenszyklus. Drei Aufsätze. Frankfurt am Main (in German)

Fischer, R.; Schmid, M.; Winiwarter, V.; Veichtlbauer, O. (2008): SIproVI – Studium Integrale pro-VISION. Grundsätzliche Überlegungen zu einer vorsorgenden Gesellschaft und der Rolle von Wissenschaft. Vienna (IFF – Institut für Wissenschaftskommunikation und Hochschulforschung der Alpen-Adria-Universität Klagenfurt-Graz-Wien) (in German)

Fleig, J. (2000): Zukunftsfähige Kreislaufwirtschaft. Mit Nutzenverkauf, Langlebigkeit und Aufarbeitung ökonomisch und ökologisch wirtschaften. Stuttgart (in German)

Fromm, E. (1976): Haben oder Sein. Die seelischen Grundlagen einer neuen Gesellschaft. Munich (in German)

Giarini, O.; Stahel, W. R. (2000): Die Performance-Gesellschaft. Chancen und Risken beim Übergang zur Service Economy. Marburg (in German)

Gross, P. (1994): Die Multioptionsgesellschaft. Frankfurt am Main (in German)

Gross, P. (1999): Ich-Jagd. Im Unabhängigkeitsjahrhundert. Frankfurt am Main (in German)

Heintel, P. (1999): Innehalten. Gegen die Beschleunigung – für eine andere Zeitkultur. Freiburg im Breisgau a.o. (in German)

Heintel, P. (2007): Über Nachhaltigkeit. Geschichtsphilosophische Reflexionen. In: Krainer, L.; Trattnig, R. (eds.): Kulturelle Nachhaltigkeit. Konzepte, Perspektiven, Positionen. Munich, pp. 37-167 (in German)

Howanietz, F.; Spohn, F. (1990): Anstelle eines Vorworts. In: Gruber, E. (ed.): Kult und Magie. Ausstellungskatalog. Vienna, pp. 11-14 (in German)

Hübner, B. (1991): Der de-projizierte Mensch – Metaphysik der Langeweile. Vienna (in German)

Hübner, R. (2010): Die Magie der Dinge: Güter und der Umgang mit ihnen als Ausdruck von Kultur In: Parodi, O.; Banse, G.; Schaffer, A. (eds.): Wechselspiele: Kultur und Nachhaltigkeit. Annäherungen an ein Spannungsfeld. Berlin, pp. 119-150 (in German)

Hübner, R.; Himpelmann, M.; Melnitzky, S.; Stahel, W. R.; Hübner, H. (2005): Reprocessing gebrauchter Güter. Eine Strategie der Nachhaltigkeit und ihre Auswirkungen auf die Lieferketten in einer Fabrik der Zukunft. Vienna (Bundesministeriums für Verkehr, Innovation und Technologie (ed.): Berichte aus Energie- und Umweltforschung, No. 33/2006) (in German)

Hübner, R.; Lung, A.; Himpelmann, M. (2007): FUTURE. Die Wiedernutzung von Gütern – Strategien für Wirtschaft und Kommune. Vienna (in German)

Jung, C. G. (1933): Die Beziehungen zwischen dem Ich und dem Unbewußten. Zürich (in German)

Liessmann, K. P. (1999): Denken und Leben I. CD-ROM. Vienna (ORF) (in German)

Nuber, U. (1995): Die ungeheure Last des Überflüssigen. In: Psychologie heute, Vol. 22, No. 4 (April), pp. 20-27 (in German)

Paech, N. (2007): Effizienz versus Konsistenz. Der Weg zum nachhaltigen Produkt- und Systemdesign. Vortrag im Rahmen der VHB-Konferenz „Umweltwirtschaft – international, interdisziplinär und innovativ" an der Wirtschaftsuniversität Wien (in German)

Precht, R. D. (2007): Wer bin ich – und wenn ja wie viele? Eine philosophische Reise. Munich (in German)

Reisinger, H.; Krammer, H.-J. (2007): Weißbuch. Abfallvermeidung und -verwertung in Österreich. Vienna (Umweltbundesamt, REP-0083) (in German)

Rifkin, J. (2000): Access. Das Verschwinden des Eigentums. Warum wir weniger besitzen und mehr ausgeben werden. Frankfurt am Main a.o. (in German)

Ropohl, G. (1999): Allgemeine Technologie. Eine Systemtheorie der Technik. 2nd ed. Munich/ Vienna (in German)

Scherhorn, G. (1997): Revision des Gebrauchs. In: Schmidt-Bleek, F. (ed.): Öko-intelligentes Produzieren und Konsumieren. Berlin a.o., pp. 25-40 (in German)

Schütz, A. (2003): Theorie der Lebenswelt. Teil 1: Die pragmatische Schichtung der Lebenswelt [1937]. Konstanz (in German)

Sorgo, G. (2006): Der Markt: Weder Gott noch Teufel. In: Wiener Zeitung Extra, 26. August 2006 (in German)

Stahel, W. R. (2004): Ressourcenproduktivität durch Nutzungsintensivierung und Lebensdauerverlängerung. 10 Jahre Good Practice Beispiele. Norderstedt (in German)

Stross, A. M. (1991): Ich-Identität zwischen Fiktion und Konstruktion. Berlin (in German)

Wittgenstein, L. (1984): Tractatus logico-philosophicus [1921]. Frankfurt am Main (in German)

Zweig, St. (1976): Die Monotonisierung der Welt. Aufsätze und Vorträge ausgewählt von Volker Michels. Frankfurt am Main (in German)

On the Way to a Culture of Sustainable Decisions

Larissa Krainer

1   The Concept of Culture Caught in a Web of Contradictions

A survey of current publications about the relations between sustainability and culture shows many of the texts referring to one of the three levels or subjects listed below:

- *Firstly*, an interesting debate about the concept of culture can be found in cultural studies, but also in a variety of other disciplines (cf. especially Hauser/Banse 2009).
- *Secondly*, treatments of the concept of culture can be found under various perspectives of sustainability (cf. e.g. Kopfmüller 2009; Parodi 2009; Stahmer 2009).
- *Thirdly*, some of these references also contain studies of the concept of culture in disciplines other than cultural studies, such as technology (cf. Parodi 2009) or economics (cf. Hübner 2009).

Studies of the concept of culture and its variations over time, in my mind, clearly show the historical development of cultural thinking, the challenges it confronted, and the way in which concepts may be opposed to each other. A few of these opposites will be listed below. Culture can be

- thought of in a very broad (comprehensive) sense or in a narrower sense (relating to a specific cultural phenomenon);
- considered an absolute constant of mankind or expressed in relative or relational terms;
- described as a historical constant or as a phenomenon permanently changing;
- seen as something concrete existing in the world, or else as "something not to be discovered" in the world in concrete terms;
- something permeating all our actions or something to be found only in specific areas of action or practice;
- sketched as a culture of what exists or also as a culture of what does not exist, i.e. a culture of things not existing;
- considered both a precondition and a result of our actions according to the principle of the hen and the egg;

- seen as describing an active achievement (a cultural act) or a phenomenon always preceding such actions;
- deliberately reflected upon or describe a subconscious phenomenon;
- considered something which can be influenced (deliberately) or something existing independent of our actions, something which cannot be influenced or queried;
- considered mouldable or immutable;
- laid down permanently (as a taboo) or subject to negotiation;
- in need of permanent adaptation (by the trial-and-error model) or constitute a habit all people can learn;
- -discussed as theory or practice;
- considered a subjective or an objective phenomenon;
- declared part of the internal glue holding society together, in the absence of which society would disintegrate, or considered something without which we could well live, something replaceable;
- regarded as something creating unity or rather as something which permanently gives rise to differences.

A similarly contradictory pattern is shown by cultural differences. They can relate to very different dimensions, very close and very distant ones (recognizable within any social culture, for instance in the differences between genders or generations or between different societies), and mostly give rise to the question whether different cultures should be treated neutral with respect to value, or whether upgrading or downgrading is permitted.

The list above, which was compiled from the Proceedings of the 9th Weimar Colloquy of 2008, shows that these are contradictions, but that it is easily possible to cite reasons for the respective poles and regard them as plausible. Obviously, it is not possible in this case to decide in accordance with concepts of logic; instead, we are more inclined to resort to answers allowing both aspects of the contradiction (roughly in the "that depends" or "both and" modes).

This allows a number of important findings to be derived:

- *Firstly*: Culture seems to be ambiguous, sometimes stubbornly stable and then, again, flexible, relative (considered in constants of time and space), it can be modified, influenced, even eradicated, as our history has demonstrated repeatedly, and yet again and again comes back as a cultural asset long thought to be forgotten. It generally tends to establish hierarchies of differences and, at the same time, to want to negate them, all of which can have a meaning or no meaning.
- *Secondly*: If these different arguments can apply to culture, culture obviously cannot be considered in a logical and linear sense. The only alternative available seems to be dialectics. This makes culture a dialectic phenomenon, a stable anchor *and* a procedural event, a precondition *and* a result of our existence, an uncon-

scious anthropological fundamental constant of mankind *and* also a cultural achievement of our species which can be reflected upon and which can be shaped. This idea will be taken up again below.

2 The Concept of Culture in the Context of the Sustainability Debate

The papers dealing with the concept of culture from a sustainability point of view provided me with many interesting aspects, but also left me slightly confused in the face of several contradictions and dichotomies.

- *Firstly*: *Culture as an inexistent or abstract, at any rate unspecific, dimension of sustainability.* Jürgen Kopfmüller, after a detailed analysis of a variety of national (especially German) and international documents about sustainability and sustainable development, respectively, arrives at the astounding conclusion that matters of culture either do not exist in these contexts at all or, where they exist,[1] more often postulate abstract values than give any indications of their practical implementation (cf. Kopfmüller 2009, pp. 27f.). This refers to the divergence between abstract norms and empirical, practical usefulness in this concept. Immanuel Kant circumscribed this phenomenon by the term "regulative ideas" which "would never be of any constitutive use" (cf. Kant 1974, p. 565; cf. also Heintel 2000). Peter Heintel, recurring to Kant, emphasized the dual character and its purpose with respect to various values of our society. Accordingly, abstract norms must always be preserved as such for use as general indicators for our specific actions. At the same time, specific actions can be considered specific forms of their implementation and can be measured accordingly. Consequently, regulative ideas are guidelines for orientation which must not be given up as such; they serve as individual and collective backdrops for reflecting and verifying what is wanted by society and what has been achieved in practice by comparison (cf. Heintel 2000).
- *Secondly: Culture in contrast to the specific implementation of sustainable development.* Kopfmüller mentions another interesting phenomenon: In referring to a study, "Brot für die Welt" ("Bread for the World"), he quotes the "cultural helplessness" term which, in that context, primarily relates to the question how cultural societal patterns can prevent sustainable aspects from taking effect (cf. Kopfmüller 2009, p. 27). In this concept, culture can be seen as a programme pre-

---

1   Culture occasionally is established as an individual pillar, for instance, by the United Nations Commission on Sustainable Development, or, together with education, considered a cross sectional matter, such as in the final report by the Committee of Inquiry of the 13th German Federal Parliament about "Protecting Man and the Environment" (cf. Kopfmüller 2009, pp. 25ff.).

venting or, at least, contradicting sustainability. The same idea is taken up by other authors, for instance when asking why there have been discussions about sustainability and presentations of potentials of sustainable development for such a long time while, on the other hand, so little progress can be perceived in the same matter, which makes them feel that we seem to be living in a non-sustainable culture (cf. Krainer/Trattnigg 2007). However, if sustainability and culture initially are considered conflicting phenomena, this again is based on a concept of culture considered largely stable, evoking the question how processes of cultural change could be initiated.

- *Thirdly: Preserving culture is sustainable and non-sustainable at the same time.* No less contradictory is the attempt to preserve cultural assets sustainably, if one follows the ideas proposed by Caroline Y. Robertson-von Trotha who shows how environmental problems on the one hand, and problematic historical re-interpretations on the other hand make the protection and preservation of sites of historical importance a rather dubious affair (cf. Robertson-von Trotha 2009).

Reading these studies once again shows that we are surrounded by a large number of contradictions when dealing with the subject of culture as well as that of sustainability. As far as sustainability is concerned, it should be added that most ideal concepts, which can be taken from the classical three-pillar model of the sustainability debate (ecological, economic, social), can also contradict each other or describe internal areas of tension of sustainability (cf. Krainer et al. 2009).

It is not surprising, therefore, that many authors find the sustainability concept difficult enough as it is and suggest that one should not complicate matters by including the concept of culture. However, this is precisely what we had in mind, and so we will continue along this line.

3   Culture in a Conflict among Scientific Disciplines

We still know very little about the different meanings of culture in different scientific disciplines and the consequences this could have for an interdisciplinary discourse (which seems to be absolutely imperative in the light of the topic of sustainability as well as that of culture). For instance, what does an economist mean by "culture", and what is the meaning, in the otherwise seemingly rational world of the science of money and the markets, of such terms as economic *culture*, corporate *culture*, or market *culture*? What is the meaning of clamouring for a change of these cultures? What does an engineer mean by speaking about culture and referring to *technological cultures,* what is in her mind when she thinks about "culture of technology?" What do scientists mean by referring to "culture" and talking, for instance, about bacterial *cultures* whose pure *cultures* are of special importance? What kind of culture is referred to by plant sociologists speaking of plant *cultures*? What do students of the Vienna University of Soil Culture mean by culture when discussing *aquaculture*? What culture is the subject of their studies of *cultural* technology? What cultures are meant by universities suddenly planning to introduce quality *culture* in their ranks? Are they really intimating that universities had neither quality nor culture before?

I dare say that almost all sciences incorporate a concept of culture. At the same time, I dare doubt that members of different disciplines even remotely mean the same thing when referring to culture. I am unable to estimate what we would gain by knowing what scientists say, think, feel when they speak of culture; I think this kind of dialogue, of interdisciplinary and thus intercultural learning could always be interesting. I also guess that this could be used to generate other interesting areas of contradiction (for instance, when considering the difference between cultures artificially generated or grown by people in a laboratory and those in which we ourselves live, which we are).

However, I think it is just as important at this point to draw attention to different *science cultures* which, because of very different fundamental axioms, elect very different approaches to their studies and, consequently, also have very different ways of interfering with social connections, with very different consequences and highly divergent outcomes and results. Scientific methods not only reflect criteria of a technically or scientifically "correct" approach, but are also expressions of a certain concept of the world which also includes cultural dimensions. Those who think they could understand the world and its innermost connections by decomposing that world into the smallest possible parts, per se think that world different from somebody who feels able, at best, to fathom it by observation. Those working in laboratories and, in a way, inviting the outside world into those labs (or reproducing it artificially), are exposed to a different working culture than those who operate "in the field", hoping to find the outside world there (in a virgin state, if possible). Those who dig in the ground to collect old cultural assets want to reconstruct past culture by present findings; those who therapeutically encourage individuals to remember their own past in order to better be able to shape their present, place hope in an individual change which, frequently, implies the change of certain patterns in the lives of people; and what are patterns of life other than phenomena of a culture of life? Those whose study and search for technical innovations, as a rule (and despite knowing extensive debates about technology assessment) initially do not ask for their potential cultural implications but tend to consider technical development something which is neutral in terms of value, and has better or worse consequences only as a result of the "right" or "wrong" use by others. Depending on how sciences see the world, or want to understand it, they design the appropriate methods for doing so. Whether they measure, decompose, produce experimental setups, resort to the "sources," test, write opinions, try out designs, observe, interview, draft questionnaires – in doing so, they always constitute a culture of research and science which is not without impact on the "objects of research" – be they inorganic or organic in nature, animals, or persons.

Different science cultures also are reflected in very different publication cultures and guidelines, be they monographs or articles for journals, written in national languages or the dominating science language, English, written for a scientific readership or for the general public.

Another important cultural topic within the sciences stems from the question whether work is carried out in a disciplinary, interdisciplinary, or transdisciplinary fashion, with interdisciplinary, in my mind, meaning co-operation among various sciences on one topic, while transdisciplinary means conducting research in a joint effort with practitioners in the respective research area. In both cases, co-operative ventures are started which are not always easy to manage. Interdisciplinary work requires communication across disciplines, which does not arise automatically (because all too often the meaning of concepts is too divergent, and methodological ideas are too heterogeneous, etc.). Co-operation in research processes with practitioners allows participative research processes to be conducted from which both sides, science and practice, can learn, but also takes careful processes to ensure a meeting of minds and build up trust, confidence, and a spirit of co-operation (cf. Ukowitz 2006).

As so many different dimensions of culture can be discerned in the sciences, how then can science be seriously assumed to define, or at least describe exactly, what is meant by culture? Let me again formulate the problem as a paradox: Sciences are expected to be institutions at the same time *influencing* and *understanding* culture. They are supposed to explain the phenomenon in the most comprehensive fashion possible although only very few have learned to look comprehensively enough (otherwise there would not be any frontiers of disciplines). And there is still hope that, being neutral agencies, they would stand a better chance of looking through structures of cultural value.

However, this also evidences that the different science cultures will have to be studied in greater detail with respect to their consequences in terms of sustainability and sustainability research, and that another topic to be discussed is the existence of science cultures with respect to our topic, where they match, and where they contradict each other.

4   Comments on Culture as an Integral Part of Human Existence

The question what is characteristic of man in contradistinction to nature, for instance, has been raised repeatedly in history and is not without difficulties because, for plausible reasons, there are some who want the line separating nature and culture to be removed, which is why they are against such polarizing divisions as explained, for instance, by Oliver Parodi (cf. Parodi 2009, pp. 55f.). Even more difficult is the question what distinguishes people from others especially where differences are established on the basis of cultural evaluations in an effort to upgrade some cultures and downgrade others. There are still too vivid memories of regimes declaring one group superhuman and another group subhuman, and not hesitating to destroy other cultures. Yet, I think it is also problematic to not mention any differences and deny those difficulties which become apparent again and again in the "clash of civilizations" (cf. Huntington 1998).

From my point of view, three things are indispensable to the existence of human beings as cultural beings:

- *Firstly,* the ability to communicate on the basis of symbols. This alone allows agreements to be reached and fulfilled. This is closely related to the ability for social interaction, which is the definition of communication by Symbolic Interactionism as developed by Herbert Blumer after George Herbert Mead (cf. Blumer 2004). Now that we have learned from Paul Watzlawick and his colleagues that persons "are unable not to communicate", it is evident that communication has always been a part of human existence (cf. Watzlawick et al. 1980). My reason for emphasizing the ability for agreements is that, to my mind, the debates about sustainability, and the efforts to achieve it, again and again seem to revolve about the question how collective social agreements can be entered into which will make binding what is considered meaningful and sustainable.
- *Secondly,* I think the ability to reflect and the associated possibility to develop self-awareness are key human capabilities characterizing all human beings. To Georg Wilhelm Friedrich Hegel, the ability to differentiate (relative to oneself and to others) is a major characteristic of distinction between humans and animals. This subject will be covered in greater detail below.
- *Thirdly,* I think the ability for social control and control of social subsystems, respectively, on the basis of reflection and collective decision-making constitutes an enormous potential on the road to a culture of sustainability. Although this ability still seems to be in its infancy, it does represent a potential rooted in human beings and collectives. This can already be observed in specific expressions of civil society, also in the broader debates about good governance, it was observed within the framework of a five-year mediation procedure about the Vienna-Schwechat airport (cf. Falk et al. 2006). Modern societies are more and more looking for new ways to solve conflicts, but also for participative decision-making structures enabling as many members of society as possible to contribute to decisions, the outcomes of which are going to affect them in the future.

And now for some problem areas associated with the question of culture as a prerequisite of human existence. Globally, it is seen very quickly that we have to do with very different traditions (I deliberately do not say abilities) of reflection. Right now, we can observe very different degrees of execution and exercise of reflection for various reasons, I think:

- *Firstly*, there are various historic traditions of tabooing which, to this day, have resulted in bans on reflection. From the Stone Age to our present time (found especially in tribes living under near-natural conditions), there have been implicit normative rules of co-existence which should not and must not be queried, because such querying of practiced rules, rights, and traditions could have a socially destabilizing effect. So, there are bans on reflection because of taboos.
- *Secondly,* we know of institutionalized bans on reflection and the associated long tradition of authoritarian governments or dictatorships. Let me illustrate this by the example of freedom of the press. The Freedom House NGO annually produces a report about the situation of freedom of the press in the world (cf. Freedom House 2009). The map of the world shows a colourful picture of states, with those marked green which have freedom of the press, while yellow denotes those which are referred to as partly free and where freedom of the press applies only partly, and then there are those countries, marked blue, where there is no freedom of the press. North America, Europe, and Australia by and large (though not completely) are marked green, South America is mostly yellow, Asia is mostly blue, while Africa can offer all of this, but mainly blue states. 2009 country statistics shows that 70 countries (36%) guarantee a system of freedom of the press, 61 states (31%) have a partly free system, while 64 states (33%) guarantee no freedom of the press. When related to the number of people living in those countries, the picture is even more drastic: Only 17% of the people worldwide live in countries where there is freedom of the press, while 41% live in systems with part freedom of the press, and 42% of the population must live without any free structures of the press. Now, freedom of the press is not necessarily an indication of any competence or tradition of reflection, but it is a symbol of the possibility to discuss publicly ideas about reflection, have discussions, establish a critical difference to regimes, or even take collective decisions, organize them, or participate in them. Where freedom of opinion is restricted, this mostly applies also to freedom of assembly which, as a rule, is important where people are to organize on their own.

In the light of all these aspects, I do not think too much of considering all cultures "equivalent" – not because I would like to refer to some as being higher and others as being lower, but because I feel that a deliberate decision in favor of specific cultures (such as a culture of sustainability) requires the freedom to make those decisions. Consequently, freedom can be described the way Immanuel Kant did, as "the key to explaining the autonomy of will" (Kant 1998, pp. 81f.), in order for a culture of sustainability to grow. Now, of course, the objection could be raised that especially authoritarian regimes have a much better chance to impose sustainability "top down".

This may be true. Apart from the fact that, right now, I know of very few totalitarian leaders expressing such commands, I also doubt whether sustainability ordered top down would have a long-term perspective. So far, the collapse of dictatorships as a rule resulted in nearly everything being discarded that had been in place before even if it had some positive aspects upon closer consideration (such as parts of a planned economy, which can quite well meet sustainability criteria).

5   About the Connection between Culture and Reflection

Kant wrote the famous sentence, "enlightenment is the escape of people from their self-inflicted dependence" (Kant 1977, p. 9). The philosopher started from the idea that human beings had a special ability, namely that of individual reflection (for which he demanded the freedom which Frederick II., Frederick the Great, ultimately offered), and he called conscience an "inner court of justice of a person" (cf. Kant 1997, p. 573). Hegel associated the difference between persons and nature directly with the human ability to reflect: "Humans are animals, but even in their animal functions they do not stay in a passive role, like animals, but become conscious of themselves, recognizing and elevating them, such as the process of digestion, to a science aware of itself. In this way, a person overcomes the barrier of his unreflected existence, implying that just because he knows that he is an animal he stops being an animal and turns this knowledge into spirit" (Hegel 1970b, p. 112).

Reflection is always a step establishing a difference. It allows for the possibility of querying actions, persons, organizations, institutions, conditions, states and, finally, themselves. This latter effect directly results in a related capability, namely that of self-observation. According to group dynamics findings, a successful change of action and reflection (self-observation) ultimately can result in the potential for self-control in groups. Although this does not yet explain how these capabilities can be transferred to larger collectives, it is safe to say that it is possible for people to learn something like autonomous control or self-control through reflection and self-observation of internal processes (above and beyond the existing individual competence). This ability for differentiation to me seems to be a particularly important core of what distinguishes man.

While Kant's interest still centred around individual enlightenment, the Klagenfurt philosopher and group dynamicist, Peter Heintel, asks how "collective autonomy" (Heintel 1998, p. 41) could be achieved, meaning precisely the ability for reflective self-control of collectives which is to go beyond the level of group information.

The connection with the subject of culture is easily explained: Those who credit persons with enlightened behaviour also credit them with the possibility to query anything and submit counter-designs (which, however, always need approval by the others, if we think in democratic structures). However, this also means that it must be possible to observe, reflect upon, criticize, query and, if necessary, change culture and cultural patterns. If we consider culture only as a static, immutable phenomenon, we give up the possibility to regard it as our product, our design potential. That cultural patterns are not easily translated into terms of enlightenment, because they stem from historically grown cultural and, incidentally, religious practices, which have been handed down and are appreciated, and were able to survive partly only because they were not allowed to be reflected upon (see taboos), must be accepted, but does not mean that it would not be possible in principle. Consequently, reflection may shake some taboos, may have to be started with caution, may also be dangerous (at least to individuals), but it is not impossible.

And now for another aspect. A key basis of the ability for self-control is the ability to take conscious and reflected decisions in a collective. This is a subject which we have looked into in Klagenfurt for a longer time and in a very comprehensive way. The last part of this contribution is to be focused on this subject, although the statements made above give rise to more comprehensive concepts and consequences which, however, cannot be detailed for lack of space. Let us therefore turn to the question of how we take decisions.

6   On the Way to Sustainable Decisions

In a study about "knowledge and decision-making, informing and documentation, control, leadership, and co-operation" we conducted, a total of 43 qualitative interviews with entrepreneurs (most of them from small and medium-sized enterprises) were held in Carinthia in 2003 in which we also asked interviewees how they took decisions in their companies and organized the associated procedures. The very question, "how do you decide?", made the persons interviewed hesitate or stutter – not because decision-making was not part of their daily business, nor because there had been no clear decision-making structures in their companies. Most of them simply had never thought about this problem. We decide on numerous questions every day, have acquired routines in doing so and obviously are not used to thinking about how we do it – both individually and collectively.

What emerged from these interviews were mainly two poles of decision-making in business: To one group, decisions are a main duty of management (i.e. themselves): *"Well, I set out the basic criteria and then I say: 'Now, Mr. Production Manger, you see how you can produce those quantities!'"* was a characteristic quotation of that group. The members of the other group see decision-making more as a process at various levels of management (sometimes up to involving all staff members). In that case, the duty of management would be to ensure the organization of these processes:

"Ultimately it is efficient because, if a decision is supported by all, the objective will be reached in a much better and easier way", said one representative of that at view. Another difference we were able to see was that between the so-called "rational decisions", mostly based on key performance indicators, and the so-called "gut feeling" decisions. The latter, as we learned in this study, are in no way irrational decisions but are made mostly on the basis of the broad horizon of experience of people. Incidentally, the entrepreneurs consistently referred to personnel and investment decisions as those most difficult to make (cf. Heintel et al. 2004, p. 27).

Decision-making can be associated with a variety of difficulties, some of them very grave. A few of them will be briefly mentioned below (cf. Heintel 1986; Krainer 2007):

- Decisions must always be taken about open points (otherwise no decision would be necessary).
- Deciding always means inclusion and exclusion, means to decide in favour of something and against something else.
- Decisions include the need to move from uncertainty and indeterminacy to certainty and determination.
- At the same time, the correctness of the decision also remains open, needs continuous observation and, where necessary, revision.
- Good decisions take time; in actual fact, however, decisions in a company must very often be taken under strong pressure of time.
- Decisions frequently include risks. Where the consequences of decisions are incalculable, risk assessment is particularly difficult, which is why decisions about major investments probably are so hard to make.

It is also evident that decisions do not arrive out of the blue, i.e. that they must be made by us. At the same time, it is important to emphasize that they do not constitute facts on which there is no going back, i.e. as a rule, they can also be modified (even if some of them cannot be reversed).

As far as matters of sustainability are concerned, the following questions must be raised:

- How can decision-making processes be established which allow as many stakeholders as possible to participate in decisions (in bringing about those decisions)?
- How can these processes also be designed in such a way that they will incorporate criteria of sustainability?
- How can sustainable decisions be made which keep open the possibility of quick revision of wrong decisions (see biofuel)?

It has been found meaningful to distinguish first between decisions resulting from a decision-making process, and decision-making as an action. I treated this subject in more detail elsewhere (cf. Krainer 2007); here are some extracts:

- Decisions are sustainable if, in the process of decision-making, all stakeholders stand a chance to be heard, understood, and taken into account, when decisions can be taken in such a way that conflicting interests can be balanced out in those decisions and the outcome is such that all stakeholders can (just) live with them.
- Decisions have sustainable effects if their implementation is ensured and their execution is subjected to regular inspection (by those affected by them), i.e. when there is a possibility to adapt them to changed conditions and new challenges or query them as a matter of principle.
- As a rule, decisions require looking for a balance. Aristotle, more than 2000 years ago, proposed a procedure which can be found under the term of Mesotes doctrine, i.e. doctrine of the Golden Mean, in his Nicomachean Ethics. Aristotle considered it not meaningful to solve the problem arithmetically instead of looking for a position in the middle to be determined in the light of the situation and adapted to the circumstances (cf. Aristotle 1995, p. 43).

Most situations in which we have difficulties taking decisions are those in which conflicts become apparent. The subject of sustainability is full of such points. As a matter of principle, conflicts are necessary, meaningful, and good. We learn from conflicts, most of which are based on unresolvable contradictions. This stems from a comprehensive theory of contradictions which cannot be discussed in greater detail at this point (cf. Krainer/Heintel 2010). The basic assumption is that all relevant subjects we have to decide upon do not offer unambiguous decisions along the lines of "right or wrong". In most cases, good arguments can be found for doing one thing and leaving the other and vice versa. This can be said also of all requirements of sustainable development. In every case, interests and lobbies can be found which hold different views, pursue different objectives which, at a closer look, also cannot be rejected offhand. Or could we treat those countries which have just got started on their way towards achieving a certain level of prosperity, on which we have been resting for a long time already, by forbidding them seriously to want to reach that prosperity (even if it is evident that that would be associated with extremely negative impacts on the environment)?

Also international climate conferences clearly show the conflicts existing in this field. Those who want to be re-elected in their own countries cannot afford to make too many promises; those who have already been elected, cannot always guarantee that they will be able to turn their own intentions into political majorities at home.

And even where such conflicts are fed into a consensus procedure in an effort to strike a balance, it can be seen that the road to consensus is hard to go. We therefore should not suffer any naïve delusions, hoping for insight into the superior normative knowledge of others, even if all stakeholders are fully convinced that they represent the ethically "right" position.

Between 2001 and 2005, we had an opportunity to accompany, as researchers, the largest mediation procedure so far known in the literature. It was held at the Vienna-Schwechat airport; negotiations dealt with the construction of a third take-off and landing strip as well as innumerable measures alleviating the impact on the population nearby. On the whole, some 60 stakeholders took part in a permanent fight for decisions based on economic interests, on the one hand (construction of a third take-off and landing strip), and private cares and concerns, on the other hand (noise pollution, environmental subjects), and faced the tremendous challenge of having to take decisions which will impact the next generation (cf. Falk et al. 2006). Merely to illustrate by one example the contradictions negotiated there: One position held was that future young generations should be given chances of mobility (i.e. build the strip), while the opposite position was that natural resources had to be protected and preserved for coming generations (i.e. not build the strip). That there were some arguments in favour of both points is evident. Judged by today's standards, the future will be for mobility, while a future worth living will be achievable only by protecting resources.

7   A Sustainable Culture is a Deliberate Decision-making Culture

As a summary of my presentation I would like to offer the following ideas: As a result of the many findings from the field of the sustainability movement, but also from accompanying research projects, I have increasing doubt that sustainable development will arise all by itself. This is contradicted not only by too many powerful interests; undoubtedly, it is also contradicted by the current dominating value concepts and cultural patterns, accurately described by Heintel as "new era model" (cf. Heintel 2004), which either support, or stem from, a dominance of the economic-technical model. As I consider culture a phenomenon which can be reflected upon, shaped, and modified, my thinking is primarily about the question how the way there can be started. This requires, first of all, to find out who has to decide whether, and which ways of, sustainable development will be opened in the future and how, other than the classical representative structures by elected representatives of the people, decision-making processes can be established in which representatives of various sustainability perspectives can agree on measures striking a balance. Many proposals towards this end have been made and some first steps in participation procedures, all of which should be utilized, are being tested in many places. However, further downstream, it should be clarified who is responsible for monitoring the decisions made and for their evaluation. This undoubtedly will result in new roles both for those bearing government responsibility and for the members of the civil society, sciences, etc.

In a nutshell: To me, demanding, initiating, and organizing binding participative decision-making procedures constitutes the greatest potential for fighting the cultural conflict between sustainable and non-sustainable lifestyles, sustainable and non-sustainable development, sustainable and non-sustainable changes, and bring them into a meaningful balance enabling, where possible, all stakeholders to (at least just) support the decisions made.

A brief personal footnote: Several colleagues rejected the concept of "cultural sustainability" on grounds of their suspicion that this meant a new fourth, fifth, or sixth pillar or dimension of sustainability. Alternative proposals are being submitted in concepts such as "sustainability culture" or "culture of sustainability". From my point of view, this has a semantic connotation, but primarily also a pragmatic one, if we ask ourselves: What do we want to achieve by using these words, what do we want to indicate or do? I, for my part, subscribe to all those who are in favour of wanting to recognize by what cultural patterns non-sustainable behaviour functions, and how a switch can be made towards a culture embodying the opportunity to be sustainable, which I would then refer to as both cultural sustainability or sustainable culture.

[This article has already been published in German in Parodi, O.; Banse, G.; Schaffer, A. (eds.): Wechselspiele: Kultur und Nachhaltigkeit. Annäherungen an ein Spannungsfeld. Berlin 2010, pp. 79-96.]

References

Aristoteles (1995): Nikomachische Ethik. Hamburg (in German)

Banse, G.; Parodi, O.; Schaffer, A. (eds.) (2009): Interdependenzen zwischen kulturellem Wandel und nachhaltiger Entwicklung. Karlsruhe (Forschungszentrum) (in German)

Blumer, H. (2004): Der methodische Standpunkt des symbolischen Interaktionismus. In: Burkart, R.; Hömberg, W. (eds.): Kommunikationstheorien. Vienna, pp. 24-41 (in German)

Falk, G.; Heintel, P.; Krainer, L. (2006): Das Mediationsverfahren am Flughafen Wien-Schwechat. Dokumentation, Analyse, Hintergrundtheorien. Wiesbaden (in German)

Freedom-House (2009): Map of Press Freedom. – URL: http://www.freedomhouse.org/template.cfm?page=251&year=2009 [17.02.2009]

Hauser, R.; Banse, G. (2009): Kultur und Kulturalität – Annäherungen an ein vielschichtiges Konzept. In: Banse, G.; Parodi, O.; Schaffer, A. (eds.): Interdependenzen zwischen kulturellem Wandel und nachhaltiger Entwicklung. Karlsruhe (Forschungszentrum), pp. 7-23 (in German)

Hegel, G. W. F. (1970a): Enzyklopädie der philosophischen Wissenschaften im Grundrisse [1817]. Frankfurt am Main (in German)

Hegel, G. W. F. (1970b): Vorlesungen über Ästhetik I. Frankfurt am Main 1970 (Theorie Werkausgabe, Vol. 13) (in German)

Heintel, P. (1986): Über Entscheidung. In: Wiener Jahrbuch für Philosophie, Vol. 18, pp. 149-69 (in German)

Heintel, P. (1998) Abendländische Rationalität – Welche Ethik für die Wissenschaften? Unpublished manuscript. Klagenfurt; short version published in: Heintel, P.: Wissenschaftskritik als rationaler Prozess. In: Liessmann, K. P.; Weinberger, G. (eds.): Perspektiven Europa. Modelle für das 21. Jahrhundert. Vienna 1999, pp. 57-81 (in German)

Heintel, P. (2000) Systemtranszendenz und die Selbststeuerung von Systemen. Klagenfurt (Klagenfurter Beiträge zur Technikdiskussion. Ed. by A. Bammé, P. Baumgartner, W. Berger, E. Kotzmann, Bd. 94) (in German)

Heintel, P. (2004): Das Modell Neuzeit. In: Initiative Global Marshall Plan (ed.): Welt in Balance. Ulm, pp. 60-81 (in German)

Heintel, P.; Krainer, L.; Erlacher, W.; Goldmann, H.; Hanschitz, R.; Lerchster, R.; Lesjak, B.; Paul-Horn, I.; Schmidt, E.; Schöffmann, K.; Ukowitz, M. (2004): Wissen und Entscheiden, Informieren und Dokumentieren, Steuern, Führen und Kooperieren. Abschlussbericht im Rahmen des KWF-Förderprogramms "Regionales Programm für innovative Maßnahmen für Kärnten". Klagenfurt (in German)

Hübner, R. (2009): Die Magie der Dinge – Materielle Güter, Identität und Metaphysische Lücke. In: Banse, G.; Parodi, O.; Schaffer, A. (eds.): Interdependenzen zwischen kulturellem Wandel und nachhaltiger Entwicklung. Karlsruhe (Forschungszentrum), pp. 85-107 (in German)

Huntington, S. Ph. (1998): Clash of Civilizations and the Remaking of World Order. New York

Kant, I. (1974): Kritik der reinen Vernunft [1781 (A) / 1787 (B)]. In: Kant, I.: Gesammelte Werke. Ed. by W. Weischedel. Vols. III/IV. Frankfurt am Main (in German)

Kant, I. (1977): Beantwortung der Frage: Was ist Aufklärung [1784]. In: Bahr, E. (ed.): Was ist Aufklärung? Thesen und Definitionen. Stuttgart, pp. 9-17

Kant, I. (1997): Die Metaphysik der Sitten [1797]. In: Kant, I.: Gesammelte Werke. Ed. by W. Weischedel. Vol. VIII. Frankfurt am Main (in German)

Kant, I. (1998): Grundlegung zur Metaphysik der Sitten [1785]. In: Kant, I.: Gesammelte Werke. Ed. by W. Weischedel. Vol. VII. Frankfurt am Main (in German)

Kopfmüller, J. (2009): Von der kulturellen Dimension nachhaltiger Entwicklung zur Kultur nachhaltiger Entwicklung. In: Banse, G.; Parodi, O.; Schaffer, A. (eds.): Interdependenzen zwischen kulturellem Wandel und nachhaltiger Entwicklung. Karlsruhe (Forschungszentrum), pp. 25-37 (in German)

Krainer, L. (2007): Nachhaltige Entscheidungen. Zur Organisation demokratisch-partizipativer Entscheidungsfindungsprozesse. In: Krainer, L.; Trattnigg, R. (eds.): Kulturelle Nachhaltigkeit. Konzepte, Perspektiven, Positionen. Munich, pp. 169-99 (in German)

Krainer, L.; Heintel, P. (2010): Prozessethik. Zur Organisation ethischer Entscheidungsprozesse. Wiesbaden (in German)

Krainer, L.; Hipfl, B.; Pirker, B.; Terkl, I. (2009): Medien und Nachhaltigkeit. Klagenfurt (in German)

Krainer, L.; Trattnigg, R. (2007): Nachhaltigkeit ist eine Frage der Kultur. In: Krainer, L.; Trattnigg, R. (eds.): Kulturelle Nachhaltigkeit. Konzepte, Perspektiven, Positionen. Munich, pp. 9-25 (in German)

Parodi, O. (2009): Drei Schritte in Richtung einer Kultur der Nachhaltigkeit. In: Banse, G.; Parodi, O.; Schaffer, A. (eds.): Interdependenzen zwischen kulturellem Wandel und nachhaltiger Entwicklung. Karlsruhe (Forschungszentrum), pp. 55-69 (in German)

Robertson-von Throtha, C. Y. (2009): Kulturerbe: Dilemmata des Bewahrens im Wandel. In: Banse, G.; Parodi, O.; Schaffer, A. (eds.): Interdependenzen zwischen kulturellem Wandel und nachhaltiger Entwicklung. Karlsruhe (Forschungszentrum), pp. 71-84 (in German)

Stahmer, C. (2009): Kulturelle Nachhaltigkeit – Vom magischen Dreieck zum magischen Viereck. In: Banse, G.; Parodi, O.; Schaffer, A. (eds.): Interdependenzen zwischen kulturellem Wandel und nachhaltiger Entwicklung. Karlsruhe (Forschungszentrum), pp. 39-54 (in German)

Ukowitz, M. (2006): Am Weg zu kollektiver Autonomie. Vertrauen im ethischen Diskurs. In: Heintel, P.; Krainer, L.; Ukowitz, M. (eds.): Beratung und Ethik. Berlin, pp. 71-91 (in German)

Watzlawick, P.; Beavin, J. H.; Jackson, D. D. (1980): Menschliche Kommunikation. Formen, Störungen, Paradoxien. Berne/Stuttgart/Vienna (in German)

On Substantiating the Conception of Strong Sustainability

Konrad Ott

1   Historic Review

The idea of sustainability can first be found in 1713 and has since been firmly fixed in German forestry theory. It was later incorporated in the forestry legislation of several countries. During the 19th century, issues of the finitude of natural resources and problems of environmental friendly land use were intensively discussed in Germany. At the beginning of the 20th century, we find a number of proto-ecological guiding visions (garden city, social hygiene, homeland protection ("Heimatschutz"), preservation of natural monuments ("Naturdenkmalpflege") that supplement the forestry principle of sustainability (cf. Ott 2008a). During the time of the Weimar Republic, these principles were summarized in the comprehensive concept of landscape management ("Landespflege"). After 1970, the paradigm of environmental protection focussing on the central environmental media of water, soil, and air was established in Western Germany.

The term "sustainable development" was coined anew in 1987 by the so-called Brundtland commission (cf. WCED 1987). In this report, we also find the often-quoted definition: "Sustainable Development is development that meets the needs of the present without compromising the ability of future generations to meet their own needs" (WCED, p. 43). This definition includes a principle according to which every human being has a moral right to satisfy basic needs. Furthermore, the definition includes a principle of intergenerational fairness. According to a less well-known phrasing of the Brundtland report, sustainable development is "a process of change in which the exploitation of resources, the direction of investments, the orientation of technological development and institutional change [...] enhance both current and future potential to meet human needs and aspirations" (WCED, p. 46). This is an enhanced definition adhering to the idea of progress.

On closer inspection, these definitional stipulations constituted a formula compromise of the WCED which disguised many conflicts that arose between the conflicting priorities of economic models of development ("postponed industrialization" versus "limits of growth"), ecological concerns referring to the overexploitation and destruction of natural systems and social-ethical issues (poverty alleviation, distributive justice, political emancipation in a post-colonial situation, etc). Probably precisely because of its vagueness, the concept called "sustainable development" took hold surprisingly quickly worldwide. Since the Rio Summit of 1992, the idea of a sustainable development has been among the established principles of international environmental and development policy. It entered countless documents and statements. However, this apparently impressive success story went hand in hand with an inflation and loss of contours which were basically already laid out in the compromise formula. Since nobody can directly oppose sustainable development, many stakeholders try to shade the term strategically according to their interests. This extension of the term is associated with a loss of intension because terms with a large scope necessarily lose meaning.

Since the 1990s, it can be observed that the discussion on sustainability shifts into the system of politics as well as into the system of scientific disciplines. The respective logic of different social systems (cf. Luhmann 1984) necessarily leads to different models. In the political system, the so-called **three pillar model** came out on top. This model entails a number of initial advantages for political stakeholders. Hence, the three pillar model is open to affiliations and it gives the system of politics flexibility to connect different programmes and strategies to the idea of sustainability thereby legitimising them.

Here, only a crucial shortcoming of this model is to be named: the three pillar model postulates the equal ranking of the three pillars (economy, social issues, and ecology). In this sense, the model is normative. However, it does not say whether this equal ranking factually exists or whether it would first have to be achieved due to existing, historically explainable imbalances. The popular visualizations of the pillars suggest an existing equal ranking which concerning the ecological dimension may well be doubted with good reason. Therefore, it would be misleading if the three pillar model presupposed an equal ranking as a factual given that would first have to be achieved through sustainability policy (cf. Paech 2006, p. 58). Moreover, the three pillar model is conceptually open for basically arbitrary interpretations of all three pillars. Therefore, it rather counteracts the postulate of equal ranking and runs the risk of becoming a legitimising **juste milieu** concept. Furthermore, in debates it acts as a benchmark for evaluating all other theories of sustainability, including those that were conceptualized in a completely different way. Hence, the concept of "strong" sustainability is often blamed for being only a "one pillar concept" and therefore essentially deficient since two pillars are obviously missing. A closer look at the concept of strong sustainability would uncover the absurdity of such claims.

2   Observation and Participation: A Methodical Remark

The political debate as well as the scientific discourse can be experienced with different basic attitudes, either with the attitude of neutral discourse observers or interested discourse participants. Observers (political scientists and sociologists of science) can assess who said what when and how concerning a topic, and also how framings and networks of stakeholders originate and change over time. Participants, on the other hand, contribute to discourses with which they ipso facto raise certain claims. Hence, politicians can claim to contribute to the progress of a national sustainability strategy by establishing new emphases and, for instance, integrating a biodiversity strategy into the sustainability strategy, as (fortunately) was the case in Germany. In the scientific discourse, contributions were made as well. There are various theoretical drafts claiming to assess more closely the idea of sustainability in a terminological, normative, analytical, and conceptual way. These drafts originated in the academic environment of economy, philosophy, technology assessment, and social sciences. Sustainability theories necessarily operate in areas of overlap and are therefore essentially transdisciplinary (cf. Ziegler/Ott 2011).

3   Contributions of the Environmental Advisory Council (SRU) to the German Sustainability Debate

The SRU does not only observe environmental policy making, but also claims to contribute to the orientation and specific advancement of environmental policy making. In two of its main reports (1994, 2002), the SRU theoretically dealt with the idea of sustainability. In the report ("Umweltgutachten", UG) of 1994, the SRU builds a bridge between environmental ethics and sustainability which is termed "dauerhaft umweltgerechte Entwicklung". The terms retinity (interconnectedness) and weighing are prominent in UG 1994. Retinity is understood as an expression of the overall interconnectedness of activities of human civilization with the "carrying" environment and as a principle of action. In my opinion, however, retinity is not a direct principle of action but rather an epistemic principle that compels especially political executives to take into account the effects of their decisions and programmes on natural systems on different time scales.

UG 2002 focuses on the controversy between the competing basic concepts of "weak" and "strong" sustainability. No. 28 of UG 2002 draws the conclusion of this investigation. The multifunctionality of ecological systems, the uncertainty concerning future preferences and the precautionary principle lead to the "policy of keeping the natural capital constant over time". This policy corresponds to the so-called Constant Natural Capital Rule (CNCR) which can be regarded as the centrepiece of the conception of strong sustainability. Rules generally are prescriptions that ought to be observed. In this sense, the CNCR is a restriction that is imposed on economic and social development. Therefore, the economic, cultural, and social development can only be regarded as sustainable if this rule is observed at the same time. The rationale as given in UG 2002 is highly compressed. From an ethical point of view, however, the rationale behind such rules are crucial; rules have to be observed only if the justification is convincing (insightful, plausible). Therefore, it makes sense to ascertain the justification of the CNCR. This is to be done in the course of this article.

4   Problems of Justification

The domination of the present over the future is the starting point of the debate. This domination is given through the direction and irreversibility of the passage of time, therefore through a basal non-moral structure of the human existence. During the time bestowed on them, the people living in the present transform possibilities into future reality and thereby change the state of the future world for the better or the worse. A future world beyond our life expectancy is not better or worse for us but for other people whose values, schemes of life, and convictions beyond elementary needs (for air, nourishment, water, shelter, etc.) we can only make assumptions about. Future generations depend on us in a fundamentally different way than we depend on them. Given our current knowledge on the substantial human interventions in natural systems we can no longer naively assume – as in the "classic" belief in progress – that the transformation of present possibilities into future realities automatically benefits future generations.

The common normative starting point of the controversy between the competing concepts of strong and weak sustainability is a comparative-egalitarian standard of a future responsibility. The Economist Robert Solow (1993, p. 180) defines this standard as an obligation "to conduct ourselves so that we leave to the future a generalized capacity to be as well off as we are" (Solow 1993, p. 180). This means that (average) members of future generations should (all in all) not be worse off than those of the present generation. The underlying benefit or welfare concept is to be understood in such a way that everything that can give people some form of satisfaction of their preferences or interests counts as benefit. Negative benefits are unpleasant events of any kind which can range from slight frustrations to intensively experienced pain, evil, suffering, and sorrow. The comparative-egalitarian standard therefore has to take into account the entire balance of positive and negative benefits.

Advocates of both conceptions accept that present generations cannot directly create the fortune of single members of future generations but that their responsibility concerns a fair bequest package of various goods that in all conscience should allow for future welfare levels to be kept at least constant which includes prevention of suffering. Therefore, a crucial question of the sustainability debate is how many and which natural goods this bequest package should contain.

The main thesis of weak sustainability is that an additive or aggregative conservation of all capital stocks of a society is sufficient for fulfilling the comparative-egalitarian standard of intertemporal responsibility. This thesis implies that natural capital can be reduced at will if investments in other forms of capital are made in return. In this case, the loss of natural capital does not constitute an injustice to future generations (cf. Solow 1974). This substitutability paradigm is deeply embedded in the axiomatic framework of neoclassical growth theory. The main thesis of weak sustainability conceptually implies that more societal and economic states can be dubbed to be "sustainable" while strong sustainability is more restrictive. From this purely conceptual implication one cannot derive that weak sustainability is "more convincing" than its opponent. Any suggestion that "less restrictive" implies "more convincing" is flawed.

In contrast, strong sustainability claims that the set of natural goods should not be reduced or diminished over time but overall kept constant or even increased. This is demanded by the CNCR which concerning its normative status has a hybrid position. This hybrid status results from the fact that the rule has not been enforced and observed over a long period of time. The CNCR on the one hand is a rule which is to be followed, while on the other hand it is a collective goal for a transformation period that is to be achieved. The CNCR is a rule that constitutes a "land ethics" in a specific sense: A land ethics comprises a set of rules and objectives that secure the overall stocks and funds of natural capital with reference to the many resources, services, and cultural values of nature.

For the purpose of justification, a general relation of preference ("x is better than y") is appropriately specified as "Cx overall is discourse-rationally preferable to Cy", with "C" being a certain conception of sustainability and discourses being a network of arguments. This relation of preference hence is no relation between private preferences. The preferability therefore has to be evaluated from a perspective being detached from private preferences and referring to a collective long-term interest. Such interests were traditionally termed common good ("bonum commune") in political philosophy.

The prerequisites of the justification are the following: First of all, there is a competition between theories which, however, cannot be decided on empirical grounds, since sustainability concepts are normative conceptions. Analogies with the competition between sustainability conceptions can rather be found in philosophy and theoretical sociology, e.g. the competition between ethical theories, truth-theories and theories in general sociology. Such a competition between theories should of course not be undecidable and the decision should not be made at random. Therefore, there is no obvious alternative to a discourse-rational evaluation in the medium of a critical comparison (cf. Neumayer 1999). The question of the adequate or satisfactory depth of justification cannot be answered in advance in the case of a discursive evaluation that includes comparative elements as well as objections, replies, concessions, and the like.

An advocate of the conception of strong sustainability has to assume the following: There "is" a set S of reasons R which individually and especially in combination "speak for" the adoption of the CNCR:

$$S\{R\} : (R1, R2, R3, \ldots, Rn) \rightarrow CNCR.$$

The set S may contain reasons brought forward against the competing approach which should have the potential of invalidating. An advocate of the conception of weak sustainability has the right to endeavour the same.

The ultimate goal of such justification is the adoption and implementation of the overall preferable concept by the political system in the form of a long-term, institutionally well anchored strategy. This political ambition is not presumptuous at all; it equals the claims of all other normative theories such as the theory of justice.

5   Arguments in Favour of "Strong" Sustainability

5.1 A first line of argumentation in favour of the CNCR refers to the confrontation with the concept of weak sustainability. It is based on the ideal of internal criticism. The validity claim that should be met in the medium of immanent criticism reads as follows: The conception of weak sustainability makes dogmatic and uncritical use of contested economic special concepts. The criticism does not refer to these concepts as such because matters of substitutability, discounting, compensability and the direction of technological progress are undoubtedly of great importance for long-term decision-making. The criticism refers much more to the quantifications and models conditioning and operationalizing these concepts.

In the case of the elasticity of substitution between forms of capital, the quantification being used is mostly a Cobb-Douglas function with the figure $\sigma = 1$. In the case of discounting future benefits for evaluating the net present value, the discount rate δ is often determined through the assumed pure time preference and the growth of consumption, i.e. the GDP. That way, future damages are minimized. Remote catastrophes do not affect the net present value very much. In the case of compensation for external effects, the Kaldor Hicks criterion is often applied which states that the benefit from a project only has to be high enough so that the losers could be reimbursed.

These operationalizations are not empirically confirmed at all, partly counter-intuitive to our lifeworld convictions and do not at all correspond to common sense. Partly, they are morally precarious and repugnant (cf. Ott/Döring 2008, esp. chap. 3).

Concerning e.g. the elasticity of substitution of capital stocks, the value σ = 1 which states that the input of natural resources into production can become infinitely small was (only) called a "best guess at the moment" in an influential article by Robert Solow (cf. Solow 1974). Solow does not say what this "best guess" is based on; therefore, it is at best backed by Solow's authority. From the point of view of its opponents, this position overlooks the elementary dependencies (reliance) of human activities on a constant beneficial exchange with nature as well as the various cultural values referring to nature. Furthermore, this position is based on a homogenization of all capital stocks which is contested in capital theory.

Concerning the discount rate, it was shown various times that pure myopia might be an explanation of human behaviour but cannot serve as a justification. Moreover, the choice of discount rates highly depends on how one thinks about future scarcities and capacities for problem solving (cf. Hampicke 2003). A general discounting above long-term growth rates is to be discarded. In cases where long-term scarcities are to be expected, a negative discount rate would be appropriate. From the perspective of strong sustainability, the conditions for justifying the discounting of natural capital would first have to be created anew (through investments in natural capital). A more balanced approach to discounting is proposed by Konrad Ott (cf. Ott 2003) and Ulrich Hampicke (cf. Hampicke 2003).

The "Environmental Kuznets Curve" (EKC) is often used as a supplementary model of weak sustainability. However, the status of this curve is unclear. It is not an economic regularity. If advocates of weak sustainability take EKC as a general economic law, they would have to face the objection that EKC is only empirically confirmed for a few environmental pollutants and that an upgrading to a law-like regularity would be a pars-pro-toto argumentation.

In summary, the argument for "invalidation" is that the conception of weak sustainability only reaches its aim by quantifying and modelling its key concepts in highly questionable ways. As soon as these dogmatic quantifications are scrutinized in discourse, advocates of weak sustainability often feel compelled to make concessions. These concessions often lead to acknowledging a "Safe Minimum Standard" (SMS) concerning natural capital. However, it is difficult to reconcile this standard with the general substitutability optimism of weak sustainability since it puts a restriction on the aggregative formula. Furthermore, concerning the interpretation of the SMS, it is debatable how safe is safe enough, which might lead to further concessions. If, for precautionary reasons, advocates of weak sustainability asserted the CNCR at this point, they would make a concession which as a consequence proves right the opponent. In any case, the concession of the SMS (or even more restrictions on substitutability for the sake of precaution) is aggravating for weak sustainability.

Weak sustainability is faced with the alternative of either uncritically adhering to dogmatic quantifications of its own key terms or making substantial concessions. Ultimately, this leads to advocates of weak sustainability having to adhere to and at the same time modify their additive formula. This could prove to be a true conceptual dilemma.

This criticism of substitution optimism ultimately does not leave untouched the entire paradigm the concept of weak sustainability originated in, namely the paradigm of the "neoclassical" welfare and growth theory. Doubts are raised as to whether a paradigm that requires the maximization of the net present value and defines intelligent egoism (maximizing personal utility) as "rational" behaviour is suitable as a basis for intra- and intergenerational justice with some emphasis on fair distribution of goods and fair access to sources of welfare.

5.2 Supporters of strong sustainability have to concede some points. It is to be conceded that the reasons by which CNCR are backed by Herman Daly (cf. Daly 1996) are not very convincing. Daly's examples for the complementarity of man-made and natural capital (fish and boats, forests and sawmills) cannot be generalized in support of the thesis that natural and real capital are complementary with respect to production. The argument by Ekins et al. also has its flaws: "The important point is, starting from a strong sustainability assumption of non-substitutability in general; it is possible to shift to a weak sustainability position where that is shown to be appropriate. But starting from a weak sustainability assumption permits no such insights to enable exceptions to be identified" (Ekins et al. 2003, p. 168). This argument would only be substantive if weak sustainability is based in a theoretically more fundamental way on the Cobb Douglas function than strong sustainability is set on the CNCR, meaning that there is a deep asymmetry concerning the possibilities to make concessions. This, however, is not the case. Choosing any of the two concepts leaves the possibility to make concessions.

5.3 A first substantial argument in favour of strong sustainability refers to the specific properties of natural capital. It says that natural capital must not be subsumed under a homogenous general stock of capital. Phrased in an Aristotelian way, the contemplation of natural capital is not a question of the genus proximum but the differentiae specificae. These properties concern the status of many forms of natural capital as collective goods or primary values, the multifunctionality of many ecological systems (e.g. forests, marshland, grassland), their retinity which makes a separation into goods worth conserving and those dispensable difficult if not impossible. Moreover, specific relationships between "stocks" and "flows", the often existing relation of complementarity with man-made capital and the diverse services the value of which we would only fully be aware of on their failure (e.g. pollination by bees). The specific properties of living funds (so-called renewable resources) should not be taken for granted but should be paid close attention. Living beings are nested funds having intrinsic capacities for reproduction and ecological resilience. One of the greatest conceptual flaws is to treat living funds as if they were stocks that might be diminished efficiently.

5.4 Another argument in favour of the CNCR is that nature does not only deliver resource inputs for production but is connected in various ways to human experiences that go way beyond the sphere of human existence which can be represented by production functions (input → production → consumption → waste). In the "Millennium Ecosystem Assessment", these experiences are represented in the category of cultural values. However, this category needs a stronger ethical differentiation (cf. Ott 2007, 2010). In a nutshell, this category includes

- nature aesthetics in its different forms (contemplative, corresponsive, imaginative; cf. Seel 1991) and historical expressions (from romanticism to contemporary LandArt);
- recreation in nature extending to forms of bodily-mental recovery ("salutogenesis");
- familiarity with and safety in the native landscape ("Heimat", "ethics of place");
- (biophilic) fascination with living organisms and systems;
- spiritual approaches to some sort of sacred items and occurrences in nature to which is alluded with different religious codes.

The many different individual accentuations embedded in differing cultural lifestyles change nothing about the importance of this cultural sphere of nature. Speaking in ethical terms, the cultural values of nature constitute a "deep" anthropocentrism (cf. Ott 2010) which is compatible with different solutions of the demarcation problem. Elsewhere, I have argued that a step even beyond sentientism might be reasonable (cf. Ott 2008b).

The importance of nature for a meaningful human existence can hardly be monetized appropriately. Contingent valuation studies show that at least in Western societies the demand for nature is higher than the present supply (cf. Degenhardt et al. 1998). This counts as an economic argument in favour of the CNCR and even of the additional rule of increasingly investing in natural capital in the future.

5.5 Certainly, we can at present not know future preferences, values, convictions and therefore the specificity of future individual welfare functions. An extension of our benefit functions into the future is not permissible. The question arises which conception of sustainability takes this uncertainty more seriously. It would be "misplaced concreteness" to rely on narrative evidences ("My children are only interested in their Game Boys.") in this point. Furthermore, we do not know the future marginal benefit of an additional unit of consumer goods and the future importance of the cultural importance of nature. From such "ignoramus", it cannot be concluded that the future benefit functions will be fundamentally different from our own and that they will well adapt to a denaturalized, highly artificial world. There are two ways to deal with this uncertainty: One can either refer to basic needs and furthermore add the argument that e.g. through the research on the biophilia hypothesis of Edward O. Wilson (cf. Wilson

1984) we learned that human beings have an anthropologically anchored biophilic inclination. Therefore, one attempts to reduce uncertainties through plausible assumptions ("There is high confidence that they will like nature too"). The other strategy takes these uncertainties seriously up to the possibility that future human beings might take pleasure in either an existence as hunters and gatherers, shepherd nomads, subsistence-oriented village communities, or an existence spent mostly in virtual-artificial worlds. Why should we exclude the possibility that many future persons might prefer Thoreau-like lifestyles or like to perform nature-restoring activities (to the ethics of restoration, cf. Ott 2009)?

Both strategies lead to similar results. If the biophilia hypotheses were true, it would be anthropologically fatal to reduce natural capital. Presupposing a comparative-egalitarian standard, taking the uncertainties seriously implies the strategy of option conservation as a form of future responsibility (cf. Hubig 1993). The aim of conserving options speaks in favour of the CNCR. In this sense, strong sustainability is the more liberal conception (cf. Weikard 1999). I would like to add an argument that refers to environmental education. The UNESCO organized a decade of "Education for Sustainable Development" (ESD). This decade has the aim of introducing and circulating the idea of sustainability in the pedagogic system of society and as a consequence in the values and convictions of the younger generation. The ESD process only rarely explicitly addresses the controversy between strong and weak sustainability, but implicitly it rather advocates stronger versions of the sustainability principle. Various authors emphasize the importance of nature education within the scope of the ESD. It would be strange if educational policies promoted ESD while economic policies operated on the basis of weak sustainability. Given that pedagogic efforts should have been successful, this bifurcation between pedagogical ideals and the ways our "fabric of society" works would lead to the result that a generation of young adults in the phase of raising their own children would be confronted with a situation where natural goods would have further declined. Therefore, we would counteract our own pedagogic efforts and thereby likely create future frustrations, disappointments, sensations of failure, and even anger. Observing the CNCR is more coherent with ESD.

5.6 The next argument in favour of strong sustainability refers to a criterion of risk assessment that is usually presented in the form of a four-field matrix. It is always a question of which action would be better in the face of the fact that it is always possible that one errs empirically. We can formulate the following uncertainties as hypothesis that might prove to be either true or false:

- the elasticity of substitution of natural capital is high (Solow's "best guess": $\sigma = 1$);
- future generations will not be interested in the cultural dimension of nature;
- the biophilia hypothesis is wrong;

- future generations will not adopt the values that are presented to them by environmental education.

The question is how "bad" it would be to have acted on the basis of hypotheses that might prove to be false. Any answer to this question presupposes that the comparative-egalitarian standard is taken seriously. If in a future world, the substitution optimism of weak sustainability should prove to be true and if future generations honestly preferred computer games, museums, cinema, virtual reality, etc. to nature experiences, we would have acted too cautiously by observing the CNCR. How much this possibly excessive caution would cost us crucially depends on how strong observing the CNCR would benefit us. With low opportunity costs and a high present relevance, it would still be wise to accept the CNCR. People who already have adopted deep anthropocentrism will not face opportunity costs in preserving, conserving, and restoring nature.

In the opposite case, however, the situation would be different. If the elasticity of substitution were small, the biophilia hypothesis were true and nature experiences highly benefited future generations, one would have strongly violated the comparative-egalitarian standard by implementing weak sustainability. Therefore, advocates of weak sustainability should accept a burden of proof for imposing a risk to posterity which might result from present misapprehensions and dogmatic stipulations in economic models. If the verity or falsity of our hypotheses can only become evident in the future, we better should choose a minimax strategy which ensures the comparative standard for future generations even if we committed certain errors. The vague expression "not compromising the ability of future generations" in the WCED definition could be overtaken by this minimax strategy. If so, this expression has been "grounded".

5.7 Another argument refers to a thought experiment of generalizability. At first sight, this thought experiment seems to be unproductive since everybody can welcome the generalization of one's most favourite concept. At this point, however, the advocate of strong sustainability can point out the "Nauru case", i.e. the case of a (probably irreversibly) ecologically devastated Pacific island which according to the model of weak sustainability, the so-called genuine savings (cf. Atkinson et al. 1997), temporarily was the most sustainable country in the world. The thought of a future Planet Earth as a globalized "Nauru" evokes repugnancy, horror, and disgust in advocates of "strong" sustainability. Advocates of weak sustainability have to develop a convincing reply, e.g. by saying that the "Nauru case" constitutes an anomaly but not a falsification. Or they might paint a generalized Nauru-like world as a nice and decent techno-garden with much wealth and entertainment for all.

5.8 The last aspect refers to arguments which are invoked against strong sustainability. These arguments refer to (a) unavoidable substitution processes, e.g. in the case of fossil fuels, (b) the presumed static of the nature image, (c) the extreme opportunity costs of the implementation of this conception, and (d) the objection that "strong" sustainability is morally indifferent towards the problem of poverty and would in all conflict situations rather protect species and wilderness areas than fight human misery (cf. Beckermann 1994).

Concerning (a), it is correct that the stocks of fossil fuels stricto sensu cannot be kept constant over time but can only be depleted by any form of utilization. The option value of these resources (e.g. crude oil in the chemical industry) and the limited assimilation capacities of natural sinks (atmosphere as CO_2 storage) speak for using these stocks very sparingly and substituting them with renewable resources during the period of time when they are consumed. Here, proponents of strong sustainability have to face a problem of substitution but they solve this problem well. If non-renewable resources are to be potentially substituted by renewable ones, this requires – apart from the development of renewable energy sources – to keep the stocks of nature as a whole in good condition. This speaks for the CNCR. Precisely at the point where advocates of strong sustainability have to concede that there must be substitution processes with respect to non-renewables, this backs the CNCR concerning self-renewing biotic funds.

Concerning (b), it is indeed important to deliver the discourse on natural capital with insights and concepts of ecology. Strong sustainability accepts that living creatures and natural systems are in a state of dynamic change. The first step entails giving up the idea of a homogenous stock of natural capital. Talking about a network of heterogeneous stocks in different relations to one another is much more appropriate. The conception of nature used in this context does not at all refer to nature untouched by humans ("wilderness") but extends a long way into the stocks and funds of cultivated natural capital. The CNCR and the rule of investing in natural capital allow various possibilities to undertake shifts on this "scala naturae". Observing the CNCR is supposed to revitalize and restore the natural world as a whole. Concerning this, restoration ecology can theoretically and practically contribute (cf. contributions in Zerbe/Wiegleb 2009).

Concerning (c), there are numerous studies showing that at least prosperous societies can afford a transformation towards "strong" sustainability. The opportunity costs of the goals of strong sustainability are moderate. The point is not about societal opportunity costs but rather about economic power. The demands of strong sustainability on industrial societies are certainly higher than the requirements resulting from the conception of weak sustainability. These demands, however, should not be interpreted as unacceptabilities. Demanding something can also mean thinking that a person is capable of a creditable achievement. Strong sustainability is over-demanding neither economically nor politically. In its different reports on the spheres of activity of climate and energy, agriculture and nature conservation, mobility and traffic, marine conservation, etc, the SRU has argued that ambitious goals can be achieved with moderate costs and sometimes with economic welfare gains.

Concerning (d), it is not at all clear from the outset which conception of sustainability fares better under the stipulation of reducing or eliminating absolute poverty and misery. In this respect, the problem of poverty would first have to be discussed in more detail. For instance, it would have to be discussed which effects the climate change that is substantially caused by the rich countries has on vulnerable populations. At this point, I would like to let this issue go with the following solution: On the ethical-normative level, both conceptions come out in favour of alleviating and mitigating poverty. However, they differ in the strategies since weak sustainability primarily relies on economic growth and free trade as measures of choice, while strong sustainability favours a more complex strategy which encompasses "convivial" economic management, strengthening of local economic relationships, and alternative forms of agriculture ("permaculture") and does not even rule out redistributions and land reforms. Strong sustainability is even more realistic insofar as poverty in many regions of the world cannot be simply eradicated but should rather be alleviated. Poverty and misery, quality and standard of live would have to be distinguished in any case. Be that as it may, the disagreement between the two conceptions is not of ethical but of political and strategic nature.

Both camps might agree on the following statements: The phenomenon of poverty is extremely complex and cannot be blamed on environmental and nature conservation. The economic globalization of the past two decades only reduced absolute poverty if an extremely low poverty threshold is defined ($1.25 purchasing power parity per day) (cf. Robeyns 2005). The traditional development aid with an annual volume of roughly $100 billion was unable to eliminate absolute poverty, either. Many poverty-related problems arise in the wake of urbanization, forceful appropriation of natural resources, civil wars and forced migration, the withdrawal of traditional land use rights and communal use, the spread of HIV/AIDS, etc. In the light of this, both camps should stop the polemic accusations that the opposite conception led to misery and suffering.

6   On How to Conclude

Let us now endeavour a presentation of the argumentation so far brought forward in ordinary language which takes a first step in the direction of an argument in formal language. The arguments presented above are now turned into premises. The details of the single arguments are abstracted away but remain present in the background. Therefore, the premises are not just arbitrarily chosen axioms but they have resulted out of arguing. The crucial claim of strong sustainability becomes the conclusion that is supposed to be "derived" ("inferred") from the premises or, less strictly put, it becomes a reasonable result whose status is closer to a judgement than to a proof. The argument presents itself as follows:

(1) invalidating arguments against weak sustainability (accusation of dogmatic operationalization against weak sustainability);
(2) implicit or explicit concessions of weak sustainability (e.g. SMS);
(3) argument of the specific features of natural capital (multifunctionality, retinity, teleonomic structure, status of collective goods);
(4) argument of the cultural importance of natural capital (aesthetics, recreation, home, fascination, spirituality);
(5) argument of taking seriously the uncertainty concerning future preferences; auxiliary argument of environment and nature education (ESD);
(6) argument from risk assessment under the comparative-egalitarian standard (better err on the side of caution, minimax strategy, shift of the burden of proof);
(7) thought experiment of generalization of both weak and strong sustainability (gut and repugnant feelings against a "world" of weak sustainability);
(8) reply to objections (substitution of fossil fuels, ecologic and evolutionary dynamics of natural system, low opportunity costs);
(9) *based on this (hence, thus)*: the CNCR should be adopted as general rule for policy-making.

Perhaps, not all premises are needed to reach the conclusion. If one does not share the repugnant feelings entailed in (7.) one might drop (7.) and, nevertheless, accept the conclusion in (9.). If so, the conclusion seems overdetermined. Logicians do not like such overdetermination since they prefer to reach a conclusion with the most parsimonious set of principles. This ideal of parsimony is not binding for ethical and political reasoning. Personally, I feel more comfortable (insured) with an abundance of premises.

This is the state of the conclusion for the time being. It is of course not "beyond all doubt" but it would be a false ideal to ask for certainty. If a more pragmatic concept of justification is taken as a basis (cf. Ott 2005), the depth of justification reached here can be regarded as being appropriate.

7   Result and Consequences

Let us suppose one accepts this justification and adopts (9) and thus the CNCR. The known management rules join in SRU 2002. After that, one can elaborate a system of rules supplementing the CNCR and specifying it with regard to different forms of natural capital. In any case, a prudent addition would be an investment rule applying to such countries where many stocks of natural capital were consumed and destroyed in the past. The countries of Central Europe are among these countries. Therefore, modern environmental policy should be recognizable as a policy of both the preservation of natural capital and investments in these funds of natural capital which became scarce. The CNCR is a rule of conservation and as such a prohibition against further deterioration; the investment rule is to be understood as a mandate for improvement and restoration. The prohibition for deterioration in environmental issues is by now widely accepted in Germany in the interpretation of Article 20a of the German constitution. The mandate for improvement and restoration certainly leaves a wider scope for political decision-making.

This set of rules is still rather abstract and in need of specification towards goal systems in the different spheres of activity of environmental policy. SRU has always advocated a goal-oriented approach as a conceptual progress in environmental policy making. In its main and special surveys between 2002 and 2008, the SRU concretized the concept of strong sustainability for the different issues and assigned goals (climate change, nature conservation, water, soil, oceans, traffic, agriculture, biomass cultivation). Within the general conception of strong sustainability, observing the rules and reaching the goals are to be procured in such a way that reaching the goals reasonably strengthens the assumption that the rules have been observed.

References

Atkinson, G.; Dubourg, R.; Hamilton, K.; Munasinghe, M.; Pearce, D. W.; Young, C. (1997): Measuring Sustainable Development. Cheltenham

Beckerman, W. (1994): Sustainable Development: Is it a Useful Concept? In: Environmental Values, No. 3, pp. 191-209

Daly, H. E. (1996): Beyond Growth. The Economics of Sustainable Development. Boston

Degenhardt, S.; Hampicke, U.; Holm-Müller, K.; Jaedicke, W.; Pfeiffer, C. (1998): Zahlungsbereitschaft für Naturschutzprogramme. Bonn (in German)

Ekins, P.; Simon, S.; Deutsch, L.; Folke, C.; Groot, R. de (2003): A Framework for the Practical Application of the Concepts of Critical Natural Capital and Strong Sustainability. In: Ecological Economics, Vol. 44, pp. 165-185

Hampicke, U. (2003): The Capacity to Solve Problems as a Rationale for Intertemporal Discounting. In: International Journal of Sustainable Development, No. 6, pp. 98-116

Hubig, C. (1993): Technik- und Wissenschaftsethik. Ein Leitfaden. Berlin a.o. (in German)

Luhmann, N. (1984): Soziale Systeme. Frankfurt am Main (in German)

Neumayer, E. (1999): Weak versus Strong Sustainability. Cheltenham

Ott, K. (2005): Moralbegründungen zur Einführung. 2nd ed. Hamburg (in German)

Ott, K. (2007): Zur ethischen Begründung des Schutzes von Biodiversität. In: Potthast, T. (ed.): Biodiversität – Schlüsselbegriff des Naturschutzes im 21. Jahrhundert? Bonn, pp. 89-124 (in German)

Ott, K. (2008a): Naturbeherrschung als Staatsaufgabe und die Rolle technologischer Leitbilder. In: Jahrbuch für Europäische Verwaltungsgeschichte, Vol. 20, pp. 303-316 (in German)

Ott, K. (2008b): A Modest Proposal of How to Proceed in Order to Solve the Problem of Inherent Moral Value in Nature. In: Westra, L.; Bosselmann, K.; Westra, R. (eds.): Reconciling Human Existence with Ecological Integrity. London, pp. 39-59

Ott, K. (2009): Zur ethischen Dimension von Renaturierungsökologie und Ökosystemrenaturierung. In: Zerbe, S.; Wiegleb, G. (eds.): Renaturierung von Ökosystemen in Mitteleuropa. Heidelberg, pp. 423-439 (in German)

Ott, K.; Döring, R. (2007): Soziale Nachhaltigkeit: Suffizienz zwischen Lebensstilen und politischer Ökonomie. In: Beckenbach, F.; Hampicke, U.; Leipert, C.; Meran, G.; Minsch, J.; Nutzinger, H. G.; Pfriem, R.; Weimann, J.; Wirl, F.; Witt, U. (eds.): Soziale Nachhaltigkeit. Marburg, pp. 35-71 (Jahrbuch Ökologische Ökonomik, No. 5) (in German)

Ott, K.; Döring, R. (2008): Theorie und Praxis starker Nachhaltigkeit. 2nd rev. ed. Marburg (in German)

Paech, N. (2006): Nachhaltigkeitsprinzipien jenseits des Drei-Säulen-Paradigmas. In: Natur und Kultur, Vol. 7, No. 1, pp. 42-62 (in German)

Robeyns, I. (2005): Assessing Global Poverty and Inequality: Income, Resources, and Capabilities. In: Metaphilosophy, Vol. 36, No. 1-2, pp. 30-49

Seel, M. (1991): Eine Ästhetik der Natur. Frankfurt am Main (in German)

Singer, G. M. (1975): Verallgemeinerung in der Ethik. Frankfurt am Main (in German)

Solow, R. (1974): Intergenerational Equity and Exhaustible Resources. In: Review of Economic Studies, Vol. 41, pp. 29-45

Solow, R. (1993): Sustainability: An Economist's Perspective. In: Dorfman, R.; Dorfman, N. (eds.): Economics of the Environment. New York, pp. 179-187

SRU – Sachverständigenrat für Umweltfragen (2008): Umweltgutachten 2008. Umweltschutz im Zeichen des Klimawandels. Berlin (in German)

SRU – Sachverständigenrat für Umweltfragen (2002a): Umweltgutachten 2002. Für eine neue Vorreiterrolle. Stuttgart (in German)

SRU – Sachverständigenrat für Umweltfragen (2002b): Für eine Stärkung und Neuorientierung des Naturschutzes. Sondergutachten. Stuttgart (in German)

SRU – Sachverständigenrat für Umweltfragen (1994): Umweltgutachten 1994. Für eine dauerhaft-umweltgerechte Entwicklung. Stuttgart (in German)

Stern, N. (2006): The Economics of Climate Change. The Stern Review. Cambridge

WCED – World Commission on Environment and Development (1987): Our Common Future. Oxford

Weikard, H. P. (1999): Wahlfreiheit für zukünftige Generationen. Marburg (in German)

Winter, G. (2007): Natur ist Fundament, nicht Säule. In: GAIA, Vol. 16, No. 4, pp. 255-260 (in German)

Zerbe, S.; Wiegleb, G. (eds.) (2009): Renaturierung von Ökosystemen in Mitteleuropa. Heidelberg (in German)

Ziegler, R; Ott, K. (2011): The Quality of Sustainability Science: A Philosophical Perspective. In: Sustainability: Science, Practice, and Policy (in print)

Cultural Heritage: Dilemmas of Preservation in the Midst of Change

Caroline Y. Robertson-von Trotha

This paper provides a short overview of the history of the UNESCO conventions pertaining to culture and their understanding of the cultural goods considered worthy of protection. After a conceptual shift to the more extensive term "Cultural Heritage", UNESCO now also takes the documentary and intangible cultural heritage into consideration. This paper provides an overview of the current conditions of university programmes in Germany and examines the KIT[1] research topic "Cultural Transmission – Digital". The second part of the paper considers the inner dialectic of "Preservation and Change", one that is also implicit within the UNESCO Cultural Heritage Programme. The conventions pertaining to cultural heritage are critically analysed, and some problems – or rather unwanted effects – that accompany the awarding of the title "World Cultural Heritage" are brought up.

1   Status Quo

1.1   UNESCO Conventions and Programmes Pertaining to Culture

From the beginning, the United Nations Educational, Scientific, and Cultural Organization aimed at contributing to the preservation of peace by fostering co-operation among different peoples. One primary focus of this contribution was the preservation and protection of cultural heritage. In the 1945 Constitution of UNESCO, we read in Article 1 that it is UNESCO's task to "maintain, increase and diffuse knowledge: By assuring the conservation and protection of the world's inheritance of books, works of art and monuments of history and science" (UNESCO 2001). Several conventions state this matter more precisely in the following years. In 1954, the Hague *Convention for the Protection of Cultural Property in the Event of Armed Conflict*

---

1   The Karlsruhe Institute of Technology – a university of the state of Baden-Württemberg and a national research centre in the Helmholtz Association.

was established. In 1961, the *International Convention for the Protection of Performers, Producers of Phonograms and Broadcasting Organizations* was signed. In 1970, signatories committed themselves to the *Convention on the Means of Prohibiting and Preventing the Illicit Import, Export and Transfer of Ownership of Cultural Property*.

A further important step on the way to the protection and preservation of the world cultural heritage was the 1972 convention that 185 states have now ratified or at least accepted. Central points of the World Heritage Convention are: first, the expansion of the protective activities of UNESCO; second, the explicit distinction, for the first time, between material and intangible cultural heritage; and third, the breaking up of the limited concept of "cultural property" in favour of "cultural heritage". The terminological change of direction from describing cultural goods as heritage instead of property is particularly significant (cf. Weigelt 2007). The concept of property was bound up with a Euro-American perspective that characterized cultural goods first and foremost as tradable commodities in economic markets. By contrast, the concept of cultural heritage places more emphasis on cultural goods as symbolic objects with specific, independent identities, and on their being much more than merely tradable commodities with monetary value. Protecting the cultural and natural heritage thus implies conserving the cultural good within its own tradition and preserving it in the context of a living culture.

The conceptual shift to an expanded notion of cultural heritage paved the way for increased consideration of intangible cultural goods that are entirely excluded from any notion of property.[2] With the 1992 *Memory of the World* programme, UNESCO intensified its efforts at the preservation of the documentary cultural heritage. "The Memory of the World" comprizes a register of transmitted collections of culturally significant written documents, film documents, and sound documents, so that these may first be secured and, second, be made accessible electronically. Two further conventions for the preservation of intangible cultural heritage were established at the beginning of the 21st century: the 2003 *Convention for the Safeguarding of the Intangible Cultural Heritage* and the 2005 *Convention on the Protection and Promotion of the Diversity of Cultural Expressions*.[3] Despite the somewhat paradoxical and far-reaching implications of the certification of intangible cultural goods, these conventions may be considered great successes in that they give expression to UNESCO's increased efforts regarding the world's cultural diversity (cf. Meyer-Rath 2007). Both conventions have been accepted or ratified by almost 100 states. The normative effects of the conventions are often overlooked, yet should not be underestimated. Following the conventions and

---

2   The extensive literature on the topic of intellectual property rights should be referred to here: Hafstein 2007; Kirshenblatt-Gimblett 1998, 2004; Wendland 2004.

3   Cf. for an example of immaterial cultural heritage, the "Karneval von Binche", Lefébure 1982.

the UNESCO programmes, in 1992 the European Union established the *Convention for the Protection of the Gastronomic Diversity of Europe*, which was completely revised in 2006. The EU member states are thus carrying on UNESCO's efforts at protecting the intangible cultural heritage in a thorough and independent way.

1.2   Sensitization and Education Programme

The preservation of the cultural and natural heritage, as it is freshly formulated in the 1972 Convention, is now being pursued on a second path. Since 1992, UNESCO has linked sensitization to the idea of preservation with the promotion of academic education and research. In the realm of education, the organization is working on developing a corresponding educational system. Toward this goal, in 1992 UNESCO began establishing UNESCO professorships within the framework of the UNITWIN Programme, and the holders of these posts co-operate internationally with other professors. In Germany, nine professorships have been founded since the end of the 1990s, and most recently the Professorship for the Material and Intangible Cultural Heritage of UNESCO at the University of Paderborn. Other countries – such as Spain, Sweden, or the USA – seized the opportunity to establish collaborative professorships as early as the mid-1990s.

Higher Education's Engagement with "Cultural Heritage"

Within this process, higher education began taking up the notion of "cultural heritage". The Masters programmes that are now offered in Germany reflect the many different focal topics. At the Brandenburg Technical University Cottbus, Masters degrees in "World Heritage Studies" have been offered since 2001; and at the Technical University of Dresden, Masters degrees in the "Preservation of Historical Monuments and Urban Development" have been on offer since 2003. The Masters programme in the "Preservation of Historical Monuments" has been a part of the University of Bamberg's curriculum since 2006, and the Masters in "Cultural Heritage" has been a part of the University of Paderborn's curriculum since 2008: they are the two most recent examples of UNESCO's expanded promotion of education. At the KIT's Centre for Cultural and General Studies (the ZAK), the course module "Historical Dimensions of Cultural Practice/Cultural Heritage" has been offered since 1990 within the framework of an interdisciplinary minor in Cultural Studies – which is an option for students of all majors in the KIT, as well as students of the Karlsruhe University of Arts and Design and the Karlsruhe University of Music.

Research in the Realm of "Cultural Heritage and the Dynamics of Change"

Research in Germany is also increasingly devoted to the realm of cultural heritage,[4] and takes up topics from very different disciplines.[5] Alongside the specialized research of the various disciplines, the need for interdisciplinary approaches is becoming increasingly apparent. Thus, in 2007 within the "Technology, Culture, and Society" area of competence at the Karlsruhe Institute of Technology (KIT), a focus was placed on the newly established "Cultural Heritage and Dynamics of Change" field of competence. This field of competence includes interdisciplinary aspects such as architectural theory and the history of art and architecture, as well as disciplinary research in the realms of renovation and restoration. With regard to the history of science and technology, the focus is on ethical, professional, and cultural developments, as well as on dialectical processes of preservation and change. Within this framework, the new project "Cultural Transmission – Digital" takes up the material and intangible aspects of cultural heritage with regard to preservation and transferral in the digital age. Here, the many great current and future social challenges that this process gives rise to are at the centre of the research. Legal aspects of immaterial property rights and technological issues surrounding digitalization and its consequences represent further important problem areas. Multidisciplinary research projects keep their sights on the interplay among cultural heritage, cultural diversity, the formation of modern identities (on this topic, cf. Assmann/Friese 1999; cf. also Robertson-von Trotha 2009), and conceptions of social responsibility. Here, processes of change stand in a complex relational network between constraints on the one hand and the necessity to adapt and renew on the other; between the readiness to take on the new and the responsibility of preserving the "old" cultural goods. Change thus implies a complex arrangement of conscious and unconscious processes, most of which are not controlled. The researching and prediction of intended and unintended consequences thus becomes an important task.

2   Dilemmas of Preservation in the Midst of Change

The world's cultural heritage is diverse in the forms of its expression. UNESCO thus makes the fundamental distinction between material and intangible cultural heritage. According to the 2003 UNESCO Convention, intangible cultural heritage comprises "the practices, representations, expressions, knowledge, skills – as well as the instruments, objects, artefacts and cultural spaces associated therewith – that communities,

---

4   For instance, the special fields of research "Preservation of Historically Significant Buildings" at the KIT, "Cultures of Memory" at the Justus Liebig University in Gießen, and "Literature and Anthropology" at the University of Konstanz.

5   The topic of cultural memory was discussed at an international interdisciplinary symposium conducted in co-operation with the city of Karlsruhe; cf. Dreier/Euler 2005; cf. also Assmann 2006.

groups and, in some cases, individuals recognize as part of their cultural heritage" (UNESCO 2003). By contrast, the material cultural heritage denotes those cultural goods that are of a physical nature – such as historic buildings or nature – and that have special significance. According to this, the material cultural heritage, which UNESCO would like to designate "World Cultural Heritage", should be unique and historically authentic (cf. UNESCO 1972).

Nevertheless, the material and intangible expressions of cultural heritage per se are liable to change. Changes in the environment damage buildings, and artistic forms of expression are passed on from generation to generation in different ways. The concept of preservation thus forms a tension with "natural" change. In this context, three theses are of particular significance:

- *First* of all, a symbolic increase in value occurs through UNESCO's certification of cultural heritage, something that the cultural artefact in question has never previously experienced. Such certification can lead to a rupture in the traditional way of dealing with the cultural heritage at hand. The physical appearance of a place or an object can be altered through the programme of preservation. In particular, internationalization and the effects of the media alter the perception and memory of cultural goods.
- *Second*, the certified cultural heritage often forms a tension with a culture of commemoration and a culture of tourism (a "heritage industry"), as can be seen from the example of Grimm's Fairy Tales (see below). The increased cultural tourism that comes with the distinction of being designated "world cultural heritage" can also lead to new ecological problems on the local level: the Pyramids of Giza demonstrate this quite clearly.
- *Third*, the interests of local actors – both private citizens and public figures – with regard to a cultural heritage site (and thus also to the cultural heritage certification) might very well contradict the interests of UNESCO. The cultural good becomes a symbolic venue and the site of a struggle over political interests. This point will be more closely examined with reference to the documentary cultural heritage.

2.1 The Internationalization of Memory

Since 5 November 2008, UNESCO has been officially registering intangible cultural goods in its *Representative List of the Intangible Cultural Heritage of Humanity*. As early as 1992, it began compiling the *Memory of the World* register. Being placed on either the list or the register is tantamount to being certified as a particularly unique and authentic cultural good. By being certified by UNESCO as documentary world heritage – i.e. within the process of heritage production – cultural fragments are dislodged from their integrated and habitual use. At the same time, these certified fragments experience a second life as representatives of themselves: a chosen cultural product is supposed to be an exemplar of its original cultural significance and the accompanying original culture.

This process gives rise to far-reaching problems, however – problems that can be illustrated with the example of Grimm's Fairy Tales. Grimm's "Children's and Household Tales" was included in the *Memory of the World* register as an exceptional national cultural narration, one that is exemplary of the German narrative culture. In the rationale behind this distinction, it is stated that the collection of fairy tales is "next to the Luther Bible, the most well-known and most widely distributed book worldwide of German cultural history" (UNESCO 2005). This rationale is a one-dimensional, exclusively nationalistic interpretation. Wilhelm and Jacob Grimm – who were moved by a romantic and patriotic spirit – compiled the fairy tales in two volumes in order to stylize them as the primary source of German stories. For the Brothers Grimm, the fairy tales were the remnants of ur-German myths that had been buried by history. From the beginning, the collection was therefore a revaluation of a certain cultural good, namely of stories transmitted orally in local contexts to stories that were fixed (i.e. written down) in an excessively nationalistic context. It is exactly this perspective of "authentically German" fairy tales that the Grimm Society in both the days of the German empire and the time of National Socialism eagerly encouraged and promulgated (cf. Hemme 2007, pp. 230ff.). By stressing only the national context of Grimm's Fairy Tales, the UNESCO description falls short. In being described as representatives of a single German culture, the tales undergo an evident re-interpretation.

At the same time, placing a cultural good onto the *Memory of the World* register is tantamount to an explicit internationalization of memory. The Grimm Brothers' anthology is thus consciously internationalized. At this point, the fairy tales are reinterpreted a second time. The collective memory is transformed, and transferred from the realm of "genuine" national memory to that of a more global memory. The iconic tales of an initially romantic and patriotic context became part of a national context, then a National Socialist context, and then the context of the Federal Republic, before finally becoming heritage fairy tales of a globalized world. The programme of preservation is thus also a programme of contextual change and of revaluation. In several respects, it leads to an altered reception and perception of the certified cultural good.

A further central problematic is that of the preconditions of versions that bear the mark of cultural socialization, and with which cultures observe and judge themselves. The different regional reinterpretations that could take place parallel to the internationalization of memory should be emphasized: new specific perceptions can be produced in this way, but this can also lead to the strengthening of previously existing stereotypes.

2.2   New Media and Memory

Regional and national cultural goods are now perceived globally thanks to new media, i.e. cinema, television, and the internet. The internationalization of the memory of cultural heritage can no longer be conceived of without global media. Global media cultures are part of the international boom of commemorative sites. The medialization of memory leads to a decontextualising of and a break in the traditional ways of dealing with cultural heritage. For example, the Auschwitz-Birkenau concentration camp has undergone a massive increase in worldwide visibility since it was included in UNESCO's 1979 list of world cultural heritage sites. At the same time, pop culture representations of holocaust memorials have spread across the world through mass media. These representations, which are often abbreviated and inadequate, are taken up within specific contexts of national memory, and are thus entirely bound up with these contexts. The reception of these memories thus clearly does not lead to a rich and differentiated understanding of the history of the Holocaust.

2.3   Heritage Industry: Cultural Tourism versus Ecological Sustainability

The internationalization and global medialization of cultural memory has caused new and very concrete problems that bring the dilemma of preservation in the midst of change into sharper focus. The worldwide reception of local cultural goods has in the past few decades given impetus to a form of tourism that can be subsumed under the concept of "the heritage industry". In Anglo-American research, the heritage industry is understood as a boom in the economic reception of history. It is that late modernist form of industry that offers cultural goods as reproducible products and that presents cultural sites as museums or theme parks. The problematic dimensions of the heritage industry can be seen in the history of the reception of "Grimm's Children's and Household Tales" after 1945 and the so-called "Kassel Cultural Struggle" that resulted from it.

The destruction of the Grimm Brothers' former homes and the loss of part of their estate during the Second World War brought about the founding of the Grimm Museum in Kassel in 1960. It remained "firstly a classical museum with an educational task and instructive presentations centred on texts" (Hemme 2007, p. 236). In 1975, the cultural and touristic "German Fairy Tale Route" was established. It connects the places where the Brothers Grimm lived and the locations and landscapes that are supposed to be the original homes of their fairy tales. The German Fairy Tale Route runs along 600 kilometres of tourist sites that include towers and castles, and thus follows an explicitly economic goal. The Grimm Museum found itself increasingly caught up in the wake of the Fairy Tale Route. Local political interests made the shift from the preservation and fostering of the local and regional cultural memories to the building up of a touristic entertainment culture. This had direct consequences on the Grimm Museum. Kassel's cultural budget moved in the direction of tourism, so "that the Grimm Museum began to act in a noticeably more 'touristic' fashion in order to make up for dwindling profits" (Hemme 2007, p. 239). With UNESCO's 2005 certification of Grimm's Fairy Tales, there was a marked increased in calls for better economic use of the Grimm's "global brand name". A fairy tale amusement park was publicly discussed, and economic experts drafted reports on how to best commodify the Grimm heritage. The contentious question of how the tradition and cultural heritage was to be dealt with escalated in local public life to a veritable "Kassel Cultural Struggle" (cf. Hemme 2007, pp. 240ff.).

The problems of the heritage industry are not merely ideational ones brought up in discussions of the appropriate intellectual manner in which to approach the cultural heritage. It becomes apparent that the heritage industry also causes material problems and raises questions of material and ecological sustainability. Venice and its canals, which were recognized by UNESCO as world cultural heritage in 1987, are a telling example of this. Due to rising sea levels, the canals of Venice are now 20 centimetres higher than they were at the beginning of the 20th century. The city is threatened more often than ever with flooding. Moreover, in order to address the needs of increasing tourism, the port entries were repeatedly deepened, which allowed flood tides to penetrate easily into the city canals. An expensive and ecologically controversial system of locks at the port entries now protects the city from flooding. Most of all, UNESCO's certification of Venice has led to a boom in tourism. Hundreds of private motorboats carry the daily flood of tourists through Venice. This increased traffic in the canals is clearly threatening some of the city's infrastructure. For a long time, preservationist have criticized the fact that the beating of the waves threatens the structures of the houses. The high-revving ship propellers increase oxygen levels in the water and consequently contribute to a rise in putrefactive bacteria on support pillars and the facades of buildings. The city structures are thus threatened not only by the rising sea levels but also by the ever increasing level of tourism, and especially boat traffic. The certification of Venice as a world cultural heritage site thus intensifies the problem of the sustainability and preservation of the old historical city and its canals.

The ecological sustainability of many world cultural heritage sites is in question. The Sphinx and the Pyramids of Giza are certainly among the most famous of the ancient wonders of the world. Since 1979, they have been UNESCO cultural monuments. Here too, one can see how the increased tourism resulting from this distinction can lead to a physical transformation of the site in question. Heritage tourism often lacks local sensitivity for the necessary protection of cultural sites and their surroundings. At the Pyramids, garbage and other environmental problems have been on the rise for years, and are threatening to spoil the ecological sustainability of the site. Air pollution, traffic problems, and the fact that the city of Cairo itself is drawing ever nearer to the cultural heritage site are of particular concern. Moreover, the number of tourists has grown to such an extent that increased security measures have been needed to control the rising flood of visitors and protect the Pyramids and the Sphinx. In a co-operative project implemented by the Ministry of Culture and the National Security Services, a fence was completed in 2006 to supposedly protect the plateau of this cultural heritage site, at a cost of eight billion euros. Although the Egyptian Minister of Culture has stressed that the fence does not have a negative impact on the appearance of the Giza Plateau, it does clearly alter its outward appearance. Although it would have been even more difficult to safeguard the plateau's original appearance without the fence, it is evident that the attempt at preservation does indeed lead to an alteration of the site.

2.4   Local Interests versus World Cultural Heritage

A further topic worthy of criticism is often underestimated. As a UN organization, UNESCO pursues joint international interests and thus can often end up entirely at odds with the regional or local cultural institutions, and can also find themselves in conflict with local representatives. Such a conflict situation can be seen in the discussions surrounding the building of the Waldschlösschen Bridge in Dresden.

Dresden's Elbe Valley has been on the UNESCO list of world heritage sites since July 2004. The Elbe Valley is described as an exemplar of a German cultural landscape that unites the countryside and the city, nature and architecture: "The 18th- and 19th-century cultural landscape of Dresden Elbe Valley extends some 18 km along the river from Übigau Palace and Ostragehege fields in the north-west to the Pillnitz Palace and the Elbe River Island in the south-east. It features low meadows, and is crowned by the Pillnitz Palace and the centre of Dresden with its numerous monuments and parks from the 16th to 20th centuries" (UNESCO 2008). Just two years after receiving UNESCO's honours, this wide-ranging cultural landscape was placed on the List of World Heritage in Danger – with the repeated threat of removing the Elbe Valley from the list of world heritage sites by 2009 at the latest. The cause of this was the building of the Waldschlösschen Bridge in Dresden, which was supposed to help relieve the pressure on Dresden's other bridges across the Elbe. Critics – and the UNESCO organization is one of them – view the construction as an absurd project from the traffic point of view, one that will not take pressure off the city centre's traffic but will rather increase it while also destroying the natural landscape. Since 2006, the media have been closely following this "Dresden Bridge Dispute". So far, it has been impossible to reverse the planning of the bridge politically, because the citizens of Dresden voted in favour of the construction of the bridge in a public decision. A legal complaint about the constitutionality of this vote was not taken up by the Federal Constitutional Court. In their May 2007 decision, the federal judges confirmed that the will of the voters manifested in the public decision is not superseded by international law, for the "signatory states of the Convention hold explicit sovereignty in those states in whose sovereign territory the protected sites are found, and they have recognized the existing property rights therein" (BVerfG 2009). Even as UNESCO pursues the protection of Dresden's Elbe Valley as world cultural heritage politically (through committee resolutions and certification) and in the media (through press releases), it is contradicting the fully democratic vote of the local citizens who are also the cultural representatives of the Elbe Valley. As expected, in June 2009 UNESCO took away the Elbe Valley's status as world cultural heritage and thereby reproached the local cultural representatives for not giving adequate care to their cultural goods. In such a case of a world heritage site that comprises both the city and the surrounding cultural landscape, the problem of preservation in the midst of change is especially difficult to resolve. This demonstrates the importance of UNESCO serving an educational role and the necessity of strongly linking UNESCO's programmes and conventions with its educational task.

2.5   Private versus Public Interests

A final important aspect should be mentioned. In the culture industry, various private and public players often compete on the local level over the right to interpret the collective history. Private actors in particular generate economic resources in close co-operation with the tourism industry. Such an industry can be seen at the site of *Checkpoint Charlie* in Berlin (cf. Frank 2007). The public side sees the former border checkpoint as a "cemetery" for victims of the Wall during the days of a divided Berlin, while the private side views it as a simulated touristic place where one can relive the Cold War. On the local level, private actors use *Checkpoint Charlie* for their own profit by charging for group photos with actors dressed up as Soviet soldiers. In this sense, the place is a scene where the borders between a memorial culture and an entertainment culture are constantly being traversed.

Finally, UNESCO world cultural heritage can be used as a political instrument for pushing through interests. At the moment, this can be seen in the central Spanish province of Soria and the proposal surrounding the archaeological site at Numancia (cf. The Olive Press 2008, p. 8). Numancia is the historical scene of a battle between Rome and the Celtiberians in 133 BC. Since the regional government recently approved a company's plans for constructing a residential, recreational, and commercial complex there, the local population in co-operation with Spain's Open University (UNED) is circulating an online petition in an attempt to have the UN recognize Numancia as a world cultural heritage site. The goal is to force the protection of the archaeological site by having it be declared world cultural heritage. This example emphasizes the fact that public authorities cannot be trusted always to protect the cultural heritage. On the contrary, private individuals and initiatives are often decisive.

3   The Outlook, and a Selection of Possible Questions

Cultural heritage per se finds itself in a bind between preservation on the one hand and change on the other. It is clear that UNESCO's outstanding efforts to preserve cultural memorials can bring about a change in memory as well as a change in physical appearance. If the situation continues to develop along its current lines, four main questions come up: Is UNESCO's general framework suited for the preservation of world cultural heritage in the sense of sustained development? On both the global and local levels, do UNESCO conventions lead to a greater sensitivity to dealing with cultural heritage? In the accompanying research and teachings, is the holistic approach towards material and intangible culture taken into adequate consideration? And finally: How are we to deal with disputes that arise from conflicting interests or a lack of sensitivity? – These are surely worthwhile questions for an interdisciplinary field of competence that examines cultural heritage and the dynamics of change.

[This article has already been published in German in Parodi, O.; Banse, G.; Schaffer, A. (eds.): Wechselspiele: Kultur und Nachhaltigkeit. Annäherungen an ein Spannungsfeld. Berlin 2010, pp. 263-274.]

References

Assmann, A. (2006): Der lange Schatten der Vergangenheit. Erinnerungskultur und Geschichtspolitik. Munich (in German)

Assmann, A.; Friese, H. (eds.) (1999): Identitäten. 2nd ed. Frankfurt am Main (in German)

BVerfG – Bundesverfassungsgericht (2009): Pressemitteilung Nr. 63/2007 zum Beschluss 2 BvR 695/07. – URL: www.bundesverfassungsgericht.de/pressemitteilungen/bvg07-063.html [02.11. 2010] (in German)

Dreier, Th.; Euler, E. (eds.) (2005): Kulturelles Gedächtnis im 21. Jahrhundert. Tagungsband des internationalen Symposiums, 23. April 2005. Karlsruhe (Schriften des Zentrums für angewandte Rechtswissenschaft, No. 1) (in German)

Frank, S. (2007): Grenzwerte – Zur Formation der "Heritage Industry" am Berliner Checkpoint Charlie. In: Bendix, R.; Hemme, D.; Tauschek, M. (eds.): Prädikat "HERITAGE". Wertschöpfung aus kulturellen Ressourcen. Berlin, pp. 297-322 (in German)

Hafstein, V. T. (2007): Claiming Culture: Intangible Heritage Inc., Folklore©, Traditional Knowledge™. In: Bendix, R.; Hemme, D.; Tauschek, M. (eds.): Prädikat "HERITAGE". Wertschöpfung aus kulturellen Ressourcen. Berlin, pp. 75-100

Hemme, D. (2007): "Weltmarke Grimm". Anmerkungen zum Umgang mit der Ernennung der Grimmschen Kinder- und Hausmärchen zum "Memory of the World". In: Bendix, R.; Hemme, D.; Tauschek, M. (eds.): Prädikat "HERITAGE". Wertschöpfung aus kulturellen Ressourcen. Berlin, pp. 225-251 (in German)

Kirshenblatt-Gimblett, B. (2004): Intangible Heritage as Metacultural Productions. In: Museum International, Vol. 56, No. 1-2, pp. 52-65

Kirshenblatt-Gimblett, B. (1998): Destination Culture. Tourism, Museums, and Heritage. Berkeley, CF

Lefébure, M.-C. (1982): Immaterielles Kulturerbe Karneval von Binche. – URL: http://commons.wikimedia.org/wiki/Image:Binche_MCL01.jpg?uselang=de [13.03.2009] (in German)

Meyer-Rath, A. (2007): Zeit-nah, Welt-fern? Paradoxien in der Prädikatisierung von immateriellem Kulturerbe. In: Bendix, R.; Hemme, D.; Tauschek, M. (eds.): Prädikat "HERITAGE". Wertschöpfung aus kulturellen Ressourcen. Berlin, pp. 147-176 (in German)

Robertson-von Trotha, Caroline Y. (2009): Die Dialektik der Globalisierung. Kulturelle Nivellierung bei gleichzeitiger Verstärkung kultureller Differenz. Karlsruhe (in German)

The Olive Press (2008): Veni, Vidi, Construxi. Roman and Celtoiberian Settlement threatened by Development Plans. – URL: http://www.theolivepress.es/2008/08/14/veni-vidi-construxi/ [02.11.2010]

UNESCO – United Nations Educational, Scientific and Cultural Organization (1972): Übereinkommen zum Schutz des Kultur- und Naturerbes der Welt. – URL: http://www.unesco.de/welterbe-konvention.html?&L=0 [02.11.2010] (in German)

UNESCO – United Nations Educational, Scientific and Cultural Organization (2001): Constitution of the United Nations Educational, Scientific and Cultural Organization, adopted in London on 16 November 1945. – URL: http://portal.unesco.org/en/ev.php-URL_ID=15244&URL_DO=DO_TOPIC&URL_SECTION=201.html [02.11.2010]

UNESCO – United Nations Educational, Scientific and Cultural Organization (2003): Text of the Convention for the Safeguarding of Intangible Cultural Heritage, Paris 17 October 2003. – URL: http://www.unesco.org/culture/ich/index.php?lg=en&pg=00006 [02.11.2010]

UNESCO – United Nations Educational, Scientific and Cultural Organization (2005): Memory of the World. Kinder- und Hausmärchen. Children's and Household Tales. – URL: http://portal.unesco.org/ci/en/ev.php-URL_ID=23214&URL_DO=DO_TOPIC&URL_SECTION=201. html [02.11.2010]

UNESCO – United Nations Educational, Scientific and Cultural Organization (2008): World Heritage List. Dresden Elbe Valley. – URL: http://whc.unesco.org/en/list/1156 [02.11.2010]

Weigelt, F. A. (2007): Von "Cultural Property" zu "Cultural Heritage". Die UNESCO-Konzeption im Wandel der Zeit. In: Bendix, R.; Hemme, D.; Tauschek, M. (eds.): Prädikat "HERITAGE". Wertschöpfung aus kulturellen Ressourcen. Berlin, pp. 129-146 (in German)

Wendland, W. (2004): Intangible Heritage and Intellectual Property: Challenges and Future Prospects. In: Museum International, Vol. 56, No. 1-2, pp. 97-107

Education and Communication as Prerequisites for and Components of Sustainable Development
Reflections for Policies, Conceptual Work, and Theory, Based on Previous Practises

Ute Stoltenberg, Verena Holz

More than a decade after the first attempts in the domains of education theory and education policy, whose goals were the comprehensive establishment of an educational programme adhering to the guidelines of Agenda 21, enough experience has been made to formulate several consequences for further work on this task. As expected, from those beginnings to the present day, a lively discourse has developed about the contents and methods of educational offerings, a discourse in which people from a multitude of educational domains and institutions are participating.

The topics under constant discussion primarily touch on the innovative character and the integrative capacities of an educational programme for sustainable development with regard to social and educational practises. Various interpretations of the concept of sustainability and its relevance for different social realms play an important role here.

In the following essay, we will sketch out in what way education for sustainable development is present in both society and educational institutions. We will demonstrate approaches for further work based on several telling observations under the headwords: common everyday knowledge and education for sustainable development; foundational value orientation; dealing with complexity and openness.

1 Social Perception and Reception of the Programme of Education for Sustainable Development

Since 2002, Germany has been following a sustainability strategy with goals, indicators, and initiatives (cf. Die Bundesregierung 2002; RNE 2009). Sustainable development as the model for future policies and social praxis has established itself in political discourse through the programmes of various state institutions with wide-ranging public relations work and the inclusion of civil society, as well as through initiatives by key players from civil society. Parallel to the public campaigns and initiatives, corresponding educational programmes have been set up, for education plays a key role in the implementation of the central ideas of sustainable development.

Education for sustainable development (ESD) is thus more than merely a separate point in the work programme of the Council for Sustainable Development 2010 - 2013. "Social Understanding", "Wide-ranging Communication Relating to Sustainability", and the question of the role of "Knowledge, Science, and Responsibility" are perceived as key problems of fundamental importance.[1] Or, to cite the example of a national initiative for sustainable development: The "National Strategy on Biological Diversity" describes education as an important arena (cf. BMU 2007, pp. 87ff.) and names both the measures and the participants that are to be included.

With regard to the domain of education itself, initiatives were taken on the national level even before an official vote on a national strategy for sustainability. In 1998, the Bund-Länder Commission for Educational Planning and Research Promotion (BLK) adopted the framework of "Education for Sustainable Development" and facilitated the practical implementation of the educational goals formulated in Agenda 21 in two programmes that feed into one another: BLK-21 (1999 - 2004) and the subsequent Transfer-21 (2004 - 2008). Similarly, the European Rectors' Conference adopted the COPERNICUS Charter in 1993 in order to emphasize higher education's responsibilities with regard to sustainable development. Since then, the network of universities which signed the COPERNICUS Charter increased to 326 by the year 2005. After some years of reduced activities and finally a breakup, several universities joined in 2009 to form a Copernicus Network.[2] With the memorandum "Rethinking Universities" (cf. Gruppe 2004), the Lübeck declaration "Universities and Sustainability" (Lübecker Erklärung „Hochschulen und Nachhaltigkeit" 2005), and the "Universities for Sustainable Development" declaration adopted at the beginning of 2010 by the German Rectors' Conference and by the German UNESCO Commission, programmatic statements about the – sustainable – development of universities have become available.

In Germany, the UN Decade "Education for Sustainable Development" – through its organising via the German National Committee (established in 2004) and via roundtable discussions that have led to working groups on various educational domains and tasks – has been a very important stimulus (cf. UNESCO 2006). Thus, education for sustainable development was seen, for the first time, as a task that also applies to the primary and elementary levels of education (cf. Stoltenberg 2008). The significance of informal education in this domain was also fleshed out (cf. Brodowski et al. 2009). In 2010, the working group on biodiversity, which is composed of experts from various fields, produced a comprehensive educational programme on "Biological Diversity and Education for Sustainable Development" (Biologische Vielfalt 2010).

---

1   Cf. www.nachhaltigkeitsrat.de.
2   Cf. www.copernicus-alliance.org.

Within the framework of sustainability initiatives of various German federal states, ESD is taken up as its own domain but also as accompanying initiative being supported.[3] Political concerns are communicated publicly through forums or conferences on education for sustainable development.

On its German website, UNESCO provides information material (some of which is internationally oriented) and also points to networking possibilities[4]. "Good examples" are published twice a year. In the list of exemplary projects in the domain of education for sustainable development, very different protagonists have been included – from nursery schools (= Kindergarten) to universities, from NGOs and smaller initiatives to cities and districts. In addition to this, a large amount of educational material has been produced and made available free of charge on the websites of Federal Ministries, Federal Offices, UNESCO, Transfer-21, and numerous NGOs as well.

Businesses (such as the Hipp Group and the OttoGroup) have also begun not only to advertise their commitment to sustainability, but also to make that commitment transparent through information and explanatory material. Activities relating to Corporate Social Responsibility (CSR) are on the increase and are currently orienting themselves towards education for sustainable development. The "FONA" website of the Federal Ministry for Education and Research is a platform for various institutions that take up the concept of sustainability either theoretically or practically.[5]

The Deutsche Bundesstiftung Umwelt (German Environmental Foundation) is an outstanding organization that encourages sustainable projects in private industry, communities, but also especially in various spheres of education.

The 2008 UNESCO World Conference on Education for Sustainable Development in Germany not only called on the media to take up ideas of sustainability more forcefully, but also shifted the focus of the discussion. To cite just one example, the need to train teachers with regards to education for sustainable development was emphasized.

Moreover, there are now more means than ever of living a sustainable lifestyle – from transportation to organic food to ecological homes.

The basic conditions for effectively implementing the central ideas of sustainable development in everyday life have never been more favourable. 82% of those polled in a recent representative study on environmental consciousness in Germany (cf. BMU/UBA 2010) associate environmentally friendly behaviour with a better quality of life rather than with personal sacrifice. The percentage of people who recognize the Fair Trade seal, rose from 30% to 56% (cf. BMU/UBA 2010, p. 46). Yet different social milieus also lead to great differences in attitudes towards the environment, and this can be attributed to different levels of income and education.

---

3 Cf. http://www.bne-portal.de/coremedia/generator/unesco/de/02__UN-Dekade_20BNE/02__
   UN__Dekade__Deutschland/03__Bundesl_C3_A4nder/Bundesl_C3_A4nder. html.
4 Cf. www.bne-portal.de.
5 Cf. www.fona.de; FONA: Forschung für Nachhaltige Entwicklung/Research for Sustainable Development.

2   The Institutional Establishment of Education for Sustainable Development in Educational Domains

The goal of the BLK educational programme for schools was the implementation of education for sustainable development in at least 10% of German schools in 2008. Since then, the programme was introduced in 12.1% of schools, and in some German states the number is even higher (cf. Transfer-21 w/o year). Nevertheless, a large deficit in secondary education has been reported – whether because the classes in grammar school (= Gymnasium) have very specific subject matters and thus provide few opportunities for an integrative approach, or because the approach is seen as being too complex for pupils attending the less academic general secondary school (= Hauptschule).

On the level of early education, many new initiatives have been launched, yet they are predominantly classically oriented: examples include "learning democracy" (conceptualized as preventive) or "basic scientific education" (understood as preparation for the classroom). Over the past few years, offers relating specifically to education for sustainable development (e.g., through the ecological programmes of Ökoprojekt Mobilspiel e. V. or S.O.F. Umweltstiftung) which make it easier for nursery schools to adopt the programme through co-operation, training, and consultation have only been available on the regional level. On the national level, an initiative to implement education for sustainable development was started in the realm of early education with the Leuchtpol project.6

Very few universities have taken up the institutional task of contributing to sustainable development. The Leuphana University Lüneburg is a pioneer here, as it started a programme of sustainable development in 1998 that encompasses all university domains (cf. Michelsen 2009; Stoltenberg 2010). Within the framework of this programme, an introductory semester with a focus on sustainable development is compulsory for all students since 2007. Moreover, in 2010, a new faculty named "Sustainability" was established at the university. The term "sustainability" becomes increasingly part of the names of several academic institutions and is taken as a basis for establishing innovative courses and curricula in Higher Education.

Vocational training has taken up the challenges of the programme, in particular through initiatives of the Federal Institute for Vocational Education and Training (BIBB), and often in co-operation with practical vocational experience. With regard to adult education in Germany, the programme has not made much headway (cf. Michelsen 2005) – with the exception of individual projects and organizations such as Tu-Was e. V. Large deficits exist in social groups such as parents, early school leavers, migrants, the elderly, employees of public institutions, and also various instructors in educational institutes.

---

6   Cf. www.leuchtpol.de.

3 Current Challenges and Stimuli for Further Work on Education for Sustainable Development

With regard to education policy, a key task is to bring about the basic conditions needed to align formal and informal education with a programme of education for sustainable development. This cannot be done by simply "rewriting" current frameworks or curricula. Rather the structure of the entire educational system – where "education" is understood in the sense of lifelong learning – must be altered to do justice to an educational programme that is oriented towards interdisciplinary and transdisciplinary thought and work. Greater weight should be placed on the principles of participation, regional co-operation, and global learning in practical international co-operation. Currently, providing continuing education for sustainable development for instructors at all levels of education should have priority. Separate initiatives and pilot projects should be developed and financed for so far neglected educational domains and target groups.

These preliminary remarks on educational policy are necessary. In spite of many programmatic declarations professing to orient the educational system towards education for sustainable development, there has yet to be any true support of this programme in practice. Currently, specific political issues like international competitiveness or the abolition of the Hauptschule dominate the discussion without relating them to educational concepts like ESD. It is neither perceived that ESD could be a driving force for structural innovations.

The challenges for science and educational praxis that we will consider in this article can re-emphasize the potential of education for sustainable development, particularly with regard to an educational policy that is well-equipped for the future.

3.1 Common Knowledge and Education for Sustainable Development

The terms "sustainable" and "sustainable development" have increasingly become part of common knowledge. On the one hand, this is due to the increased presence of the concept of sustainability in the public domain. On the other hand, the objectives of sustainable development such as "providing a good life", "social security", "preserving nature", or "peaceful coexistence" are very close to people's own subjective needs. The study that the Federal Environmental Agency regularly conducts on environmental consciousness and questions of sustainable development provides insight into different forms of common everyday knowledge about sustainable development. An integrative understanding of sustainability – one that takes into account the interaction of the economic, ecological, social, and cultural dimension of decisions for sustainable development – is the exception here. It is not surprising that groups of people that have different levels of access to education and financial security also develop different attitudes towards social participation (cf. Bandura 1995). Educational pro-cesses can have a greater impact on people when they take people's respective views into serious consideration and integrate them into ongoing thought processes and recon-ceptualizations. We would briefly make note of accounts offered in constructivist epistemology and learning theory (cf. Dewey 1985; Gerstenmeier/Mandel 1995) and in sociological models of understanding differences in attitudes and behaviour (cf. Bernstein 1961; Grundmann et al. 2006; Kuckartz 1999). We know from these theo-ries that common knowledge (in which facts, attitudes, and intentions are bundled to-gether) differs regarding the understanding of sustainable development, the readiness to do something that is considered sustainable, and one's actual proximity to the concept.

Only one aspect can be considered here, but it holds significance for all educa-tional target groups. It justifies itself not didactically, but rather via the understanding of education for sustainable development that we have established here. The starting point is the observation that people who already have an initial understanding of sus-tainable development as well as those who are confronted with the idea for the first time both react in a defensive manner. For example, all students of the Leuphana Uni-versity Lüneburg attend a course entitled "Academia Bears Responsibility" in their first semester in which, as noted above, they take up the concept of sustainability. Many of the students consider this a form of "top-down indoctrination". Another ex-ample: Hauptschule students as well as parents of kindergarten students (in addition to high school students and teachers – the list could go on and on) often react to the men-tion of organic food in the following way: "It's not practical" or "I can't afford it" (thereby rejecting the entire concept outright). Even when the arguments are quite subtle and have several layers to them, in all cases the idea and the concept of sustain-able development is misunderstood as a demand. This is not surprising, since formal educational institutions are generally understood as instructive authorities rather than educational facilities. Education for sustainable development can push back against this. First of all, educational processes should be introduced into real situations and should take up serious tasks that all parties involved can identify with. This requires considerable guidance and assistance, but also the self-organization of the students, the search for partners outside the educational institution, and communication among members of a group that are all tackling the same question. Within the framework of seminars on topics relevant to sustainable development, the Lüneburg students are therefore asked to work in small groups on projects that they choose themselves and whose results could be of importance to others as well (cf. Barth/Godemann 2006). Even Hauptschule students can take courage to face their own future when they real-ize that "organic" products are within their means, are healthy, and taste good (cf. Stoltenberg et al. 2007). Parents will be won over to ideas of sustainability when they realize how buying seasonal and regional foods benefits both their children and them-selves while also supporting regional producers and the regional economy. In all cases, it is not only actions taken that are of significance, but also integrating people's ideas and attitudes into educational processes, i.e., into information, communication, and reflection processes.

Secondly, the defensive attitude towards sustainable development can be tackled by providing occasions for informal learning on sustainable development. The sustainable renovation of buildings or responsible use of energy and water can be used as examples. In such situations, one can expect the message to hit its mark when comparisons are made with non-sustainable situations, when access to the necessary information is provided, and when a participatory element is involved.

Last but not least, education for sustainable development should be understood as political education in the sense of citizenship education and participation. This understanding of the concept should have consequences in educational practice, provided that (constructivist) models of a self-determined education are taken as a basis (cf. Arnstein 1969; Hart 1997). In this case, study settings and educational opportunities need profound restructuring. Yet in the educational institution of the school in particular, the dominant teaching conventions still stand in the way of this. Such a reorientation would also entail rethinking the role of the teacher as well as modifying the existing grading systems.

Many key decisions about sustainable development are made in political and economic realms. Education for sustainable development cannot simply mean implementing a new programme politically. Access to the concept of sustainable development as well as organizational possibilities and the responsibility that comes with them require an open discussion about the interpretation and acceptance of the value framework. They require knowing one's own interests, one's limits, and the degree to which one is affected. They also require knowing the resistance that sustainable development can expect to meet on the individual and societal level. There must be space for all of this – not only through thoughtful and supportive teachers, but also through institutional measures.

3.2 Value Orientation as a Foundation

People act morally because they are free to choose to do so. They are aware of their responsibilities, whether with regard to their family, or to a particular social group, or to humanity as a whole, or even to other creatures – all of these are decisions that depend on their perception and reflection, and ultimately on how they value the relationships they are part of.

Human dignity, preserving the environment, and justice – the fundamental values of sustainable development – are very general principles that become more concrete when one asks "What do they mean for us?" "How should we live in the future?" "What coexistence of man and nature is possible on this one planet of ours?"

Here, too, observations from educational work provide occasions to establish the relations between values and education for sustainable development as a further important field of work. Teachers and instructors, who tend to argue in a moral way, feel responsible for their clients and their clients' futures. From here, it is easy to arrive at an interpretation of everyday values as rules and norms. A common example is energy conservation in kindergartens and primary schools – conservation that is legitimized through the use of competitions and "energy detectives". Yet the relation between "energy conservation", the type of energy used, and the effects of generating that energy, etc. threatens to fall out of the picture. Another example shows insecurities in dealing with values: the current discussion about migration/identity/integration in Europe is an example for changing values. The interpretation of values and the way one deals with them should therefore be an integral component of education for sustainable development. In order to understand and appreciate these relations, we need an exchange of knowledge and an exchange of values and the consequences that result from them.

Sustainable development is an objective based on certain values, yet it is also a mission that can only be accomplished through a transformation of values. The ethical foundation of sustainable development – and the educational efforts that can contribute to it – is the linking together of human dignity, preservation of nature, and justice with regard to the life opportunities for people today and for future generations. This stakes out a value framework with regard to sustainable development that practically the entire world can agree on. The concretization of these values in the process of sustainable development is an issue that demands for cultural and situational advancement. The international community can already draw on global values that have been concretely formulated and that emerged from a common process of deliberation. This exists as a political foundation in the UN's Universal Declaration of Human Rights, as well as the "Towards a Global Ethic" declaration by the Parliament of the World's Religions (in Chicago, 1992). In the Constitution of the Federal Republic of Germany, these values are expressed in the first twenty (inalienable) articles. UN conventions such as those on biodiversity, cultural diversity, and especially on child rights also offer value orientations.

An important foundation for sustainable development and the future of this one planet is the Earth Charter, which began to be drafted in 1994 by civil society groups in a process of international dialogue. It has also had a large influence on the work of UNESCO with regard to the international development of education for sustainable development.

Values that we adhere to are based on facts that are important to us as humans. When we consider the preservation of the environment as a value, we know about the necessity of ecological balances, about the limits of natural resources, about the significance of biodiversity, and about our basic dependence on nature. When we think about justice, we think about the opportunities that people have for development and co-operation, and about people's freedom to make choices about their own lives (cf. Nussbaum 2000; Nussbaum/Sen 1993; Sen 1985, 2010).

Values depend on people's life experiences: What was preserved? Where did the values prove themselves to be of practical use for social life? Different cultures have developed different answers and therefore different value systems. Some of these value systems are beyond the comprehension of the international community – for example, when the caste system in India includes extreme discrimination, or when women's participation in politics is condemned as being contrary to traditional values.

This last example can show us that the transformation of values must be brought about by civil society, and that the courage of individuals can play an immense role here – individuals, who often act against those who were up to that point profiting from the former values. Equal rights between men and women have been written into German law since 1 July 1958. This would not have been possible without the courageous woman Elisabeth Selbert, who fought doggedly – with the support of women's organizations – to anchor this into the 1948 Constitution, against resistance from within the "Parliamentary Council", which had drafted Germany's Constitution. Values are transformed by social developments which we can influence. Values can be transformed if these transformations are justified, and if one has the necessary allies to do so.

Education for sustainable development can open our eyes to the fact that everyone can contribute to the formation of general values. But it can also show us that many measures must come from politics and private industry, as well as from international agreements. Yet individuals are not only capable of changing things in their own everyday lives; they can also become politically active. Education for sustainable development is always simultaneously a form of political education, and it takes up values that are politically relevant.

Since values aim at social consensus, since they should be a form of orientation for coexistence, and since they should be subject to change when they are no longer suitable as foundational values, they should always remain subject to scrutiny. The meaning and function of values should be justified and comprehensible, so that people can adopt them. Therefore, the value horizon in which people in an educational institute work is not a question of individual responsibility. Rather, it should be a matter of an agreement among all relevant parties in that institution. This is necessary because an educational institution is always a part of the larger community too, in which it must position and orient itself.

Values cannot be invented, prescribed, or exercised. Values must be experienced as meaningful orientations in connection with both concrete actions and hard facts. If you prescribe a moral orientation to people, then you can count on resistance (and this applies to older children, young people, and adults). In the educational domain, we should therefore avoid all moral conclusions that are not supported by the facts – for example, the statement, "when we save water, we are helping children in Africa". Reflecting on values – on those values that enable the international community to

develop a common future, on those that bind communities together, and on those that
are questionable – is a key component of education for sustainable development.

3.3   Dealing with Complexity and Openness

An ecological understanding of sustainable development is the one most easily adapt-
able to everyday ideas and pedagogical programmes. It is heavily inspired by the ideas
of protecting the environment and living a healthy life, as well as by an idealized understanding of nature. There is no question that sensitivity to natural processes or
awareness of natural resources as a condition for our existence is an important requirement for being able to tackle the challenges of sustainable development. As a
field of action, ecology (or rather, environmental education and environmental policy)
can obscure our view of many other fields of action that relate to sustainable development, for it cannot do justice to the complex global challenges of sustainable development; this can be clearly seen from Agenda 21.

Rather than an observation, current empirical findings will be our starting point
here. A comprehensive quantitative study of educational institutes (non-formal sector)
in Germany – institutes that are raising awareness of sustainable development policies
– shows how widespread the ecological approach still is in educational work: 55% of
those surveyed consider their work to be rooted in environmental education, followed
by 33% that view their work as coming out of Agenda 21 and thus see themselves as
representatives of education for sustainable development, and 32% who consider
themselves to be working in the domain of general education (cf. Rode/Wendler 2009,
p. 4). The over-representation of institutions that position themselves within the realm
of environmental education leads one to suspect that this orientation is also present in
the content of their course offerings. Indeed, the fields of nature and technology are by
far the most listed in terms of content (cf. Rode/Wendler 2009, p. 16). The further development of the education programme of sustainable development should not remain
a culturally specific field, and by this we mean that each individual institution should
refrain from taking up and teaching only those topics of sustainable development that
are relevant to their specific academic focuses. Antoinetta di Giulio also attests to this:
Many "programmes define the skills to be developed not on the basis of the idea itself,
but on the basis of concrete targets of sustainable development without critically reflecting on the underlying function of education in the context of sustainable development" (Giulio 2006, p. 62). The often-raised objection that the programme is too
complex can be relativized. The aforementioned study also shows that after engaging
with the programme in a long-term and comprehensive manner, the hurdles associated
with its implementation are viewed as significantly less problematic (cf. Rode/Wend-
ler 2009, p. 12).

The potential of the sustainability programme lies in the consideration of complex interdependencies of different dimensions of social action. They should be identified on the local/regional and global levels, as well as in the crossover between these levels. In order to analyse these relations in educational processes, a model is used that attempts to bring to the fore the economic, social, cultural, and ecological dimensions of a particular set of problems (cf. Stoltenberg 2009; Stoltenberg/Michelsen 1999). In those dimensions, certain protagonists with (often contradictory) interests can be identified. These fields should also be understood as fields of action in a common sustainability strategy: One can therefore ask, for example, what dealing sustainably with the soil could mean in its ecological, economic, social, and cultural dimensions. Negotiation processes (and with them the concretization of values) are oriented towards the value framework of sustainable development (discussed earlier in this article) that is non-negotiable with regard to its principles: human dignity, preserving natural resources, and fair life opportunities for all people. One question that could be negotiated in this realm would be whether one should start from an anthropocentric worldview or a biocentric worldview, and what justifications can be given for one perspective or the other. Even the question of universal criteria for human dignity and human rights often leads to controversial discussions on Eurocentrism and provides an occasion to reflect on global social transformation. Such reflection processes are a prerequisite for adopting one's own viewpoints; they are a part of educational processes and also a part of the social communication that is necessary for sustainable development (cf. Holz 2010). We therefore call upon educational institutions to organize their engagement with sustainable development as part of a critical public as well.

On the organizational level, one could counter the inadequate complexity of educational approaches with strengthened co-operation among education providers. They could work together on one topic from different sustainability perspectives, yet still communicate the integrative approach through information exchanges and complementary course offerings. Such thematic educational networks (cf. Stoltenberg 2009) could make the integration of actions relating to sustainable development comprehensible, and also trace out possible lines of conflict among protagonists.

In the theoretical work on the programme of education for sustainable development, great significance is attached to the underlying understanding of nature on the one hand, and to understanding sustainable development as a cultural project on the other hand.

Education for sustainable development can contribute to a reassessment of the supposed opposition between man and nature that has taken root in everyday understanding and in less enlightened milieus. Correspondingly, a critical examination of the supposed opposition between nature and culture can cast light on cultural diversity and its significance for sustainable development as well as the relation between nature and culture that we ourselves must take responsibility for.

The cultural dimension of sustainable development (which usually comes up in models of sustainable development in its "socio-cultural" dimension) offers theoretical constructs and methods of analysing non-sustainable developments and drafting sustainability strategies (cf. Holz/Stoltenberg 2011). It outlines a system of meanings, knowledge, worldviews, lifestyles, and material concerns that can effectively organize social life within a framework of values. Thus, the cultural dimension of sustainable development can play a role in critical-constructivist analysis; such a perspective is indispensable in view of the current challenges of the discourses surrounding religious freedom, "cosmopolitan culture" (cf. Beck 2000), "mondialité" (cf. Glissant et al. 2010, cited in Naiir 2010, p. 17). Yet it can also be viewed as a specific level of action and organization, if one considers cultural forms of expression that reveal the complexity of the concept of sustainable development. This is possible through aesthetic education and joint projects with artists.

4   Concluding Remarks

For the further development of the educational programme, we will list three starting points here that, against the backdrop of efforts towards education for sustainable development, should be given more prominence as elements of the educational programme – in all educational domains and for all target groups. First of all, we need to confront the common understanding of "sustainability" and the defensive attitude that people often have towards it, which in the realm of education is due to the false belief that "sustainable development" is a prescriptive task, whose parameters are set in stone. Another misinterpretation that educational practice can correct lies in the interpretation of values as norms and regulations. Finally, by focusing on ecology as the field of action and analysis, the general understanding of sustainability is narrowed and diminished. These developments are certainly comprehensible, for sustainable development is an open process, and there are many different points of view as to how it should be structured. It is thus even more important for education for sustainable development to make accessible the undoubted framework of values, as well as the knowledge about the guardrails of our action insofar as they exist through insights into and open questions about the ecological, economic, social, and cultural aspects of problems. In addition, educational processes should provide spaces for organization and the exchange of experiences that would allow for a responsible discussion of values, and that would turn the organizational views of all individuals (at all levels of action) as well as those of the community and national and international institutions and organizations – with all their limits and opportunities – into objects of reflection.

References

Arnstein, Sh. (1969): A Ladder of Citizen Participation. In: Journal of the American Institute of Planners, No. 4, pp. 216-224

Bandura, A. (ed.) (1995): Self-Efficacy in Changing Societies. Cambridge

Barth, M.; Godemann, J. (2006): Study Programme Sustainability – a Way to Impart Competencies for Handling Sustainability? In: Adomssent, M.; Godemann, J.; Leicht, A.; Busch, A. (eds.): Higher Education for Sustainability. New Challenges from a Global Perspective. Frankfurt am Main, pp. 198-207

Beck, U. (2000): The Cosmopolitan Perspective. Sociology of the Second Age of Modernity. In: The British Journal of Sociology, Vol. 51, No. 1, pp. 79-105

Bernstein, B. (1961): Social Structure, Language and Learning. In: Journal of Educational Research, No. 3, pp. 163-176

Biologische Vielfalt und Bildung für nachhaltige Entwicklung (2010), erarbeitet von der Arbeitsgruppe Biologische Vielfalt; edited by: Die deutsche UNESCO-Kommission e. V. Bonn (in German)

BMU – Bundesministerium für Umwelt, Naturschutz und Reaktorsicherheit (2007): Nationale Strategie zur biologischen Vielfalt. Berlin (in German)

BMU – Bundesministerium für Umwelt, Naturschutz und Reaktorsicherheit; UBA – Umweltbundesamt (eds.) (2010): Umweltbewusstsein in Deutschland 2010. Berlin/Dessau-Roßlau (in German)

Brodowski, M.; Devers-Kanoglu, U.; Overwien, B.; Rohs, M.; Salinger, S.; Walser, M. (eds.) (2009): Informelles Lernen und Bildung für eine nachhaltige Entwicklung. Beiträge aus Theorie und Praxis. Opladen/Farmington Hills (in German)

Bundesregierung (2002): Perspektiven für Deutschland. Unsere Strategie für eine nachhaltige Entwicklung. Berlin (in German)

Dewey, J. (1985): Democracy and Education. In: Dewey, J.: The Middle Works 1899 – 1924. Carbondale/Edwardsville, SI, Vol. 9, pp. 4-58; 331-355

Gerstenmaier, J.; Mandl, H. (1995): Wissenserwerb unter konstruktivistischer Perspektive. In: Zeitschrift für Pädagogik, Vol. 41, No. 6, pp. 867-888 (in German)

Giulio, A. di (2006): Education for Sustainable Development – What Does it Mean and What Should Students Learn? In: Adomssent, M.; Godemann, J.; Leicht, A.; Busch, A. (eds.) (2006): Higher Education for Sustainability. New Challenges from a Global Perspective. Frankfurt am Main, pp. 60-66

Glissant, É.; Séma, S.; Thill, B. (2010): Das magnetische Land. Die Irrfahrt der Osterinsel Rapa Nui. Heidelberg (in German)

Grundmann, M.; Bittlingmayer, U. H.; Dravenau, D.; Edelstein, W. (eds.) (2006): Bildungsmilieus und Handlungsbefähigung. Zur Analyse milieuspezifischer Alltagspraktiken und ihrer Ungleichheitsrelevanz. Münster (in German)

Gruppe 2004 (2004): Hochschule neu denken. Neuorientierung im Horizont der Nachhaltigkeit. Ein Memorandum. Frankfurt am Main (in German)

Hart, R. (1997): Children's Participation. The Theory and Practice of Involving Young Citizens in Community Development and Environmental Care. New York (Unicef [et al.])

Holz, V. (2010): Transkulturalität, Hybridität und neue Ethnizitäten im Spiegel der Diskussion um "Kulturelle Vielfalt" im Rahmen einer Bildung für nachhaltige Entwicklung. In: Parodi, O.;

Banse, G.; Schaffer, A. (eds.): Wechselspiele. Kultur und Nachhaltigkeit. Annäherungen an ein Spannungsfeld. Berlin, pp. 275-291 (in German)

Holz, V.; Stoltenberg, U. (2011): Mit dem kulturellen Blick auf den Weg zu einer nachhaltigen Entwicklung. In: Sorgo, G.; Forum Umweltbildung (eds.): Die unsichtbare Dimension. Die Bedeutung impliziter Kulturalität für eine Bildung für nachhaltige Entwicklung. Wien (in print) (in German)

Kuckartz, U. (1999): Lebensstile und Umweltbildung. Folgerungen aus der Lebensstilforschung. In: NNA-Berichte, Vol. 12, No. 1, pp. 14-20 (in German)

Lübecker Erklärung „Hochschulen und Nachhaltigkeit" (2005), verabschiedet im Rahmen der Konferenz der Norddeutschen Partnerschaft zur Unterstützung der UN-Dekade Bildung für Nachhaltige Entwicklung (BNE) 2005-1014 (NUN) in Lübeck (in German)

Michelsen, G. (2005): Verpasst die Weiterbildung einen wichtigen Diskurs? Erwachsenenbildung für eine nachhaltige Entwicklung. In: DIE Zeitschrift für Erwachsenenbildung, Vol. 4, pp. 31-34 (in German)

Michelsen, G. (2009): Hochschulen im Horizont einer Bildung für nachhaltige Entwicklung. In: Kerschner, F.; Büchl-Krammerstätter, K.; Funk, B.-Chr.; Priewasser, R. (eds.): Bildung für eine nachhaltige Entwicklung. Manz/Wien, pp. 3-18 (in German)

Naiir, S. (2010): Europa wird mestizisch. In: Lettre international, No. 91, pp. 15-20 (in German)

Nussbaum, M. (2000): Women and Human Development. The Capabilities Approach. Cambridge, MA

Nussbaum, M.; Sen, A. (eds.) (1993): The Quality of Life. Oxford

RNE – Rat für Nachhaltige Entwicklung (ed.) (2009): Peer Review der deutschen Nachhaltigkeitspolitik. Berlin (in German)

Rode, H.; Wendler, M. (2009): „Früher nannten wir es Umwelterziehung". Kommentierte Grundauszählung zur quantitativen Befragung zur außerschulischen Bildung für Nachhaltige Entwicklung – ausgewählte Ergebnisse (as yet unpublished) (in German)

Sen, A. (1985): Commodities and Capabilities. Oxford

Sen, A. (2010): Die Idee der Gerechtigkeit. München (in German)

Stoltenberg, U. (2008): Bildungspläne im Elementarbereich. Ein Beitrag zur Bildung für nachhaltige Entwicklung? Bonn (Deutsche UNESCO-Kommission) (in German), p.2

Stoltenberg, U. (2009): Mensch und Wald. Theorie und Praxis einer Bildung für eine nachhaltige Entwicklung am Beispiel des Themenfelds Wald. München (in German)

Stoltenberg, U. (2010): Sustainable Development Discourse – Challenges for Universities. In: Akdemir, A.; Koc, O. (ed.): Canakkale Onsekiz Mart University: 2010 World Universities Congress. Proceedings I. Canakkale, Turkey, pp. 327-342

Stoltenberg, U.; Bartsch, A.; Wüllner, C. (2007): Zukunftscamp Future Now. Lüneburg (in German)

Stoltenberg, U.; Michelsen, G. (1999): Lernen nach der Agenda 21. Überlegungen zu einem Bildungskonzept für eine nachhaltige Entwicklung. In: Stoltenberg, U.; Michelsen, G.; Schreiner, J. (eds.): Umweltbildung – den Möglichkeitssinn wecken. NNA Berichte. Vol. 12, No. 1, pp. 45-54 (in German)

Transfer-21 (w/o year): Programm Transfer-21. Bildung für eine nachhaltige Entwicklung. Abschlussbericht des Programmträgers. Berlin (in German)

UNESCO (2006): UN-Dekade „Bildung für nachhaltige Entwicklung". In: UNESCO heute, Vol. 1

Sustainability, Uncertainty, and Environmental Ethics

Teresa Kwiatkowska, Wojciech Szatzschneider

"Most people […] take refuge in theory and think they are being philosophers and will become good this way, behaving like patients who listen attentively to their doctors, but do none of the things they are ordered to do. As the latter will not be made well in body by such a course of treatment, the former will not be made well in soul by such a course of philosophy."

(Aristotle 2002, 1105b, 15)

1 Remarks about Sustainability

If we scan our horizon these days we detect a huge labyrinth of ecological, climatic, economic, and social challenges that drives us into disoriented changes at unprecedented speed. This myriad of swingings often without simple cause or solution has brought on the evolution of new concepts, including that of sustainable development as a basis for overcoming the environmental and economic challenges (cf. Mebratu 1998).

The publication of the UN-sponsored report *Our Common Future* (1987) opened the door to this ambiguous concept that became highly instrumental in developing a "global view" of our planet's future. Indeed, some of the local successful outcomes paved the way to discussions about global policies that are thought to cope with the vast environmental challenges worldwide. This catch phrase has become part of many policy documents, ending in a wide variety of definitions and interpretations. As Sharachchandra M. Lele fittingly affirmed: "[Sustainable development] is a 'metafix' that will unite everybody from the profit minded industrialist and risk minimizing subsistence farmer to the equity seeking social worker, the pollution concerned or wildlife loving First Worlder, the growth maximizing policy maker, the goal-oriented bureaucrat and, therefore the vote-counting politician" (Lele 1991, p. 607). The flexibility of the uses of this concept raises questions about its diverse meanings hidden behind widespread green rhetoric.

Although the historical and conceptual antecedents of the concept of sustainability are well known, many practical questions have been arising. Herman Daly, challenging the trendy and fluid nature of sustainability concept, pointed out that "this term – touted by many and even institutionalized in some places – is still dangerously vague" (Daly 1996, p. 1). Many politicians believe that their decisions concerning global environment rely on robust and secure scientific knowledge, a voice of the natural world. However, there are good reasons to question our optimism about scientific knowledge mainly when it is applied to complex climate and environmental problems. Therefore, the false impression that we have a clear scientific elucidation of "sustainability" carries on countless unexpected ecological, social, and economic consequences.

Without doubt, all the definitions go around the severe environmental crisis we are facing and point out the necessity of clean and fair economic growth. Therefore, the sustainability concept has to be woven out of the rich fabric of theory and practice. Each of different formulations of "sustainability" makes a distinct and noteworthy contribution to our understanding of this notion, but also suggest that we are not really in position to comprehend and apply this "science" until we have recognized all differences among various perspectives. Some authors assume that sustainable human society with "good quality of life for all" can be achieved by changing consumers' habits and promoting "green" development programmes with appropriate technologies (cf. Sinha/Greenway 2004). At the same time, we face countless problems of extensive floods or droughts, rising food prices followed by social unrest, deepening poverty, and spreading diseases over many places of our Earth community. Hence, if the science of sustainability pretends to be more than a mere theoretical fanfare, it should avoid a partial view of one aspect of the world in highly abstract and reduced terms (cf. Holdrege 2008, p. 326).

The contemporary environmental debate is mostly associated with growing pollution, dwindling natural resources and biodiversity loss. With a good reason, for history gives us mounting evidence that numerous ancient societies may have collapsed because of environmental degradation. Back then, however, many of the perilous changes have been to slow to be noticed during the individual human life. In contrast, in the course of the last two centuries, the economic growth and globalization have inevitably led us to point of various critical environmental thresholds.

As the German poet Johann Wolfgang von Goethe pointed out: "If we want to achieve a living understanding of nature, we must follow her example and become as mobile and flexible as nature herself" (Goethe 1977, p. 48). Shall we adjust social and economic structures to natural systems, re-conceptualize the whole theory of development, or develop an environmental "way of thinking" at the community level to meet basic needs of local populations? "The Romans", wrote Martin Heidegger, "called a matter for discourse res […] Res publica means, not the state, but that which, known to everyone, contains everybody and is deliberated in public" (Heidegger 1971, p. 175).

Expert knowledge, based upon theories of science of Earth systems and space, will in due course generate regulatory practices of governance and the concepts of sustainability that suit uniform ideals of law, justice, and society of a central state. The practice of dwelling within the region with its *res publica* characterized by a long tradition rooted in customs and convention, will, on the other hand, tend to create an ideal of policy that emphasizes local idiosyncrasy, diversity, and look after local community interests. One can morally act only on policies that could be truly universalized in the sense of being freely adopted by all who could be affected by them.

2 Private Morality and Public Policy

We have to begin by explaining the concept of morality. How can we morally condemn certain acts of injury to plants, animals, or ecosystems unless we are clear on what constitutes morality? Here we also note that moral rules exceed legal norms. Countless human actions may be rejected or encouraged but they cannot be part of any legal system. A moral rule such as Aldo Leopold's famous pronouncement ("A thing is right when it tends to preserve the integrity, stability, and beauty of the biotic community. It is wrong when it tends otherwise.", Leopold 1949, p. 262) is a recommendation to act in a certain way, a recommendation established by experience (science comes in handy), which has been shown to promote personal, social, and natural well-being better than others. And "well-being" can only imply something empirical like self-development, happiness, a more pleasant life, an aesthetically pleasing environment, spiritual enjoyment, a sympathetic connection with other living things, and so on. Morality, as Aristotle indicates, is strictly a personal affair. It is a matter of each person's independent judgments.

Ludwig Wittgenstein once said: "Only from the consciousness of the uniqueness of my life arise religion, science, and art" (Wittgensten 1979, p. 79e). We can equally apply his thought to morality. The way we act depends on what life we would like to live. This is a territory where environmental ethics can play a leading role in shaping our values and our moral fiber into a way of understanding that preservation of nature is a necessary condition for developing human possibilities. But, as Aristotle rightly noted in *Nicomachean Ethics*: "[…] if arguments were in themselves enough to make man good, they would […] have won very great rewards […]; but as things are, […] they are not able to encourage the many to nobility and goodness" (Aristotle 2002, 1179a, 1-5). So here lurk difficulties grounded in our lives as social beings. Our values and their origins are embedded in inherited human cultural contexts. Private choices operate within social codes or customs. Given the fact that environmental values are rooted more in ethical discourse than in social or political practice, the protection and conservation of vulnerable biological riches requires a collective form of response that involves regulatory and legislative principles, and political decisions. It is through the government that we have to mediate human-nature relationships. It was again Aristotle who pointed out that it is politics that uses the rest of sciences, and it legislates as to what we are to do and what we are to abstain from.

By making decisions that directly affect the anonymous public, our acts acquire another character. We cannot disregard this when we make a decision concerning the environment beyond our own back yard; we act as social or political agents, regardless of our deepest ethical or religious intentions. If one designs and decrees a certain natural area as a national park or biosphere reserve, he or she acts as a political agent, not as moral one. Most environmental decisions and initiatives are in large sense " political" since they consist in advice as to what should be done. However, policy though usually based on how people behave, can also be proscriptive and normative. Environmental values (frugality, care, intergenerational justice, compassion, and respect for nature) like all the other qualities can be thought and learned. Together with the experience and comprehension of the non-human world they might instill a new moral disposition and change old habits, and thereby traditional features of social ethics and political decision-making. The new quality of culture that reflects and promotes the goodness of character can, in time, convert the quality of the environment into the political priority. However, it is worth to remember the words of Aristotle that "most people obey necessity rather than argument, and punishments rather than the sense of what is noble" (Aristotle 2002, 1179b, 35).

At the same time, one of the most disquieting features of the more radical solutions to ecological and social problems is their tendency to become authoritarian in the face of the pre-supposed total environmental (climatic) destruction. Such concern leads to proposals for "ecological guardians" to advise the sustainable society on the "just" or moral use of natural resources. We should not fail to remember that there are ways in which the coercive protection of wildlife and ecosystems ostensibly for public good and the intangible benefits of conservation can actually damage the environment and reinforce the political power of the state. The dangers of the state that thinks it knows what is good for us are not alien to our history, and we should be wary of this in environmental affairs. We must guard against telling others what their morally good decision ought to be, or what their "interests" are, as opposed to the interests they think they have. Paternalism is a vice in environmental policy.

Various critics of contemporary policies offer visions of a free and ecological society that can transform our relationship with each other and with the world. There are parallels more recently in the longing for eco-socialism or eco-communism that seemingly connects the good of the humanity with the Earth Democracy. In our quest for the better future we should be searching for a viable alternative to the present development models, but not for a new utopia. For whilst utopia is only a vision of a world without suffering, without conflict, without poverty and with justice for all, while it is just an intellectual or philosophical exercise, it is inoffensive and painless. When it becomes an instrument to convert our wishful thinking into practice, it sacrifices everything and everybody on its way to reach its goal. Wherever we look for the Earth

Democracy that reunites the human being with the environment, and offers the likelihood for dignified life for everyone, it can not be found in projects that unleashed human and environmental horrors before, for they can unleash them again.

3   What Uncertainty Are We Talking About?

"I have praised folly, but not altogether foolishly."

(Erasmus 2008, p. 7)

At the present time most physicists are indifferent to humanistic discourse on the subject of Heisenberg's concept. Paradoxically, philosophers, literary theorists, anthropologists and many others from the social sciences have enthusiastically appropriated the attractive and slippery expression of *uncertainty*, only to confuse its real meaning with whatever sort of arranged fictitious connotation they found fitting. Science, they assumed, no different than the arts and humanities, offers us models, images, and metaphors of the world, and there is no reason why the layman should not make use of these models in his or her dealings with the world, without having to become a nuclear physicist to do so. In a majority of cases this kind of elucidation is, generally speaking, plain nonsense from the scientific point of view. While there is understanding of probabilities and uncertainty in the hard sciences, particularly in mathematics or physics, there is little understanding of such concepts in the social sciences in spite of the appearance of "experts". If we were dealing with a deterministic world, the universe stripped of randomness, the pattern of the series would reveal predictive information. But we live in a world that is not well charted, and time gone by teaches us to avoid the brand of naïve empiricism that consists of learning from casual historical facts. The sad truth is that quite often in soft sciences people confuse science and scientists, who are biased as we all are.

Recently, an entire industry of "risk measurers" has emerged, specializing in assessing risks in different scenarios. These ideas go back to the concept of Knightian uncertainty. In his seminal work that deals explicitly with decision-making under conditions of uncertainty, *Risk, Uncertainty, and Profit,* economist Frank Knight wrote: "Uncertainty must be taken in a sense radically distinct from the familiar notion of risk, from which it has never been properly separated. [...] The essential fact is that 'risk' means in some cases a quantity susceptible of measurement, while at other times it is something distinctly not of this character; and there are far-reaching and crucial differences in the bearings of the phenomena depending on which of the two is really present and operating [...] It will appear that a *measurable* uncertainty, or 'risk' proper [...] is so far different from an *unmeasurable* one that it is not in effect an uncertainty at all" (Knight 2002, p. 19).

Much has been made of Knight's famous distinction between "risk" and "uncertainty". In his interpretation, "risk" refers to situations where the decision-maker can assign mathematical probabilities to the randomness which he is faced with. In contrast, "uncertainty" refers to situations when this randomness cannot be expressed in terms of specific mathematical probabilities. (Knight's uncertainty arises from the difficulty of predicting the future.)

Knight's distinction between uncertainty and risk is quite well preserved in classical decision theory (cf. Luce/Raiffa 1989). A decision is made under risk when the probability of each end result is known, and under uncertainty if the outcomes of the alternatives are known, but the probabilities of these outcomes are "completely unknown or are not even meaningful" (Knight 2002, p. 13). Many economists argue that Knightian risk and uncertainty is one and the same thing. In particular, the distinction is challenged by Bayesian decision theory. Central in this theory is the idea that a subjective probability, or degree of belief, can be assigned to any state of affairs. The Bayesian approach enters as a massive avalanche into environmental studies (cf. Beven 2009). However, to take full advantage of modern Bayesian statistics, these studies should consider losses or gains as outcomes of human actions that hardly could be assessed. Others assume that there are actually no probabilities out there to be "known" since probabilities are just individual expressions of our beliefs and have no connection to the blurry randomness of the "real world". If one cannot construct a well-defined stochastic model, the correct quantitative parameterization is even more difficult. In some situation one can adjust the model to present situation but any forecast of future events (in climate change, natural catastrophes, political and social change etc.) is clearly more elusive. "There has been a tremendous improvement in the three-dimensional numerical models of climate over the last two to three decades in terms of resolution, processes included and accuracy of simulation of present-day climate and variability. However, the uncertainties in the prediction of climate change have changed little in that time, even excluding the additional uncertainties arising from modelling chemical and biological processes" (Mitchell 2004, p. 2355).

All decisions about environmental impacts generally fall into the category of decisions under high risk. The solutions depend on science, engineering, logistics, and economic and moral assumptions about what is good and bad for humans or other life forms. In spite of the growing interest of the general public in nature and wildlife, it may be that the arguments of conservationists must be ultimately framed in cost-benefit terms since governments will always determine their policies against the background of money they have to spend, and, sometimes, the priorities accepted by their electorates.

Recently, some have suggested that all kinds of non-market benefits (preserving a species, aesthetic appreciation of forests, and scientific values of biodiversity, recreational or spiritual pleasures) be included in cost-benefit analysis. The idea of this more extended kind of analysis in the environmental context is to compare the benefits (immediate and diffuse, monetary and non-monetary) of a decision (such as preserving wilderness, alleviating poverty and equity) to the costs (direct or potential). It has to be stated that a lot of policy-related research develops increasingly complex models that generate a never-ending debate about their applicability. We do not refer only to famous Schrödinger's phrase that "nature resists imitations through models" (Schrödinger 1980, p. 323), but to the fact that models entries can hardly be observed or estimated. The use of statistics is hampered by the lack of specified knowledge about the ways the ecosystem works and its spatial and temporal changes. This combined with scarce information about the social factors that contribute to the degradation of ecosystems make sound decision-making particularly difficult.

Randomness does not exclude regularities in the hierarchical pattern of special and/or temporal variations in natural systems (cf. Kwiatkowska 2001). Stochastic models with time factor involved – even the most symmetric – exhibit the possibility of large excursions from the actual state. The simplest, most popular, and for probability people most beautiful, continuous time and continuous paths stochastic model is Brownian motion that although symmetric and recurrent, can produce very large displacements, positive or negative. Roughly speaking Brownian motion is characterized by Gaussian symmetric distribution and independent increments of past history. In environmental topics there is large unstructured uncertainty generated by external factors. In addition, things are complicated because the stochastic mechanism behind them is not autonomous, meaning that models must depend intrinsically on time factor. Any serious analysis and subsequently predictions must be given in terms of probability of occurrence of specific results; hence, if the model or its parameters are practically unknown, these predictions are fuzzy and dimmer with increasing time horizon.

4   A Step towards Realistic Answer

"Act so that you use humanity, whether in your own person or in the person of any other, always at the same time as an end, never merely as a means."

(Kant 2002, p. 429)

"When politicians, industrialists, and environmentalists run out of practical advice, they often take refuge in appeals for a new vision, new values, a new commitment, and a new ethic. Such calls often ring hollow and rhetorical. This is the crux of the problem of sustainable development, and perhaps the main reason why there has been acceptance in principle, but less concrete actions to put into practice."

(Selvam 2007, p. 6)

Until now, various recommendations to bring together ecologically sound ways of living with the call for renewing growth to alleviate poverty in the developing world have scarcely brought the required results. The conjecture that once the site was designated as a "nature reserve", its biodiversity was preserved proved short-sighted. The shelter of its legal status did not resolve the problems of land tenures and speculation, or stopped the harmful agricultural activities. Furthermore, none of the proposals including the Kyoto Protocol with its Clean Development Mechanism and permits to pollute is aimed at stopping deforestation.

Environmentalists thought that a strong case can be made for conservation based on the local, regional, and global values of forests to be incorporated into decisions on "sustainable" management of this important resource. The idea was to help forest dwellers and rural settlers profit from the wilderness without destroying it. However, in many developing countries, it did not stop the destruction; selective timber harvesting proved costly and inefficient. Ecologically friendly activities such as collecting wild fruits, rubber, nuts (non-timber products), including pharmaceutically active substances are either money-loosing propositions or push some plant species to the brink of extinction. Many of well meant "sustainable" programmes lost touch with the development necessities of the communities. They focused exclusively on the alternative activities like industrial reforestation or intensive, multi-crop land use that may appeal to the healthy self-interest of the local people by providing trees and harvests of value to them. But they missed the real connection between the complex community problems, external market pressures and biodiversity loss. As Arturo Gómez-Pompa and Andrea Kaus rightly observed: "All the terracing, green mulching, selective harvesting, field rotation, crop diversity, and reforesting in the world cannot help if the external consumption of natural resources continues to outpace local sustainable practices and to offer economic incentives that out-compete long-term conservation benefits" (Gómez-Pompa/Kaus 1999, p. 5984).

The overwhelming majority of proposals to conciliate economic progress and quality of life with the necessities of biological conservation have financial incentives attached to them. Until now disbursement of the funds public or private has often been insufficient or sporadic, and frequently derailed. On the one hand, the governmental subsidies (local and national) frequently have been bringing more harm than benefit. On the other hand, the international fund-lending institutions tend to promote unrestrained development directly threatening biological, ecological, and cultural diversity. The aid has also been used by power groups without changing local ideas and uses of the environment. Many conservation proposals have only succeeded in enormous squander of money. The subsidizing agencies never visualized the complex interactions between protection of biodiversity, requirements of development and the community life. Nor have they analyzed the direct connections between the local activities and the possible reduction of deforestation or other environmental pressures. As Alexander N. James, Kevin J. Gaston and Andrew Balmford pointed out: "Governments could safeguard the world's biodiversity with a small fraction of the money they spend on environmentally harmful subsidies" (James et al. 1999, p. 323).

All agree with Aldo Leopold that "system of conservation based solely on economic self-interest is hopelessly lopsided" (Leopold 1949, p. 214), yet the question of financial incentives that can alleviate the poverty, and indicate the alternative to the environmentally damaging practices, has to be addressed promptly. According to some views expressed at the European Conference on the Biodiversity (2004) one of the main reasons of continuing biodiversity loss has been a market failure to play a fundamental role in halting deforestation and overall environmental degradation. Benefits associated with conserving biodiversity are mainly of use for the society as a whole and most of the time not covered by the market. Many ecosystem functions and services defy monetarization as their contribution to our well-being, present and future, is unknown or difficult to asses. Most of the non-material life support functions represent "collective goods". Intrinsic values by definition have no price, and many other values, as for instance unpredictable preferences of future generation, escape monetary evaluation. "Freely functioning markets are based on narrow self-interest. The upstream polluter has no incentive to account for the cost he imposes on a downstream user of the river. The non-consideration of such 'externalities' – the third party costs – may lead to decisions that are 'wise' for the individual now, but 'unwise' for the society as a whole (and that may also be harmful to the individual). This is a market failure" (Jooston/Clark 2002, p. 138).

Conceivably, the monetary valuation can play a supportive role in environmental policy in spite of many objections, but its multiple practical and normative problems have to be considered when using such a method. However, the comprehensive approach to conservation of the entire biological diversity requires a strategy that goes beyond economic cost-benefit valuation. A number of proposals like permits to pollute or transferable development rights are essentially market approaches that set limits on environmentally harmful activities. However, as observed by Allen Blackman and Winston Harrington in reference to developing countries "tradable permits are generally not practical" (Blackman/Harrington 2000, p. 5).

It is important to stress that we do not pretend to price environment by endowing it with market value. What we propose is the direct market out of *environmental improvements*, always when high reliability measurement of actual state could be ensured: for example the number of wind turbines. The "conditional carrot" approach using "Principal-Agent" methodology (cf. Laffont/Martimort 2002) might be the only way to deal with the most serious environmental crisis. In fact, this approach has been already under way in combating pollution, like opening of high-occupancy vehicle lines or promoting hybrids. However, it poses different optimization problems because initial customer's decision remains stable over time.

On the whole, the Principal-Agent method (Nature being the Principal *represented by a financial institution*) aims at creating new investment opportunities that will stimulate economic development of the region, benefit local communities, and the wildlife. Agent could be anyone who buys the certificate or, in situations involving reforestation, these certificates could be given free of charge to the inhabitants of a community. In another words, agents are people, some of them with null participation. Participation means the ownership of corresponding certificates. It also offers transparency in handling conservation funds that will be created from taxes, or voluntary contributions, offsetting (compulsorily or voluntarily) environmentally harmful actions. It can be taken for granted that the main problem of any environmental decision is not how to impose additional taxes, but how to use the collected money wisely. The fund creation offers more efficient ways to improve and protect the environment than spending millions of dollars in organizing panels of experts who conclude (with fuzzy estimation of probabilities) that degradation is caused by human activities.

A different approach with the use of Principal-Agent method has been considered by Laurent Franckx and Alessio D'Amato. They wrote: "We have considered there the regulation of a (private or public) agent by an EPA (Environmental Protection Agency). This EPA is constrained to basing its incentive scheme (both rewards and punishments) on environmental performance, and allocate funds to alternative projects with environmental benefits. The private agent can allocate its effort either to environmental protection or to its core task" (Franckx/Amato 2003, p. 15). While we consider only environmental improvements, we go further in co-operation topics. At the same time, our approach does not need precise specification of parameters, as the quoted above study requires.

It is also known that rural communities in undeveloped countries mostly have a hierarchical structure controlled by powerful individuals. Some authors see it as a main reason of their failure to stop deforestation of the regions in question. According to our strategy their inhabitants could act positively if sufficiently rewarded. "Good" environmental certificates[1] would recompense planting trees or decreasing pollutant levels. We would like to stress that our method is not aiming at valuation of environmental goods nor would the proposed market lead toward this direction.

The precise optimality of such certificates – *Principal optimization problem* – depends on the given models. After using this method for a while, we can consider more exact models to get precise optimality stemming from the strict application of the Principal-Agent method. It is worth to bear in mind that modern finance applications often anticipate theories, models, and theorems. Usual cost-benefits analysis compares Nash competitive equilibria with collusive ones. Well-known mismatch between these two (depending heavily on parameters chosen) does not have an easy

---

1   Good certificate is meant to stimulate and encourage positive environmental actions like reforestation, restoration, conservation of biodiversity, or reduction of pollutants. These certificates can be freely bought by all interested agents.

solution, and is linked to coalition creation and eventual renegotiation through the theory of repeated games (cf. Ray 2001).

Our approach is qualitatively different. With the use of certificates of improvements that could any temporal mean of some convex function of pollutants (for example square function) we are able to create the co-operation using the concept of fusion.

Let us explain the difference between collusive and fusion. In a collusive approach a certificate that pays more for smaller pollution levels embraces, let us say, two "domains", for example countries, states, or local communities; each agent can make improvements in his or her own domain only. In the fusion case an agent can make improvements in the other agent's land. This could result in the transfer of technologies or any other form of real co-operation. (In fact, recent conferences on climate change stress the transfer of technologies as one of the most significant parts of the future political agenda.) Mathematical analysis of certificates of improvement is non trivial (cf. Kwiatkowska/Szatzschneider 2009). The good news is that our project can start with the issue of ANY good environmental certificate. Instead of diffuse promises of cutting pollution that could put poor countries (if compromised) back to dark ages, we should consider bona fide co-operation, which can be accomplished by properly using Principal-Agent methodology.

References

Aristotle (2002): Nicomachean Ethics. Engl. Transl. Oxford, UK

Beven, K. (2009): Environmental Modelling: An Uncertain Future? An Introduction to Techniques for Uncertainty Estimation in Environmental Prediction. London/New York

Blackman, A.; Harrington, W. (2000): The Use of Economic Incentives in Developing Countries. Lessons from International Experience with Industrial Air Pollution. In: Journal of Environment and Development, Vol. 9, No. 1, pp. 5-44

Daly, H. (1996): Beyond Growth. The Economics of Sustainable Development. Boston, MA

Erasmus, D. (2008): The Praise of Folly [1511]. Rockville, MD

Franckx, L.; D'Amato, A. (2003): Environmental Policy as a Multi-task Principal-Agent Problem. Leuven, Belgium (Energy, Transport and Environment Working Papers Series, no. 2003-12)

Goethe, J. W. (1977): Zur Morphologie [1817]. In: Goethe, J. W.: Schriften zur Naturwissenschaft. Stuttgart, pp. 45-174 (in German)

Gómez-Pompa, A.; Kaus, A. (1999): From Pre-Hispanic to Future Conservation Alternatives: Lessons from Mexico. In: PNAS – Proceeding of the National Academy of the Sciences of the United States of America, Vol. 96, No. 11 (May), pp. 5982-5986

Heidegger, M. (1971): The Thing. In: Hofstadter, A. (ed.): Poetry, Language, Thought. New York, pp.165-182

Holdrege, C. (2008): Can We See with Fresh Eyes? Beyond a Culture of Abstraction. In: Vitek, B.; Jackson, W. (eds.): The Virtues of Ignorance, Complexity, Sustainability, and the Limits of Knowledge. Lexington, KY, pp. 323-333

James, A. N.; Gaston, K. J.; Balmford, A. (1999): Balancing the Earth's Accounts. In: Nature, Vol. 401, 23 September, pp. 323-324

Joosten, H.; Clark, D. (2002): The Wise Use of Mires and Peat Lands. Background and Principles Including a Framework for Decision Making. Jyväskylä, Finland (IPS – International Peat Society)

Kant, I. (2002): Groundwork of the Metaphysics and Morals [1785]. Oxford/New York

Knight, F. (2002): Risk, Uncertainty, and Profit [1921]. Reprint. Washington, D.C.

Kwiatkowska, T. (2001): Beyond Uncertainties: Some Open Questions about Chaos and Ethics. In: Ethics and the Environment, Vol. 6, No. 1 (Spring), pp. 96-116

Kwiatkowska, T.; Szatzschneider, W. (2009): How to Rescue the Environment: The Uncommon Idea. In: China-USA Business Review, Vol. 8, No. 9 (September), pp. 58-65

Laffont, J. J.; Martimort, D. (2002): The Theory of Incentives. The Principal Agent Model. Princeton, NJ

Lele, S. M (1991): Sustainable Development: A Critical Review. In: World Development, Vol. 19, No. 6, pp. 607-621

Leopold, A. (1949): A Sand County Almanac, and Sketches here and there. New York

Luce, R. D.; Raiffa, H. (1989): Games and Decisions. Introduction and Critical Survey [1957]. New York

Mebratu, D. (1998): Sustainability and Sustainable Development: Historical and Conceptual Review. In: Environmental Impact Assessment Review, Vol. 18, pp. 493-520

Mitchell, J. F. B. (2004): Can We Believe Predictions of Climate Change? In: Quarterly Journal of the Royal Meteorological Society, Vol. 130, No.602 (October), pp. 2341-2360

Ray, R. (2001): Economic Value Added: Theory, Evidence, a Missing Link. In: Review of Business, Spring. – URL: http://www.entrepreneur.com/tradejournals/article/76941377.html [2010/01/30]

Schrödinger, E. (1980): The Present Situation in Quantum Mechanics [1935]. A Translation of Schrödinger's "Cat Paradox Paper". Transl. by J. D. Trimmer. In: Proceedings of the American Philosophical Society, Vol. 124, pp. 323-338

Selvam, A. M. (2007): Chaotic Climate Dynamics. Beckington, UK

Sinha, R. K.; Greenway, M. (2004): Green Technologies for Environmental Management and Sustainable Development. New Delhi, India

Wittgenstein, L. (1979): Notebooks: 1914 – 1916. Engl. Transl. Oxford

Science, Responsibility and Global Sustainability: Steps toward a New Ethical Paradigm?

Ignacio Ayestaran

1 Introduction: The Catastrophic Convergence and the Tropic of Chaos

Global crisis is not a technical problem, nor even an economic problem. It is, fundamentally, a cultural and political problem, where we need new epistemological and ethical tools. Climate change has arrived in a world primed for global crisis. The dislocations of unsustainable change intersect with the already-existing crisis of poverty, resources, and violence. Christian Parenti has called this collision of political, economic, and environmental disasters "the catastrophic convergence" (Parenti 2011, p. 7). By catastrophic convergence, he does not merely mean that several disasters happen simultaneously, one problem atop another. Rather, he argues that problems compound and amplify each other, one expressing itself through another. Disruptive climate change now joins these natural and social crises, acting as an accelerant, as a threat multiplier. All across the planet, extreme weather and water scarcity now inflame and escalate existing political and cultural conflicts.

Between the Tropic of Capricorn and the Tropic of Cancer lies what Parenti has called "the Tropic of Chaos" (Parenti 2011, p. 9), a belt of economically and politically battered post-colonial states girding the planet's mid-latitudes. In this band, the societies are very vulnerable to shifts in weather patterns. In this belt, the climate crisis pushes the Third World into chaos. This chaos fuels violence and collapse in the form of the catastrophic convergence.

Western military planners and political leaders recognize the dangers in the convergence of political disorder and climate change. Instead of worrying about conventional wars, they see an emerging geography of climatologically driven civil war, refugee flows, pogroms, and social breakdowns. This is the geography of chaos and the entropy of global industrialism. The Tropic of Chaos is on the front lines of the Cold War and of neoliberal economic restructuring. As a result, in this belt we find clustered most of the failed and semifailed states of the developing world.

The multilayered crisis of the globalisation is upon us. The metabolism of the world economy is "out of sync" with that of nature – or in Hamlet's own words, our global time is "out of joint". The pre-existing crises of poverty and violence, which are the legacies of Cold War militarism and neoliberal economics, converge on forms of violent adaptation in the case of anthropogenic climate change (cf. Parenti 2011, p. 225). In the Global South these take the form of: ethnic irredentism, religious fanaticism, rebellion, banditry, narcotics trafficking, and small-scale resource wars. In the Global North these take the form of the politics and ethics of the "armed lifeboat": the preparations for open-ended counterinsurgency, militarised borders, aggressive anti-immigrant policing, and proliferation of rightwing xenophobia. The combination of these factors, their imbrications and mutual acceleration, is the new catastrophic convergence. This is not natural and inevitable. Rather, this convergence is the unsustainable history of the Global North's use and abuse of the Global South. This is the entropy of the global chaos, the unsustainable metabolism of the global crisis, and the true cost of our oil addiction, beyond anthropogenic climate change.

If our unsustainable time is "out of joint", if there is not a sustainable future, we have to combat the disjointed globalisation in the name of a better, a more just and sustainable world for the future generations. For this reason, we need to rethink the symptoms and challenges of the metabolism of this global change from a new ethical and scientific paradigm.

2   Symptoms and Indicators of Global Change

We are living in a globalising world where transnational and planetary connections have transformed our ways of living and thinking. In the early 16th century, in a feat of daring unheard of before then, Ferdinand Magellan and Juan Sebastián Elcano took three years (1519 - 1522) to circumnavigate the world. Later, a 19th century traveller, using motorways, railways, and steamboats, needed 80 days to go around the world. In the late 20th century, jets made these same round-the-world journeys by air in just 24 hours. In the early 21st century, an astronaut circles our planet in his spaceship approximately every hour and a half. To the mind of Peter Sloterdijk, this trajectory traces a pathway taken throughout Modernity, marked by a transcendental philosophical change: the job of sketching the new image of the world has shifted from the metaphysicists to the geographers, sailors, and now pilots and astronauts (cf. Sloterdijk 2005). From the 15th to 16th centuries, the confines of the Earth shifted from the metaphycisists to the sailors, cartographers, conquerors, merchants, and missioners in a massive race to draw and depict the image of the world, which ultimately culminated in the space race of the second half of the 20th century, which lies halfway between technology and metaphysics:

The goal now is to encompass and physically go around this real Earth, like an irregularly stratified, chaotically folded body eroded by storms. For this reason, the new image of the Earth, of the globe, became a guiding icon in the modern world view. According to Sloterdijk (cf. Sloterdijk 2005, pp. 31-43), from Behaim's globe from Nuremberg in 1492 – the oldest of its kind still conserved today – to NASA's latest photograms of the Earth and the shots taken from the Mir space station, the cosmological progress of Modernity is marked by the formal changes and fine-tunings in the image of the Earth made possible by technical means. But never – not even in the age of space travel – could the boldness of visualising the Earth conceal its semi-metaphysical nature.

The technological, social, and cultural changes associated with the evolution of humanity in recent millennia or centuries are still surprising for both their boldness and their risks. When human beings invented agriculture (around 10,000 - 12,000 years ago), the world population probably hovered at between 2 and 20 million people. At that time, the population of some primates, like baboons, was higher than the human population. But with the introduction of agriculture came the first major surge in the number of human beings. The population grew much more quickly than before, probably between 10 and 1,000 times more quickly. However, its annual rise was quite slow, equivalent to tiny fractions of people (a figure equal to Indonesia or the United States today). In AD 1500, the world population had reached 400 or 500 million. Around one and a half millennia had been needed for the world population to double, and it had risen at a rate far below 0.1 percent per year. From then on, the world population kept rising steadily, reaching 700 million in around 1730. At that point, its growth started to rise sharply, triggering the prolonged expansion around one billion. In 1900 it reached 1.6 billion. And by 2000 it had reached 6 billion – we follow the historical interpretation of John R. McNeill (cf. McNeill 2000).

This process of human expansion has also come, not coincidentally, with a rise in the use of energy. Human beings' efficiency, for example, is around 18 percent. Of every 100 calories a human being consumes as food (a concentrated form of chemical energy), it only turns 18 into mechanical energy. The other calories are lost, almost always as residual heat. The advance of itinerant agriculture starting in the Neolithic probably multiplied the availability of energy to be gotten from hunting and gathering by ten; later on, stable agriculture multiplied it by ten once again.

Lately, the expansion in the energy sources handled has been an indispensable requirement in human life on a global scale. In the 19th century, the amount of energy obtained all over the world multiplied by approximately five thanks to the influence of steam and coal. In the 20th century, it multiplied by 16 with oil, natural gas (starting in 1950) and, to a lesser extent, nuclear energy. Since 1900 we have probably used more energy than all of human history before then: in the 20th century, the world consumed ten times more energy than in the thousand years prior to 1900. In the 100 centuries which range from the dawn of agriculture until 1900, humanity had consumed around two-thirds of the energy expended in the 20th century alone. The economic and demographic growth of the past two centuries would have been utterly impossible without this silent revolution in the expansion of somatic energy. In the 1990s, one human being used an average of 20 "energy slaves", that is, the equivalent of 20 human beings working for him 24 hours a day 365 days a year. The magnitude of the global changes in the past century is truly surprising.

It is obvious that *mondialization* and *globalization* have grown exponentially, while the *universalization* of values and rights have meandered along a slower pathway on a planet with symptoms of social and environmental unsustainability (cf. UNEP 2007): almost 60% of the services of the planet's ecosystems are depleted, and the average temperature on Earth has risen by 0.74°C since 1906 due to greenhouse gases. Since 1987, when the concept of "sustainable development" was coined, the world population has risen from 5 billion to 6.7 billion people, and trade had tripled by 2007. Meanwhile, 2.6 billion people lack basic facilities (sewage systems and potable water supply), and one child under the age of five dies every five seconds for reasons that are fully preventable (cf. Save the Children 2008). In view of the scientific and technological knowledge of these symptoms, which signal a systemic change on a global scale, we must wonder about the scope of our responsibility – already formulated by Hans Jonas in *Das Prinzip Verantwortung* (in 1979, cf. Jonas 1984) – and above all, we must reflect on the problem and issues for managing a global world where the ethos of the triple economic, social, and ecological accounting would be borne in mind for both today's generation and for future generations on a limited planet.

3   Two Different Earth Ethics: the Heidegger-Lévinas Clash

Having expanded his scope of action to the global scale, the human being is compelled to rethink the ancient ethical formulas. Among the different possibilities, two traditional forms clamour for attention as they posit the role of the human being with regard to his link to the planet Earth. I shall call these two positions or possibilities the *ethics of humus* and the *ethics of space*, respectively. The former is the position hinted at or sketched out by Martin Heidegger, and the latter is the position upheld by Emmanuel Lévinas.

The "ethics of humus" was suggested by Heidegger in several different sections (from 39 to 44) of his book *Being and Time*, in which he focuses on the analysis of care as the ontological-existential category of the *Dasein*. Specifically, in section 42 the German thinker explains one of the cases of care – *Sorge* – through the ancient fable 220 of Hyginus (cf. Heidegger 1962, p. 242), which features the mythological figure of Cura – the Latin term usually translated as *cure*:

"Cura cum fluvium transiret, videt cretosum lutum
sustulitque cogitabunda atque coepit fingere.
dum deliberat quid iam fecisset, Jovis intervenit.
rogat eum Cura ut det illi spiritum, et facile impetrat.
cui cum vellet Cura nomen ex sese ipsa imponere,
Jovis prohibuit suumque nomen ei dandum esse dictitat.
dum Cura et Jovis disceptant, Tellus surrexit simul
suumque nomen esse volt cui corpus praebuerit suum.
sumpserunt Saturnum iudicem, is sic aecus iudicat:
'tu Jovis quia spiritum dedisti, in morte spiritum,
tuque Tellus, quia dedisti corpus, corpus recipito,
Cura enim quia prima finxit, teneat quamdiu vixerit.
sed quae nunc de nomine eius vobis controversia est,
homo vocetur, quia videtur esse factus ex humo'."

In crossing a river, Cura (Care) saw some clay and began to mould it, engrossed in thought. As she was thinking about what she had already made, Jove appeared. Cura asked him to grant it *spiritus*, *breath* or *spirit*, and readily grants her request. Cura wanted to give it his name, but Jove refused and asked her to give it her own. While they were arguing, Tellus (Earth) appeared and desired that her own be conferred on the creature, because she had given it her body. They took equitable Saturn as their judge, who determined (cf. Heidegger 1962, p. 242): "Since you, Jupiter, have given its spirit, you shall receive that spirit at its death; and since you, Earth, have given its body, you shall receive its body. But since Cura [Care] first shaped this creature, she shall possess it as long as it lives. And because there is now a dispute among you as to its name, let it be called 'homo', for it is made out of *humus* (earth)".

Without delving any further into Heidegger's reinterpretation of this Latin fable, the crux of the matter is the reference to the etymological origin of humans: human beings (*homo*) get their name from humus, the layer of soil or earth that is generated through the decomposition of animal and plant matter and minerals. Thus, the possibility remains open of re-linking humans in their being located in a place *(Dasein)*, which is none other than the very Earth that we inhabit and dwell on, to such an extent that the human comes from the humus itself. This kind of pre-modern and pre-technological proposition may contrast with an *ethics of space*, the kind of ethics that corresponds to an age of astronauts and technological journeys through outer space. This is the claim put forth by Emmanuel Lévinas on space journeys as the shapers of a post-Heideggerian image of the world. In his essay "Heidegger, Gagarin and Us" (in Lévinas 1990, pp. 231-234), Lévinas first summarizes Heidegger's position on the image of the modern world in the following terms:

"I am thinking of Heidegger and Heideggerians. One would like man to rediscover the *world*. Men will lose the world. They will know only matter that stands before them, put forward in some way as an object to their freedom. They will know only *objects*.
To rediscover the world means to rediscover a childhood mysteriously snuggled inside the place, to open up to the light of great landscapes, the fascination of nature, and the delight of camping in the mountains. It means to follow a path that winds its way through fields, to feel the unity cre-

ated by the bridge that links the two river banks and by the architecture of buildings, the presence of the tree, the chiaroscuro of the forests, the mystery of things, of a jug, of the worn-down shoes of a peasant girl, the gleam from a carafe of wine sitting on a white tablecloth. The very Being of reality will reveal itself behind these privileged experiences, giving and trusting itself into man's keeping. And man, the keeper of Being, will derive from this grace his existence and his truth" (Lévinas 1990, pp. 231-232).

Given this ethics of humus, of place, of the pathways and clearings of the forest that shapes Heidegger's image of the world and the Earth, Lévinas contrasts the image of the world and the Earth provided to us by astronauts since Yuri Gagarin's first space journey:

"One's implementation in a landscape, one's attachment to *Place*, without which the universe would become insignificant and would scarcely exists, is the very splitting of humanity into natives and strangers. And in this light technology is less dangerous than the spirits [*génies*] of the *Place*.

Technology does away with the privileges of this enrootedness and the related sense of exile. It goes beyond this alternative. It is not a question of returning behind a landscape and a climate. Technology wrenches us out of the Heideggerian world and the superstitions surrounding *Place*. From this point on, an opportunity appears to us: to perceive men outside the situation in which they are placed, and let the human face shine in all its nudity. Socrates preferred the town, in which one meets people, to the countryside and trees. Judaism is the brother of the Socratic message.

What is admirable about Gagarin's feat is certainly not his magnificent performance at Luna Park which impresses the crowds; it is not the sporting achievement of having gone further than the others and broken the world records for height and speed. What counts more is the probable opening up of new forms of knowledge and new technological possibilities, Gagarin's personal courage and virtues, the science that made the feat possible, and everything which that in turn assumes, in the way of abnegation and sacrifice. But what perhaps counts most of all is that he left the Place. For one hour, man existed beyond any horizon – everything around him was sky or, more exactly, everything was geometrical space. A man existed in the absolute of homogeneous space" (Lévinas 1990, pp. 232f.).

In the age of globalization, from Lévinas' vantage point, the human being is no longer simple humus, because he is transhumant, he changes places and lands all over the planet, as perceived by an astronaut from a technological spaceship. Thus, we have two apparently contrasting theses: first, an ethics located in the here of the earth and forest, in the realm of the peasant provinces and native regions, which mistrusts modern science and technology, and secondly, a globalized ethics nestled in the sidereal realm, beyond all horizons and places, which does not mistrust contemporary science and technology. Both aim to think about human beings' relationship to the Earth, but one seems to drift towards the local-topographical and the other towards the global-spatial. Both point to two necessary directions in view of global change, and both surely signal contemporary applied ethics between the local and the global, or, if you will, between the global and the local, which both theses posit.

4   Science, Responsibility, and Global Sustainability

In the clash between the local and the global, the ethos of science has undergone a move towards responsibility, which entails a shift in its historical evolution since Modernity. As Janez Potõcnik, European Commissioner for Science and Research between 2004 and 2009, and current European Commissioner for the Environment, put it in his speech delivered at the *World Science Forum* in Budapest in November 2005, the development of modern science has altered the function of three historical values: truth, progress, and responsibility (cf. Potõcnik 2005). These three values, which have helped to construct our modern societies in both Europe and other parts of the world, have had diverse influences in three successive waves in the modern history of science:

- The age of truth: from the Renaissance to the Enlightenment, the period from the 16th to 18th centuries;
- the age of progress: the Industrial Revolution, basically the 19th century;
- the age of responsibility: the Knowledge Society (or Knowledge-Based Society), the second half of the 20th century.

From the historical experience of the 16th to 18th centuries, we have inherited the mission to discover the underlying laws of nature. Galileo Galilei and Johannes Kepler ushered in this new cognitive and methodological age based on observations and experiments. In it, the topmost value was epistemological, the quest for the truth aside from individual or particular beliefs, which should not interfere with science. This value was expressed in the fundamental principles of academic freedom, and it partly ensured the legitimization of the self-governance of the scientific community. Starting value of progress came to the fore by observing that scientific discoveries come with technological developments that positively affect our lives, just as positivists of all stripes had dreamt about. These impacts, which were initially positive, opened up new areas for economic activity and for the growth of industry or labour.

In the 20th century, scientific and technological developments retained their cognitive, emancipating promises, but since then the limits of the concepts of truth and progress have also been revealed. First, we have realized that scientific knowledge does not correspond to an absolute truth or a pre-existing reality, rather to efficient ways of representation that enable us to predict phenomena or interact with them. Likewise, the second half of the 20th century spurred new political and social concerns related to the limits of technological progress:

- abuse of technologies with the use of the atom bomb and other forms of mass destruction;
- sustainability problems with the first oil crisis, pollution, biodiversity, and climate change;

- ethical questions, chiefly but not exclusively related to biotechnology.

Thus, doubt was cast on the Baconian statement that knowledge is power, understood as control and prediction. These new fronts of political and ethical concern have led science to be acknowledged as an ambivalent activity that cannot be blindly associated with automatic progress, accepting that science is both part of the problem and part of the solution. In this way, the value of responsibility has come to be part of the evaluation of science and technology, compared to the traditional values of truth and progress. Science has become yet another issue on the political agenda, something that would have been unthinkable for our grandparents.

With the relationship between science and society transformed, part of the new ethos of responsible science entails wondering about this globalization of the planet Earth, and more specifically about the limits of some of the fundamental indicators. First, before getting on, it is worth recalling that if we distilled the history of the Earth into a three-hour film, our species would appear in the last second, and our history would only appear in the last hundredth of a second in that film. If an astronaut who had read Lévinas watched this film from space and blinked at this last instant, all the information on humanity would be lost. So having said this, in the last part of this last hundredth of a second, human beings have managed to travel to the Moon, but also to alter some of the thresholds and patterns in the dynamic of the Earth's system. In a recent study in *Nature*, Johan Rockström, Executive Director of the Resilience Centre at the University of Stockholm, and 28 other scientists from universities and institutes from Europe, North America, and Australia set forth the critical limits and thresholds of the planet that humans must respect in order to avoid destabilising the Earth's essential systems, as these violations might trigger abrupt, non-linear changes (cf. Rockström 2009, pp. 472-475). Based on their analysis, Rockström and his large team have detected nine key processes in the planetary dynamic:

(1) climate change;
(2) loss of biodiversity (land and sea);
(3) interference in global nitrogen and phosphorous cycles;
(4) destruction of the stratospheric ozone layer;
(5) acidification of the ocean;
(6) global consumption of fresh water;
(7) changes in land use;
(8) chemical pollution;
(9) concentration of aerosols in the air.

Three of these nine limits have already been violated beyond reasonable limits: global warming, species extinction and the nitrogen cycle. Four other processes are on the verge of being violated as well: the use or consumption of fresh water, the conversion of forest into croplands, the acidification of the oceans, and the alteration of the phosphorous cycle. The changes to the limits of the planet due to anthropogenic activities since the late 18th century – the dawning of the Industrial Revolution – are so huge that some scientists (cf. Clark et al. 2004; Schellnhuber et al. 2005) even claim that we have altered the geological chronology of the Quaternary Period and the Holocene has shifted to a new age, the Anthropocene, an age in which humanity emerges as a global geological force capable of modifying the planet's surface and atmosphere. The major challenge facing science and technology today is to investigate and act to prevent the transformations in all these critical thresholds from becoming collapses or catastrophes (cf. Costanza et al. 2007), both globally and locally.

5   Mondialization, Globalization and Universalisation

The evidence that we are experiencing a global change also merits other considerations. Thus, in a global world like today's we can claim that we are living in the "network society of information and global risk" – coupling the theses of Manuel Castells (cf. Castells 2005) and Ulrich Beck (cf. Beck 1992). This social form is experiencing an unprecedented techno-economic expansion in which three superimposed but not equivalent phenomena converge: *mondialization*, *globalization* and *universalization*.

(1) *Mondialization*: French analysts tend to talk about *mondialization*. This phenomenon is the planetarization of communications, of certain cultural connections and of the first massive migratory movements thanks to the revolution in transport and communications driven by electrical energy. In the late 19th and first half of the 20th century, railway, telegraph, the press, the telephone, the radio, television, aviation, modern marine transport, cars, lorries, film, video, and records spread far and wide. The ontology of this phenomenon: physical space and time are cut through the acceleration of speed. Its scope: the entire planet, the world.

(2) *Globalization*: English experts talk about globalization, the creation of a spatial-temporal globality beyond *mondialization*, although it supports and is based on the latter: without the *mondialization* of electrical energy and transports, globalization would not be as effective as it is. The key to this globalization lies in technology: satellite, electronic money, computers, the Internet, remote networks, faxes, digital technologies, artificial intelligence, virtual reality, bio-computing, MP4, CD-ROMs, DVDs. Part of the ontology of globalization is physical (the entire underlying foundation of *mondialization*), but another large part is virtual: a new space and time in the convergence of cyberspace and cybertime. Cyberspace is no longer physical space: I can chat with a person from Argentina and another one from Australia at the same time. And when we chat we are in neither Argentina nor Australia, nor even at the desk where I'm hooked up. Rather, we are in a new

space, tantamount to a cyber-omnipresence. Cybertime also verges on cyber-simultaneity or instantaneousness: I can send a message via email to 300 recipients in mere tenths of a second. Stock markets and financial markets, too, can earn money or crash in the space of a few minutes. This ontology is unheard of; it does not come from the physical world.

(3) *Universalization* of values and rights: Rights are proclaimed to be universal: the rights of human beings, of children, of women, of the elderly; the right to a home, to work, to freedom of expression. They are timeless and cross-cultural because any human being deserves them. However, even though they are atemporal (or timeless), universal rights have been claimed and established throughout history. They received a huge impetus in the late 18th century (the United States' Declaration of Independence and the Declaration of the Rights of Man and of the Citizen in the French Revolution, which opposes the remnants of feudalism and monarchical authoritarianism), although they were definitively consolidated in the second half of the 19th century (to offset savage industrial capitalism), and especially throughout the 20th century and in what has elapsed so far of the 21st century (to combat colonialism, totalitarianism, racism, militarism, misogyny, economic and ecological exploitation, homophobia,…).

It remains to be seen whether the old processes of *mondialization* (electricity, transportation, and massive migratory movements), the current processes of *globalization* (mainly remote technologies) and the well-founded desire for *universalization* (first, second, and third generation human rights) converge in the 21st century into a responsible, sustainable planetary management, or whether to the contrary, they lead to a situation of maximal risk, enmeshed in a financial, ecological, and social crisis.

6   The Principle of Responsibility and the Culture of Sustainability

To conclude, we must point out that all these global changes require us to reconsider some longstanding ethical formulation. Thus, for example, the Kantian categorical imperative, formulated in the context of the 18th century, needs to be revamped and updated to fit the needs of the 21st century. From its anthropocentrism, the Kantian imperative does not outline the ethical relationship with non-humans, with the terrestrial environment, with the other species on the planet, with the future we will bequeath to the forthcoming generations on the planet Earth. For this reason, Jonas suggests revamping the human ethics of the present that Immanuel Kant proposed with a planetary ethics of the future which anticipates the principle of precaution and sustainable development based on responsibility (cf. Jonas 1984, p. 11). Its ecological imperative would be: "Act so that the effects of your action are compatible with the permanence of genuine human life". Or, to express it negatively: "Act so that the effects of your action are not destructive of the future possibility of such life". Or simply: "Do not compromise the conditions for an infinite continuation of humanity on Earth". Or, again turned positive: "In your present choices, include the future wholeness of mankind among the objects of your will".

More recently, Leonardo Boff distilled Jonas' imperative into the following ethical-ecological precept: "Act in such a way that your acts do not contribute to destroying the Shared Home, the Earth, and everything that lives and coexists on it with us". Or alternatively: "Use and consume responsibly what you need so that things can still exist and meet our needs, the needs of the future generations, and the needs of all other living beings, who along with us also have the right to consume and live". Or: "Solicitously care for everything because care means that everything lasts much longer, protects and provides security" (cf. Boff 2002).

In any event, regardless of the formula adopted, what is expressed in the pathway embarked upon by both Jonas and Boff is a new relationship between human beings and the rest of the planet, including the forthcoming generations. The extension of responsibility towards other communities, both present and future, both human and non-human, both local and global, once again poses the challenge of devising a philosophy of balance between the *ethics of humus* and that *ethics of space*. This can only be accomplished if we realize that our culture has changed, and along with it our capacity for ethical and political agency has, too. This is what David Tàbara has precisely called the *culture of sustainability* (cf. Tàbara 2002, pp. 63-85). In this new culture of sustainability, our spatial, temporal, and natural dimension has grown. In the past, our agency or capacity for action had a specific spatial boundary (usually a city, a region or, more recently, a country), a limited time span (only the current generation) and a way of dealing with problems that was directly related to human beings. Today, whether we like it or not, we have extended the systemic boundaries of our moral agency. We have expanded the spatial dimension, as it no longer encompasses a city or a country but also communal or global, cross-border goods. Likewise, we have expanded the time dimension, which includes both today's generation and future generations. Last but not least, we have also raised the number of legal, ethical, and political considerations, which no longer solely include human beings but also the rights of non-human species and even some biotic communities.

To summarise and conclude, we can state the following points (see Figure 1):

(1) A globalising world presents several superimposed but not equivalent phenomena: (*mondialisation*, *globalisation* and *universalisation*), which offer different cultural aspects and methodological issues;

(2) in this globalising world we have political, ethical and epistemological problems related to the global sustainability and the metabolism of chaos;

(3) an emerging sustainability culture is needed, but ethical debates and conflicts proliferate between the local and the global, between the present and the future, between the Global South and the Global North; and

(4) the ethos of science is extended to the realm of responsibility beyond Modernity. Finally, one question: will we be able to take the next step toward global sustainability? We cannot afford another misstep.

Figure 1:   Expanded Paradigm of Sustainable Responsibility, Knowledge, and Ethics

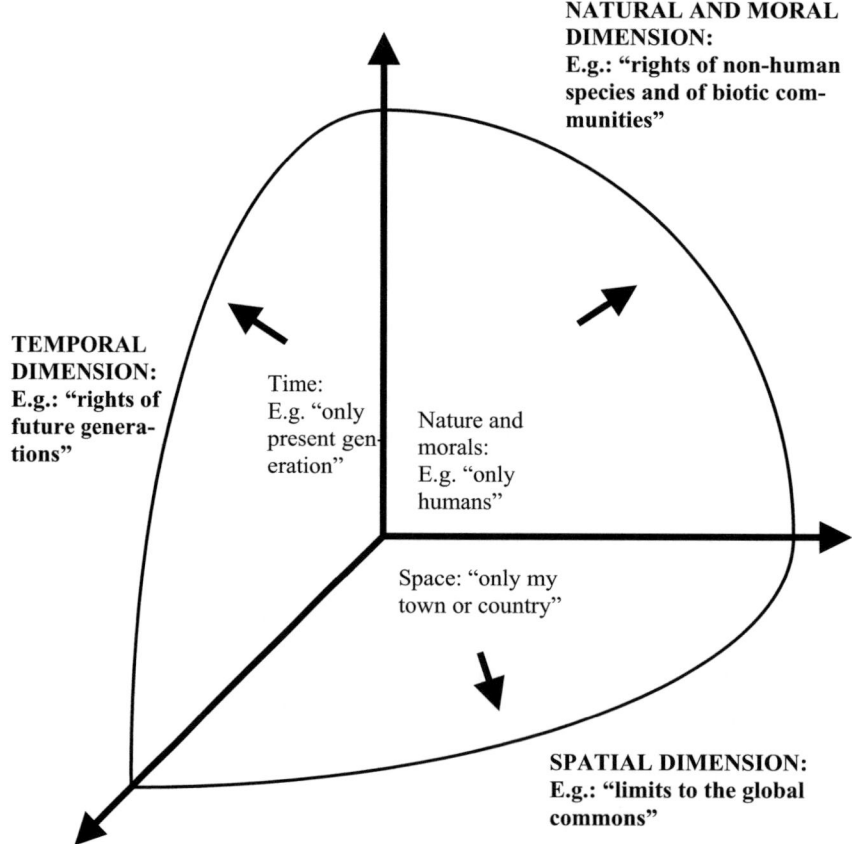

Source: Tàbara 2002, p. 74

[Acknowledgements: This article was developed in the context of the research project UNESCO 08/20, *Sustainability as post-Kuhnian paradigm*, funded by the UNESCO Chair for Sustainable Development and Environmental Education of the University of the Basque Country (UPV/EHU) and the Basque Government.]

References

Beck, U. (1992): Risk Society. Towards a New Modernity. London

Boff, L. (2002): Do iceberg à Arca de Noé. O nascimento de uma Ética Planetária [From Glacier Meltdown to Noah's Ark. On the birth of a planetary ethics]. Petrópolis (in Portuguese)

Castells, M. (ed.) (2005): The Network Society: A Cross-Cultural Perspective. Cheltenham, UK: Edward Elgar.

Clark, W. C.; Crutzen, P. J.; Schellnhuber, H. J. (2004): Science for Global Sustainability. Toward a New Paradigm. In: Crutzen, P. J.; Clark, W. C.; Claussen, M.; Held, H. (eds.): Earth System Analysis for Sustainability: Report on the 91st Dahlem Workshop. Cambridge, MA/London, pp. 1-25

Costanza, R.; Graumlich, L. J.; Will, St. (eds.) (2007): Sustainability or Collapse? An Integrated History and Future of People on Earth. Report on the 96th Dahlem Workshop. Cambridge, MA/London

Heidegger, M. (1962): Being and Time [1927]. Oxford/Cambridge

Jonas, H. (1984): The Imperative of Responsibility. In Search of an Ethics for the Technological Age [1979].Chicago/London

Lévinas, E. (1990): Difficult Freedom: Essays on Judaism [1963 & 1976]. Baltimore, MD

McNeill, J. R. (2000): Something New under the Sun. An Environmental History of the Twentieth-Century World. New York

Parenti, Ch. (2011): Tropic of Chaos: Climate Change and the New Geography of Violence. New York

Phillis, Y. A.; Koikoglou, V. S. (2009): Fuzzy Measurement of Sustainability. New York

Potŏcnik, J. (2005): Truth, Progress and Responsibility: The Key Values that Anchor Science in European Societies. World Science Forum – Knowledge, Ethics and Responsibility, Budapest, 10th of November 2005. – URL: http://ec.europa.eu/commission_barroso/potocnik/news/docs/20051110_speech_budapest.pdf

Rockström, J.; Steffen, W.; Noone, K.; Persson, Å.; Chapin III, F. St.; Lambin, E. F.; Lenton, T. M.; Scheffer, M.; Folke, C.; Schellnhuber, H. J.; Nykvist, B.; de Wit, C. A.; Hughes, T.; van der Leeuw, S.; Rodhe, H.; Sörlin, S.; Snyder, P. K.; Costanza, R.; Svedin, U.; Falkenmark, M.; Karlberg, L.; Corell, R. W.; Fabry, V. J.; Hansen, J.; Walker, B.; Liverman, D.; Richardson, K.; Crutzen, P.; Foley, J. A. (2009): A Safe Operating Space for Humanity. In: Nature, vol. 461, pp. 472-475

Save the Children (2008): State of the World's Mothers 2008: Closing the Survival Gap for Children Under 5. Westport, CT

Schellnhuber, H. J.; Crutzen, P. J.; Clark, W. C.; Hunt, J. (2005): Earth System Analysis for Sustainability. In: Environment, Vol. 47, No. 8, pp. 10-25

Sloterdijk, P. (2005): Im Weltinnenraum des Kapitals. Für eine philosophische Theorie der Globalisierung. Frankfurt am Main

Tàbara, J. D. (2002): Sustainability Culture. In: Governance for Sustainable Development. Barcelona (Institut Internacional de la Governabilitat & Generalitat de Catalunya), pp. 63-85 (Collecció Papers de Sosteniblitat, 2)

UNEP – United Nations Environment Programme (2007): Global Environment Outlook: Environment for Development (GEO-4). Malta

Authors

Ayestaran, Ignacio, Professor Dr.; Universidad del País Vasco / Euskal Herriko Unibertsitatea, Facultad de Filosofía y Ciencias de la Educación, Departamento de Filosofía / University of the Basque Country (UPV-EHU), Faculty of Philosophy and Education Science, Department of Philosophy; Donostia-San Sebastián, Spain; ignacio.ayestaran@ehu.es

Banse, Gerhard, Professor Dr.; Karlsruher Institut für Technologie (KIT), Institut für Technikfolgenabschätzung und Systemanalyse (ITAS) / Karlsruhe Institute of Technology (KIT), Institute for Technology Assessment and Systems Analysis (ITAS), Karlsruhe, Germany; gerhard.banse@kit.edu

Grunwald, Armin, Professor Dr.; Karlsruher Institut für Technologie (KIT), Institut für Technikfolgenabschätzung und Systemanalyse (ITAS) / Karlsruhe Institute of Technology (KIT), Institute for Technology Assessment and Systems Analysis (ITAS) & Büro für Technikfolgenabschätzung beim Deutschen Bundestag (TAB) / Office of Technology Assessment at the German Bundestag; Karlsruhe & Berlin, Germany; armin.grunwald@kit.edu

Hauser, Robert, Dr.; Karlsruher Institut für Technologie (KIT), Zentrum für Angewandte Kulturwissenschaften (ZAK) / Karlsruhe Institute of Technology (KIT), Centre for Cultural and General Studies (ZAK); Karlsruhe, Germany; robert.hauser@kit.edu

Holz, Verena, MA; Leuphana Universität Lüneburg, Institut für integrative Studien (infis) / Leuphana University of Lueneburg, Institute of Integrative Studies (infis); Lüneburg, Germany; verena.holz@uni.leuphana.de

Hübner, Renate, Ass.-Professor Dr.; Alpen-Adria-Universität Klagenfurt, Institut für Interventionsforschung und Kulturelle Nachhaltigkeit / University of Klagenfurt, Department of Intervention Research and Cultural Sustainability; Klagenfurt, Austria; renate.huebner@uni-klu.ac.at

Kopfmüller, Jürgen, Dipl.-Volkswirt; Karlsruher Institut für Technologie (KIT), Institut für Technikfolgenabschätzung und Systemanalyse (ITAS) / Karlsruhe Institute of Technology (KIT), Institute for Technology Assessment and Systems Analysis (ITAS); Karlsruhe, Germany; juergen.kopfmueller@kit.edu

Krainer, Larissa, Professor Dr.; Alpen-Adria-Universität Klagenfurt, Institut für Interventionsforschung und Kulturelle Nachhaltigkeit / University of Klagenfurt, Department of Intervention Research and Cultural Sustainability; Klagenfurt, Austria; larissa.krainer@uni-klu.ac.at

Kwiatkowska, Teresa, Professor Dr.; Universidad Autonoma Metropolitana-Iztapalapa, Department of Philosophy; Mexico City, Mexico; kwiat@xanum.uam.mx

Ott, Konrad, Professor Dr.; Ernst-Moritz-Arndt-Universität Greifswald, Institut für Botanik und Landschaftsökologie und Institut für Philosophie / Ernst-Moritz Arndt University of

Greifswald, Institute of Botany and Landscape Ecology and Institute of Philosophy; Greifswald, Germany; ott@uni-greifswald.de

Parodi, Oliver, Dr.; Karlsruher Institut für Technologie (KIT), Institut für Technikfolgenabschätzung und Systemanalyse (ITAS) / Karlsruhe Institute of Technology (KIT), Institute for Technology Assessment and Systems Analysis (ITAS) & KIT-Schwerpunkt Mensch und Technik / KIT Research Focus Human and Technology; Karlsruhe, Germany; oliver. Parodi @kit.edu

Poole, Alexandria, PhD Student; University of North Texas, Department of Philosophy and Religion Studies & Sub-Antarctic Biocultural Conservation Program, Associate Director of the Center for Environmental Philosophy; Denton, TX, U.S.; alexandria.poole@gmail.com

Robertson-von Trotha, Caroline Y., Professor Dr.; Karlsruher Institut für Technologie (KIT), Zentrum für Angewandte Kulturwissenschaften (ZAK) / Karlsruhe Institute of Technology (KIT), Centre for Cultural and General Studies (ZAK); Karlsruhe, Germany; caroline.robertson@kit.edu

Rozzi, Ricardo, Professor Dr.; University of North Texas, Department of Philosophy and Religion Studies & Sub-Antarctic Biocultural Conservation Program; Denton, TX, U.S., and Parque Etnobotánico Omora [Omora Ethnobotanical Park], Universidad de Magallanes and IEB – Institute of Ecology & Biodiversity)]; Puerto Williams, Chile; rozzi@unt.edu

Stoltenberg, Ute, Professor Dr.; Leuphana Universität Lüneburg, Institut für integrative Studien (infis) / Leuphana University of Lueneburg, Institute of Integrative Studies (infis); Lüneburg, Germany; ute.stoltenberg@uni-lueneburg.de

Szatzschneider, Wojciech, Professor Dr.; University Anahuac del Norte, The Actuarial School, Chairman of Graduate Studies; Mexico City, Mexico; wojciech@anahuac.mx

Karlsruher Studien Technik und Kultur
(1869-7194)

Hrsg.: G. Banse, A. Böhn, A. Grunwald, K. Möser, M. Pfadenhauer

Alle Bände sind unter www.ksp.kit.edu als PDF frei verfügbar oder als Druckausgabe bestellbar.

Band 1   Gerhard Banse / Armin Grunwald (Hrsg.)
          Technik und Kultur. Bedingungs- und Beeinflussungsverhältnisse.
          2010
          ISBN 978-3-86644-467-6

Band 2   Andreas Böhn / Kurt Möser (Hrsg.)
          Techniknostalgie und Retrotechnologie. 2010
          ISBN 978-3-86644-474-4

Band 3   Oliver Parodi / Ignacio Ayestaran / Gerhard Banse (eds.)
          Sustainable Development – Relationships to Culture, Knowledge and Ethics. 2011
          ISBN 978-3-86644-627-4